Bipolar, Not So Much

BIPOLAR, NOT SO MUCH

Understanding Your Mood Swings and Depression

CHRIS AIKEN, MD,
AND JAMES PHELPS, MD

W. W. NORTON & COMPANY
Independent Publishers Since 1923
New York • London

Important Note: *Bipolar, Not So Much* is intended to provide general information on the subject of health and well-being; it is not a substitute for medical or psychological treatment and may not be relied upon for purposes of diagnosing or treating any illness. Please seek out the care of a professional healthcare provider if you are pregnant, nursing, or experiencing symptoms of any potentially serious condition

Copyright © 2017 by Chris Aiken, MD, and James Phelps, MD

All rights reserved
Printed in the United States of America
First Edition

For information about permission to reproduce selections from this book, write to Permissions, W. W. Norton & Company, Inc., 500 Fifth Avenue, New York, NY 10110

For information about special discounts for bulk purchases, please contact W. W. Norton Special Sales at specialsales@wwnorton.com or 800-233-4830

Manufacturing by RR Donnelley Harrisonburg
Production manager: Christine Critelli

Library of Congress Cataloging-in-Publication Data

Names: Aiken, Chris, 1974– author. | Phelps, James, 1953– author.
Title: Bipolar, not so much : understanding your mood swings and depression/ Chris Aiken, M.D., James Phelps, M.D.
Description: First edition. | New York : W.W. Norton & Company, [2017] | Includes bibliographical references and index.
Identifiers: LCCN 2016024722 | ISBN 9780393711745 (hardcover)
Subjects: LCSH: Manic-depressive illness. | Manic-depressive illness—Diagnosis. | Manic-depressive illness—Treatment.
Classification: LCC RC516 .A3683 2017 | DDC 616.89/5—dc23 LC record available at https://lccn.loc.gov/2016024722

W. W. Norton & Company, Inc., 500 Fifth Avenue, New York, N.Y. 10110
www.wwnorton.com
W. W. Norton & Company Ltd., 15 Carlisle Street, London W1D 3BS

1 2 3 4 5 6 7 8 9 0

To our patients. You showed us what life is like in the mood spectrum, and we hope we got it right, or at least close, in this book.

Contents

PART THREE

TREATMENT
139

CONTENTS

Acknowledgments

We are grateful to our colleagues who donated their talents to help bring this book together: Lisa Aiken, Kirtan Coan, Mike Foley, Cheryl Goldberg, Ann McCarty, T.J. Shaffer, Kate Theall, Ali Turner and Jennifer Wittmann. And to our families, whose support helped keep us going: David, Eleanor and Lisa Aiken and Anna-Maria Phelps.

Introduction

"I would take physical pain over this any day." It's a bleak wish, but it's one we often hear from people with depression. Depression confuses the mind, strips away hope, and causes people to blame themselves for an illness they never asked for. "I must be doing something wrong because medications never work for me," said a man who had tried nine antidepressants. "Depression is making me depressed," said another who had suffered for 20 years before receiving the correct diagnosis.

If you've been in that place and found that antidepressants didn't live up to their name, then this book may be for you. We begin by bringing clarity to the diagnosis of depression. It turns out there are many types, and tests are available that can identify them just as accurately as a laboratory work-up does for medical illness. Then we walk you through treatments that can work when antidepressants haven't. Last, we talk about the most important things you and your family can do to further your recovery.

This book comes on a wave of increasing understanding of mood disorders and their treatment. Depression turns out to be caused by a very large number of genes that interact with environmental stress. These stressors lead to molecular changes inside the brain that are part of a normal process (called *neuroplasticity*) that gets carried too far in depression. The brain regions associated with depression have been so well identified that some research groups are now treating the illness with tiny amounts of electric current delivered precisely into the affected areas (a technique borrowed from the treatment of Parkinson's disease).

Meanwhile, through a literal act of Congress, pharmaceutical companies are now required to release all of their studies, including those that didn't turn out as planned. The full set of data has shown that antidepressants are often ineffective. Only about 30% of those who take an antidepressant reach full recovery; the rest respond partially, or not at all (Trivedi et al., 2006). A few people get worse on them, and we now have clues to help identify them *before* they are given an antidepressant.

Fortunately, the whole concept of depression is being reexamined and recognized to form a spectrum of problems from plain depression on one end to full bipolar disorder on the other. In between are huge numbers of people who don't have bipolar disorder but don't have plain depression either. They're in the middle of the mood spectrum. This idea of a mood or bipolar spectrum used to be hotly debated, but most mood experts now acknowledge that there is no place to put a dividing line between plain depression and bipolar disorder. This change has given researchers the green light to seek more refined treatments, and we're beginning to see the fruits of their labors.

The only good thing about depression is that it can go away completely. If *you* haven't reached full recovery, it's a good idea to look again at your diagnosis. Or if you're considering treatment for the first time, you'll also want to begin with a detailed look at all the diagnostic possibilities for someone who is depressed. We'll start there.

PART ONE

WHAT TYPE OF DEPRESSION
DO YOU HAVE?

ONE

Understanding the Mood Spectrum

Key point: *There's a spectrum of mood problems from depression to bipolar. Depressions that fall in the middle of that spectrum don't fit neatly into diagnostic categories.*

An accurate diagnosis can help you find the right treatment. There are over 30 antidepressants in the United States, but there's a type of depression that won't respond to any of them. In fact, antidepressants can even make it worse. One out of every three people who seek help for depression have it, but it's so hard to recognize that it takes—on average—10 years to accurately diagnose (Hirschfeld, 2001).

The depression we're thinking of is not bipolar disorder. It's not plain depression either, but it falls somewhere in between these two extremes. It feels like depression, but with an extra edge that's hard to describe. "Restless," "agitated," "anxious energy," "mood swings"—these are a few of the words our patients have used for it. You could call it bipolar, and some people do, but we think that word describes it . . . not so much. At least not in the sense that most people mean when they say "bipolar."

In everyday use, "bipolar" means Bipolar I Disorder, where moods cycle between depressive lows and ecstatic—but destructive—highs. Bipolar means "two poles," which are the manic and depressive sides it swings between. Plain depression is called *unipolar depression*, as it only has one pole and no trace of mania.

There's not a good word for the type of depression we have in mind, but we think you'll find it easier to understand if we let go of diagnostic labels for a moment and look at depression from a different angle. It's called the *mood spectrum*.

THE MOOD SPECTRUM

In the *mood spectrum* view, there are many variations of depression, not just unipolar and bipolar. They form a continuous spectrum with shades of gray, rather than black lines, between them:

Unipolar (depression without mania)

Bipolar (mania, with or without depression)

At the extreme ends of the spectrum are pure unipolar depression and classic bipolar disorder with full mania (called Bipolar I). Between these extremes are depressions with milder bipolar features. Though the bipolar features may be mild, the depressions in this gray zone can be severe.

The mood spectrum is not a new idea. It was first presented by Emil Kraepelin, a German physician who discovered bipolar disorders in the early 1900s. In those days, bipolar was called manic-depression, and that term applied to both ends of the spectrum. The idea of separating those poles into unipolar and bipolar categories first came about in the 1960s, and this separation became official when the third edition of the diagnostic rule book (the *Diagnostic and Statistical Manual of Mental Disorders*, or DSM for short) became widely adopted in 1980. There was good reason behind this separation, as there are significant differences in the genetics, life history, and treatment of the disorders on the extreme ends of the spectrum: unipolar depression and Bipolar I.

Lost in the transition was the large number of people who fell in the middle of the spectrum. There were more treatments for the depressive side, so most patients in the gray area were shunted into the unipolar-depressed category. It took years for psychiatrists to figure out that anti-depressants weren't working for the majority of those folks.

By the 1990s, Dr. Kraepelin's books were out of print in English, and we had to relearn what the field had forgotten. A host of researchers have spent the last two decades advancing our understanding of depression, and ironically this has brought them back to Kraepelin's original insight: that depression and mania exist on a spectrum. In this view, the diagnostic question is "Where are they on the spectrum" rather than "Do they have bipolar disorder?"

You can hardly imagine how radical it was, just 10 years ago, to talk like that. It went straight against the DSM rule book. Since then, the idea of a mood spectrum has steadily gained acceptance, and the new DSM (called DSM-5) now recognizes several disorders within the spectrum:

- Bipolar II Disorder
- Cyclothymic Disorder
- Depression with Short-Duration Hypomanias
- Depression with Mixed Features

Those categories will help a lot of people find their way to the right treatment, but we still think they are better understood through a spectrum lens rather than the corner that categories can back us into. The diagnostic question in the DSM-5 remains a black-or-white one: "Does she have bipolar disorder, or not?" Still, many leaders in the field are steering this question toward a spectrum view. Here are just a few examples:

In 2004, the Harvard-associated mood clinic started asking "How bipolar is she," and devised a rating scale to answer this question that we'll present in Chapter 5.

At the National Institute of Mental Health, the group studying complex mood disorders is now called the bipolar *spectrum* disorders section. The chief of that section, Dr. Ellen Leibenluft, has said that the cutoffs between bipolar and unipolar mood disorders are inevitably arbitrary because they are "imposed on fully continuous, smooth distributions" of mood problems (Leibenluft, 2014).

Even the chairman of the *DSM*, Dr. David Kupfer, has declared in a separate article that mood disorders are better thought of as "an affective disorders continuum"—a spectrum (Phillips & Kupfer, 2013).

To be fair, there are good reasons why the *DSM* takes a categorical, rather than a spectrum, approach, but those reasons probably don't apply to our readers. The *DSM* is not just used by psychiatrists and therapists, who see the continuum of mood disorders every day. It is also used by insurers, researchers, and lawyers, who all need diagnoses with clear cut-offs. It is always difficult to get insurers to cover mental health, and fuzzy spectrum concepts would not make that any easier. Researchers need clear definitions for specific groups of patients, even if they are only a part of a continuum. And the legal system is not set up to handle shades of gray. So for the most part, the *DSM-5* hung on to a system of cutoffs for mood disorders—despite many of the mood committee members recognizing that a spectrum model is closer to reality.

CALLING IT WHAT IT IS: STIGMA

In writing this book, we struggled over what to call the depressions in the middle of the mood spectrum. There's a lot of stigma attached to the word bipolar. It sounds too close to Bipolar I, which conjures up images of mania and the destructive behaviors it brings like spending into bankruptcy or having three affairs in a week. Many of our patients on the spectrum have a relative with Bipolar I, and they're quick to point out, "There's no way I could have bipolar—I'm nothing like my uncle Dennis."

On the other hand, we didn't want to add to the stigma by ignoring the bipolar word. So we settled on the term *depression with bipolarity,* or *bipolarity* for short. Remember, that's not the same as Bipolar Disorder, or at least not so much.

Whatever the word is, we have reason to hope that the stigma around it may start to change. The word *depression* once carried as much stigma as *bipolar* does today. That was before the 1960s, when the first medications for depression came out. Effective treatment brought greater awareness, as many brave people came forward, excited yet scared to speak up about the remarkable recoveries they experienced with antidepressants.

This is starting to happen for bipolar. (Perhaps you may play a role in reducing that stigma yet further.) There was a long wait between the first effective medicine for bipolar depression (lithium in 1949) and the second (lamotrigine (Lamictal) in 2004). Since then, around a dozen more have appeared, and as we write this book the first television ads for *bipolar* depression have aired promoting another new option. Prominent people are speaking up about their experience with bipolar, from Congress (Patrick Kennedy, Jesse Jackson, Jr.), to Hollywood (Ben Stiller, Catherine Zeta-Jones), to the world of professional sports (Darryl Strawberry, Keith O'Neil).

Before we get carried away on the bipolar bandwagon let's slow down for a word of caution. Most medications for bipolar disorder carry greater medical risks than antidepressants. One shouldn't conclude that they have bipolarity solely because antidepressants didn't work. Bipolarity is not the only reason people don't respond to antidepressants; it's just the most common.

We hope this book will help you figure out where you are on the mood spectrum: unipolar, bipolar, or somewhere in-between. We'll walk you through the symptoms, give you some diagnostic tests, and offer tips to help you share what you learn with your doctor. Whatever word you end up with in your diagnosis, keep an open mind about it. Even the best physicians and medical tests can be wrong, and the spectrum view of mood is not without flaws.

With those disclaimers in mind, let's turn now to the four key mood episodes that make up the spectrum: depression, hypomania, mania, and mixed states.

TWO

The Down Side: Depression

Key point: *Depression is a low energy state that drains motivation and slows down the mind and body.*

The next few chapters describe the major moods in the spectrum: depression, hypomania, mania, and mixed states. We'll start with depression, as nearly everyone on the mood spectrum has experienced that one. It's also the longest of the major moods. Depressions tend to linger for months or years, while hypomanic episodes tend to last a few days.

Depression is not a moral weakness. Like many health problems, it is strongly influenced by genes that people don't choose and stresses they have little control over. Unlike other health problems, depression tries to convince people that it's their own fault. The more they get convinced of that, the more depressed they become. It's a terrible loop. But that loop is not the person's fault either. A shift in brain chemistry makes such thoughts more likely.

True, some choices can make it worse: poor diet, lack of exercise, irregular sleep, impulsive risk-taking, and so forth. But even these choices are strongly affected by mood. Diet and exercise are hard enough to stick with when your mood is fine, and depression doesn't make this any easier ("Ah, what's the point? Nobody cares. I don't really care. It won't get any better anyway.").

Depressions tend to be more frequent for people with bipolarity, such as several times a year. This kind of depression can grow like a weed and even take over the whole garden. This weed feeds on vicious cycles, such as the one we just described where depression creates self-blame, which creates more depression.

If that analogy rings true, take hope. These weeds can also shrink back, and we'll give you tools to fight them in the second half of this book. But first you'll need to recognize what depression is, and what it isn't; we don't want to trample over any flowers while we're cutting back the weeds.

Depression is not the same as sadness. Severe depression can actually numb emotions to the point that people are unable to cry. When that happens, the appearance of tears may be a sign of recovery. Mistaking sadness for depression runs the risk of pathologizing normal emotions. If you've ever heard someone ask "did you take your medicine today" when you show genuine emotion, then you know what we mean by "pathologizing."

Rather than sadness, we recommend looking at energy and motivation to figure out whether you are in a depressed state. Depression tends to slow things down. Thoughts are sluggish, and energy is low. The body is impacted as much as the mind, and muscles can feel weak, heavy, and slow to move. Even the brain's sense of time grinds down, so that minutes feel like hours and hours like days.

Let's look at a few other depressive symptoms in more detail.

Self-Blame and Guilt

One aspect of depression that makes it so dangerous is self-blame, sometimes called "recrimination" or "reproach." Weird, isn't it? What possible value could this kind of thinking have? Perhaps a small dose could help people stay humble, but a big dose can pull people into a downward spiral of depression.

Severe depression can pull self-confidence down to a delusionally low level. For example, a man might think that he somehow caused a bad car accident, even though he was miles away and completely uninvolved. When it is extreme like that, it's easy for others to see the delusion. But when just a bit less extreme, poof—the idea that self-blame could be somewhat delusional is completely lost. People think terrible thoughts about themselves, and it somehow seems normal, not even close to a delusion.

For example, one of our patients was standing in her kitchen and heard her mind come up with the thought "everyone else can empty their dishwasher but me, I can't even get that done." This doesn't sound like a delusion, does it? Yet think about it. First of all, plenty of other people are slow to get their clean dishes out of the dishwasher. More importantly, this woman has emptied her dishwasher hundreds of times. But her mind is not giving her any credit for that. If your bank statement was this inaccurate, you wouldn't think, "Oh, someone made an error." You'd think, "this is utter fraud!" Our patient was amazed to realize, as her depression improved, how extreme her self-blame had been. At the time, it seemed completely appropriate.

In our psych lingo, this is called *mood congruent cognition*; in plain English, "thoughts that match your mood." The problem is that depressed thoughts don't come with a label on them saying "Made in Depression." They just come along, one after another, and seem so right. Then people try to think their way out of their depression ("I shouldn't be like this, I'm bringing everyone down, I have to get out of this"). But they don't realize they're trying to solve the problem with the same tool that caused it (their mind). It's as though they're in a deep hole, and the only tool they have to get out is a shovel, so they just keep digging themselves in deeper (Hayes, Strosahl, & Wilson, 2003).

Several forms of psychotherapy teach people new tools to get out of depression. They learn to recognize depressive thoughts for what they are: thoughts, not the truth, and to find more meaningful ways of living in the face of them. The right medication can also shift mood enough to bring those thoughts within reach of these therapies, or sometimes just stop them entirely. Bottom line: Depression can make minds lose track of truth. One of our patients calls them "depression lies." These lies can reach delusional levels.

Motivation and Pleasure

When the brain is working well, it constantly passes information between the thinking center (called the frontal lobes) and the emotional center (called the limbic system). This allows people to move easily throughout the day, staying on task, making good decisions, and keeping up with their priorities. They may even feel like their own will power is responsible for this success, and take for granted the fact that this quiet engine in their brain is really running the show.

During depression, that engine shuts down. Everyday tasks become overwhelming, and simple decisions are paralyzing. This is a big problem for someone trying to go to work, finish school, or run a household. The good news here is that effective treatment can do more than improve mood. It can help you function better, so life can get underway again.

Appetite and Weight

Depression can make appetite go up or down. People can gain or lose weight during depression, and sometimes depression can slow metabolism to the point that it's hard to lose weight even when dieting. Appetite is one of the few symptoms that can tell a little about where you are on the spectrum. There is a form of depression (called *atypical depression*) that involves dramatic increases in appetite and sleep. Atypical depression is slightly more common on the bipolar side of the spectrum, but only slightly, and not enough to make the diagnosis.

Sleep

Depression can change sleep in both directions, from too much to too little. It also alters sleep quality, so even those who oversleep during depression are unlikely to feel refreshed when they wake up.

HOW ARE BIPOLAR AND UNIPOLAR DEPRESSION DIFFERENT?

After all the fuss we've made about distinguishing bipolar and unipolar depression, it may come as a surprise that the *DSM* defines both of these depressions the same way. We agree with the *DSM* here. Depression looks pretty much the same, whether it comes from the unipolar or the bipolar side. This is partly why diagnosis is so difficult.

There are a few hints that a depression may be a bipolar type, though none of these are definitive. Bipolar depressions tend to be shorter (lasting 1 to 4 months) and come on quickly (over a few days). Unipolar depressions last longer (3 to 6 months) and start gradually. Bipolar depressions are likely to recur more frequently (e.g., two to four times a year), though that can happen in unipolar as well.

A more reliable way to tell them apart is to look at when the depression first appeared. Bipolar depressions tend to start early, between ages 15 to 20. Unipolar depressions first appear around age 30 to 40. If someone has their first depression after age 35, it's very unlikely to be a bipolar type.

We'll look at more tell-tale signs of bipolarity in Chapter 5. For now, let's move on to that elusive state of mind that officially separates bipolar from unipolar disorder: hypomania.

SIZING IT UP: A SELF-TEST FOR DEPRESSION

The Patient Health Questionnaire-9 (PHQ-9), as shown below, is one of the most widely used tests to screen for depression. You can also use it to track your progress while starting new treatments.

The PHQ-9

Over the last 2 weeks, how often have you been bothered by any of the following problems?

	Not at all	Several days	More than half the days	Nearly every day
1. Little interest or pleasure in doing things	0	1	2	3
2. Feeling down, depressed, or hopeless	0	1	2	3
3. Trouble falling or staying asleep, or sleeping too much	0	1	2	3
4. Feeling tired or having little energy	0	1	2	3
5. Poor appetite or overeating	0	1	2	3
6. Feeling bad about yourself — or that you are a failure or have let yourself or your family down	0	1	2	3
7. Trouble concentrating on things, such as reading the newspaper or watching television	0	1	2	3
8. Moving or speaking so slowly that other people could have noticed. Or the opposite—being so fidgety or restless that you have been moving around a lot more than usual	0	1	2	3
9. Thoughts that you would be better off dead or of hurting yourself in some way	0	1	2	3

If you checked off *any* problems, how *difficult* have these problems made it for you to do your work, take care of things at home, or get along with other people?

Not difficult at all	Somewhat difficult	Very difficult	Extremely difficult

Developed by Drs. Robert L. Spitzer, Janet B. W. Williams, Kurt Kroenke, and colleagues, with an educational grant from Pfizer, Inc. No permission required to reproduce, translate, display, or distribute.

Scoring

Add all the numbers in items 1 to 9 that you circled to arrive at your final score (from 0 to 27). The final item does not impact your score. It's there to remind us that it's normal to have symptoms of depression now and then, and it's unlikely to be a disorder unless it's making life difficult.

The cutoffs in Table 2.1 allow you to compare your score to the general population. These are based on averages, so it's not set in stone that your depression is mild just because you scored a 7:

TABLE 2.1: PHQ–9 Score

PHQ-9 Score	Depression level
0–4	None
5–9	Mild
10–14	Moderate
15–19	Moderately severe
20–27	Severe

THREE

The Up Side: From Hypomania to Mania, and Everything In-Between

Key point: *Mania and hypomania take many forms, but at their core, they are both states of high energy. The difference between them is one of degree. In mania, there is a significant loss of self control, while in hypomania people can still put the brakes on.*

"I was silly and giddy one minute, bursting with rage the next; running around excitedly in the afternoon but impossible to rouse out of bed in the morning."

—GOGO LIDZ, *New York Magazine*

Mania and hypomania are often called the "up side" of mood, but that doesn't mean they feel good. "I felt infinitely worse [during mania] than when in the midst of my worst depressions," wrote Kay Redfield Jamison, a psychologist who has spoken up about her own experience with bipolar disorder (Jamison, 1995). Mania turns the volume up on whatever is going on inside you, and that's not always good stuff. Anxiety can turn into uninterruptible worry and dread. Irritability can turn dangerous. There are moments where pleasure is heightened as well, but those are rare and more likely to lead to addiction than contentment. Most commonly, it's energy that goes up.

Hypomania means "a little manic." Sometimes it's so little that it almost looks normal. A little more talkative. A little more active. A little more confident. Wait, this is starting to sound like just about anyone on their best days. That's true. Every symptom of hypomania also happens to normal folks. There's a spectrum from normal to hypomanic to fully manic. The lines between them are not always clear, but we'll try to show you some guideposts in this chapter.

Hypomania is the least understood and hardest to recognize of the moods. There are at least three big reasons for that:

- Hypomania is misunderstood as a happy, euphoric state.
- Hypomania is rare and brief compared with depression.
- Self-awareness goes down during hypomania, so it's often quickly forgotten. In contrast, self-awareness goes up in depression, and painfully so.

There are many faces to hypomania, as it's a state of rapid flux. Depression tends to sit still. Its message is "don't take risks, don't bother changing anything—there's no point anyway." In contrast, hypomania is always on the go. We're going to slow it down for the rest of this chapter so you can see what's going on one symptom at a time.

HYPOMANIA: FRAME BY FRAME

Everyone's experience of hypomania is a little different, as its many symptoms can mix in various ways. The DSM-5 counts nine symptoms of hypomania, and we added a few more here. They can happen at the same time or scatter around, flickering on and off like Christmas lights. Sometimes one symptom flares up by itself, like the racing thoughts that our patients struggle to shut off (especially at night). The core feature of hypomania is increased energy. Nearly everyone will experience that in a true hypomanic state, so let's start there.

15

Increased Energy and Activity

Energy is key to understanding both depression and hypomania. In depression, energy is low, and in hypomania it's high.

Elevated energy may not stand out in the daytime. People just get things done. Students make up for depressed times when they missed class. Workers finish projects. Homemakers organize. None of this may look unusual.

But at night, when most people are winding down, this high energy becomes a bit more noticeable. One of the most common symptoms in hypomania is cleaning the house all night. People go from room to room, decorating and rearranging, often working on several areas at the same time, and finishing none. In recent years we're seeing this evening activity shift to the digital realm, as all-night social media marathons have become a common sign of hypomania.

Sometimes the excess energy is visible even in the doctor's office. Patients practically vibrate with energy, fidgeting, bouncing their knees up and down, as though they're ready to leap up and head out the door at any moment.

Bottom line: If you're wondering whether a certain phase is hypomanic, look for the energy. It will almost always be increased. This doesn't necessarily mean you're bouncing off the walls, just more energized than your usual state.

Intense Emotions

Emotions tend to be more extreme in hypomania. When they rise high it's called *euphoria*. A euphoric mood is a state of exalted joy where troubles wash away and pleasure intensifies. For some, it is a state of almost spiritual transcendence.

Euphoria is a classic symptom of hypomania, but it's also a rare one. You'll see that paradox a lot in this chapter. Many of the hallmark signs of hypomania are also the least common. More often, emotions intensify in hypomania by swinging rapidly from one extreme to another, which is called *lability*. Laughter turns to tears, and friendly cheer switches quickly into hateful scorn.

There are a lot of dark emotions that go along with hypomania. Surprisingly, anxiety is more common in hypomania than in depression (Simon et al., 2005). In another surprise, researchers once asked people with mania and hypomania what they were suffering from. The most common answer: "depression." Those patients weren't wrong, they were just answering in terms of emotions rather than energy (Kotin & Goodwin, 1972).

Feelings run deep in relationships during hypomania. You may fall in love too easily, or feel an intense connection with people you just met. It can take years to figure out that these relationships were not quite as fantastic as they first seemed (everyone is fantastic in their own way, of course, but no one is quite as fantastic as a new acquaintance who came into your life during a hypomania).

Irritability

Irritability is one of the easiest symptoms of hypomania to recognize (especially for family members). However, it's also common in many other psychiatric disorders, so it's not the most useful in making a diagnosis. Yet another reason why hypomania goes undetected.

The telltale sign of irritability is that you react with great anger over minor matters. However, those matters don't *seem* minor at the time.

For example, Jeremiah knows he's in trouble when he starts getting angry in the checkout line in the grocery store. The clerk is unbelievably slow, and his conversations with the shoppers are so bothersome. Can anyone be that dumb to think such trivia is worth putting into words? Where did they find this clown?

But Jeremiah learned the hard way that this experience in the checkout line is a warning. His last girlfriend left him after he came home from the grocery store in such a rage that he threw a can of beans across the room. She'd seen this kind of thing before, and that one was the last straw.

It's very hard to recognize your own irritability during hypomania, in part because of the way hypomania affects the mind. Self-awareness falls, so it's hard to see your own role in the problem. When Jeremiah talked to his therapist about the episode that lost him his girlfriend, he still thought the checkout clerk was the problem, not his hypomania. Hypomania also makes people single-minded and inflexible, leaving little room to compromise in an argument. Last, confidence soars, which means you know you're in the right, no matter what.

Inflated Self-Esteem

Unlike depression, hypomania is not a place of self-doubt. Confidence goes up, as does one's sense of self-importance. The easiest way to recognize this is by contrast with your usual self. Perhaps much of the time you are quite *un*-confident. Then, once in a while you feel good about yourself. You talk freely with people because you think they might be interested in your ideas.

The psychiatric term for high confidence is *grandiosity*. It's unlikely you'll think of yourself as grandiose when your confidence goes up, but for your significant others, who are on the receiving end of your hypomania, that word might seem quite accurate. When extreme, grandiosity becomes dangerous. People can take on physical risks, from reckless driving to unprotected sex. More often, it causes problems in relationships or on the job. Paul's therapist was a little concerned when he told her, "My boss isn't really my boss. I mean, I often tell her how to run the company, and she doesn't mind—she sees me as an equal." A week later, this therapist found out she had only been hearing half the story when Paul called—shocked and angry—to tell her he had just been fired.

When confidence flares, there is no sign on a person's head saying, "Don't mind me, I don't want to be like this, I'm just having some pretty extreme hypomania." So the boss probably won't think, "Paul is just not himself today." Instead, she's likely to fire him. Who would choose to put up with this guy who thinks he's so absolutely great, and seems to find everyone else too slow and incompetent? Even psychiatrists may misunderstand it (people are often diagnosed with narcissistic personality disorder during this phase of bipolar). Yet when less extreme, this very same symptom can have the opposite effect, drawing people in and impressing them. That kind of mild hypomanic confidence is not likely to be seen as abnormal unless it's compared with the meek and modest style they usually have. Tricky, huh?

Decreased Sleep

When hypomania feels good, people can get by on only a few hours of sleep. By the *DSM* definition, that's how sleep changes in hypomania: People just don't need as much of it. In our practice, we rarely hear about this symptom, perhaps because it's hard to recall. It tends to be short-lived and happens more often in the young-adult years where it might be mistaken as a normal phase of life. "We all partied and pulled all-nighters," say our patients who aren't inclined to see decreased sleep as a symptom. Is that hypomania, or youth?

More often, people with hypomania want to sleep but can't. Once the edgier side of hypomania creeps in, they know that something is wrong, and they are pretty convinced that they would be less scattered and irritable if they could just get more rest. They're right. As we'll see in Chapter 11, sleep is one of the best ways to treat hypomania.

The most common sleep problems we hear about during hypomania are:

- Difficulty falling asleep, usually because of racing thoughts that won't turn off.
- Difficulty staying asleep, most frequently waking after 3 to 4 hours and then having fitful sleep through the rest of the night.
- Waking up early and being unable to fall back asleep.

Though they are common, none of those sleep problems are in the *DSM-5* definition of hypomania. Only "decreased need for sleep" made the list, and the reason is similar to what we saw with irritability, another symptom that *DSM-5* discounts. Actually, this reason is worth a brief aside, as understanding it may help you cut through some confusion with your provider.

Here is the problem: The symptoms that are most distressing in hypomania are also common in nearly every other psychiatric disorder. Insomnia, anxiety, distraction, and irritability are key examples. Both doctors and patients may prefer to look toward other disorders to explain these symptoms, particularly those that carry less stigma than bipolar and are conveniently named after the troublesome symptom. In Generalized Anxiety Disorder (GAD), people complain of anxiety; in Major Depression, they say "I'm depressed"; and in Attention Deficit Hyperactivity Disorder (ADHD), they seek help for inattention. There is also Intermittent Explosive Disorder, which like bipolar causes random explosions of irritability.

Naturally, patients want to emphasize the symptoms that matter most to them, and an empathic provider will focus there as well. But that will usually lead to the wrong prescription if the cause is hypomania. Imagine instead that you told your provider this: "I'm tired, depressed, and anxious, but the strangest thing happened last month. I was able to get by on only 3 hours of sleep. I felt fine. I got everything done and then some—instead of sleeping I reorganized the whole garage."

A good psychiatrist would probably think of hypomania after hearing that because hypomania is the only psychiatric disorder where the *need* for sleep goes down.

Talkativeness and Pressured Speech

During hypomania, people often feel an intense need to explain whatever comes into their mind, and the ideas come so fast that others have a hard time keeping up. Being on the receiving end of this rapid, pressured speech is like being sprayed with a verbal fire hose.

In its mild form, you may simply feel like you have interesting things to say. You might find yourself talking louder than usual, or telling quick-witted jokes and puns. As with energy, this would be a shift from , --. usual quiet, reserved style.

This symptom doesn't cause much harm, though your friends may not think you're a good listener. Sometimes it's patients who recognize this; sometimes it's the relatives. "She's Chatty Cathy again." Psychiatrists gauge this pressure by noting how difficult it is to interrupt a patient (or is it just that doctors interrupt patients too much?). In recent years, we're seeing this symptom come out in the form of lengthy e-mails, texts, and Facebook posts.

Racing Thoughts

Rapid thoughts are closely linked to rapid speech. When extreme, racing thoughts can make even routine tasks difficult. People get stuck trying to think their way through simple steps because their mind is crowded with thoughts about whether to do it this way, or that way, and what will happen if it's done wrong, or how there really is a better way, and so on.

Donna got stuck like that while taking her medication. "Should I? Will it harm me? What if I didn't take it, what would happen? Is this pill really what it says it is? How would I know?" She stood there frozen while these thoughts ripped by. Soon they went on to other ideas, until the starting place was completely lost.

There is little peace when thoughts won't be still. "I've tried meditation, but my mind is crowded with thoughts that I can't slow down." People can have multiple trains of thought at the same time, "it's like a radio playing six stations at once." Perhaps it's no coincidence that Brian Wilson, the Beach Boys composer who pioneered multi-track recording, also suffered from bipolar disorder.

In its mild form, people simply think quickly, jumping from one idea to the next with speed and clarity. Working in a group or listening to a lecture can be torture: Everyone is going so s-l-o-w. But when one works alone, this aspect of hypomania is one of the most desired and exhilarating. You feel highly creative and intensely productive. Ideas come quickly and easily. When extreme, as in mania, it can lead people to find connections in unconnected ideas—think of this as creativity gone completely loose. In milder forms, the connections are still logical, and sometimes even brilliant.

When hypomania is tinged with anxiety, racing thoughts fly from one possible disaster to another, digging up evidence—again, sometimes not well connected—that the feared event will really happen. Imagine trying to fall asleep while that kind of thing is going on.

Racing thoughts are not unique to hypomania; they happen in ADHD, anxiety, and normal life. The key is to look for their opposite. If you've also had times when your mind is so sluggish that it almost comes to a halt, then it's more likely that the fluctuations in speed are due to a mood problem.

Distractibility

It's hard to keep your attention in one place when you're hypomanic. Everything seems interesting, and your focus shifts quickly to the point of distraction. Distractibility often goes hand-in-hand with racing thoughts, leading to a crowded, noisy mind that feels like a ping-pong ball is bouncing inside it.

This distraction can make people jump from project to project to the point that they don't finish any of them. They may be shopping for clothes online, rearranging the closets, and working on a photo album all at the same time. One woman described cleaning every room in the house but being unable to complete one before going on to another, leaving each room in the middle of things: Rugs taken up, furniture stacked, wash buckets ready but no mop, and so forth.

When more mild, this may take the form of daydreaming, with your mind creating fanciful stories while you're talking with the cashier at Target. Manic distractibility can look a lot like ADHD. These two conditions share many of the same symptoms. Tellingly, the most popular self-help book on ADHD, *Driven to Distraction*, has two symptoms of hypomania in its title (Hallowell & Ratey, 1995). These are only surface similarities, however, as mania and ADHD stem from very different changes in the brain.

Impulsivity

Acting without thinking. Making sudden decisions without considering the consequences. These are the hallmarks of impulsivity. Examples include spending sprees, travel, reckless driving, gambling, drug use, unwise decisions, saying things you can't take back, sexual promiscuity, and walking in dangerous areas late at night.

There is often a social aspect to the impulsivity. Other people get caught up in the excitement, and their interest fuels it on. Hypomanic spending often plays a social role, such as buying gifts for others or fashionable, attention-grabbing clothes. New relationships can form in this electrified state, some of which are later regretted. Sexually, you may find a broader range of people attractive during hypomania. Heterosexuals may experiment with bisexuality. We've even seen homosexual men who—to their bewilderment—find themselves attracted to women during hypomania. Whichever way it turns, the importance of protection can't be overstated. Research has confirmed that people with bipolarity have higher rates of HIV (Perretta et al., 1998).

The consequences of this risk-taking are much more dramatic in mania than hypomania. People can usually clean up or explain away hypomanic problems, but mania can be irreparable. Here are a few impulsive behaviors we recently saw in our hypomanic patients:

- Buying clothes that never get worn
- Flirting with coworkers
- Jumping into online relationships (in their many forms)
- Skipping class
- Buying electronics that need to be returned
- Spur of the moment travel
- Buying an old car to fix up when there are already two awaiting that same plan
- Giving lots of presents
- Sudden changes of fashion or hair color

Sense of Time

People can get so caught up in the moment during hypomania that they run late for every appointment. The brain keeps track of time, and that sense tends to flow faster during hypomania and slower in depression. This internal clock also helps us recall events in order, so we know what came first and what happened next. Psychologists call this *sequencing*, and it can fall apart in hypomania, sometimes with painful consequences (Bearden et al., 2007; Lera-Miguel et al., 2010).

Consider this example. During a hypomania, Randy's wife criticized him for staying out all night. He got a little reactive and told her "It's nobody's business when I go out. Love is freedom, and even though I wasn't messing around, I ought to be free to sleep with anyone I want to." Devastated by this outburst, his wife said "I don't know if I can love you again after hearing that." "Fine," replied Randy. "I *should* have an affair if that's how you really feel."

The next day, in an emergency marital therapy session, the story was quite different. Randy's loss of sequencing had set in. He told the therapist that he was only reacting to his wife's rejection of him. "The real problem is that she doesn't love me anymore," he said. "That's why I threatened to have an affair. I didn't mean it, but she tore me apart when she said she couldn't love me." At this point, his wife is likely to think he's a pathological liar.

Sequencing is one of the more mysterious symptoms of hypomania. Doctors often hear the arguments it stirs up after the fact. It's the families who witness it firsthand. It is hard to understand how the brain can slip up like that, or maybe it's a miracle that anyone's brain keeps track of events as well as it does.

The Five Senses

Mania can turn up the volume on the senses as well. Sounds are louder, and colors are brighter. This can feel exhilarating, overstimulating, or even annoying. The brain has a filter that dampens out irrelevant noise.

That's how we can talk at a loud restaurant without being confused by all the conversations around us. In more severe hypomania, that filter breaks down, and crowded, noisy places feel like a physical assault. Fluorescent lights, background music, the humming of a refrigerator, the sound of people chewing food—it all becomes intolerable.

In this sensory jungle, people may hear things that aren't there. As with other symptoms, there is a spectrum of severity to this. On the milder side, a hypomanic person might misinterpret things a bit, hearing someone call their name in a bustling crowd, or seeing shadows move in a dimly lit hall. In its more severe form, frightening hallucinations can appear out of nowhere. Overt hallucinations are a sign that hypomania has crossed into full mania.

HOW LONG DOES HYPOMANIA LAST?

Technically, hypomanic symptoms need to last at least 4 days in a row to qualify as a true hypomania (which in *DSM-5* would be diagnosed as Bipolar II). This is a controversial area. Most hypomanias are actually shorter than 4 days, and there are a lot of people with depression whose hypomanias never go on that long (Benazzi & Akiskal, 2006). Short hypomanias are particularly common in teenagers with bipolar disorder (Birmaher et al., 2008). There is also a phase of bipolar called *ultradian cycling* where short hypomanias alternate with depression every few days.

The *DSM-5* committee considered lowering the official limit from 4 days to 2, but in the end, they decided that we needed to learn more about these short-hypomanic folks before we start diagnosing them with full bipolar disorder. Instead, depressions with short hypomanias were moved to the back of the book under "Conditions for Further Study." They also show up in Cyclothymic Disorder, which *DSM-5* defines as brief hypomanias that cycle with brief depressions over many years.

We're glad to see those categories in *DSM-5*, but we view this duration issue as another part of the mood spectrum. Just as the intensity of hypomanic symptoms increases from the unipolar to the bipolar side of the spectrum, so does the duration. We'll turn now to the most intense form: full mania.

MANIA

The difference between mania and hypomania is one of degree. Mania brings a significant loss of self-control, causing people to act recklessly in ways that are out of character for them. In hypomania, there is only a partial loss of control, and people can usually put on the brakes before the consequences get severe.

It's hard to draw a clear line between these extremes. The DSM defines mania as causing "marked impairment" while hypomania causes "no marked impairment." As a rough guide, think of the most extreme things you did at a time when you had hypomanic symptoms. What type of problems did your impulsive action cause?

- Did it lead to significant legal problems, job loss, or bankruptcy?
- Did it lead directly to the loss of a relationship you cared about? We say "directly" because relationships may end after years of repeated hypomanic problems, but in mania we're talking about a relationship that falls apart because of one episode.
- Did you have to take off work because of the symptoms?
- Did you go to a hospital or partial hospital (day program) for the problems?

If the answer to any of those questions is yes, then it may have reached full manic severity. During mania, people can fully lose the ability to respond to feedback. Everyone is telling them to stop, but they push on knowing they're in the right. Checks start to bounce, but it's only a minor hitch: switch to credit cards. Hypomania can also be stubborn and inflexible, but eventually people with hypomania will take in feedback before things get too out of hand. The damages mania brings are often irreversible, while the ones from hypomania can usually be cleaned up with a careful apology. Once you drive that red convertible off the dealer's lot, it can't be returned. When a person with hypomania buys bags of clothes, they usually remember to save the receipt.

Culture and personal values affect how we think about these problems. In the Pennsylvania Amish, mania caused behaviors that would be normal for most people but were prohibited by their faith. The main signs were: racing a horse and buggy too fast, buying machinery, using public telephones, and vacationing during the wrong season (Egeland, Hostetter, & Eshleman, 1983).

Why do these distinctions matter? Because manic episodes can recur, and they're likely to cause the same kind of trouble again. This may not happen right away, but the risk of a repeat episode is 90% in the 5 years following a mania (Yildiz, Ruiz, & Nemeroff, 2015). So instead of just treating and preventing depression, which is the goal for most people on the bipolar spectrum, a person with a history of mania also needs to prevent the next manic episode. This shifts the treatment options a bit.

THE SPECTRUM OF HYPOMANIA

As you've now heard, hypomanic symptoms fall on a continuum from none to severe (manic), as shown in Figure 3.1.

Figure 3.1 shows a smooth continuum from normal to mania that's similar to the kind of line that researchers find when they look at manic symptoms in the general population (Angst & Dobler-Mikola, 1984). We plucked a few arbitrary points along the line and labeled them A–E. Table 3.1 gives a glimpse of how manic symptoms might appear as their intensity rises along those points.

Quite a large list, we know. We've gathered an even longer list—from our patients' own words—in Appendix A. You might want to pause for a breather here. Make sure everything we've covered so far is making sense, because we need your help to get through three more tricky concepts.

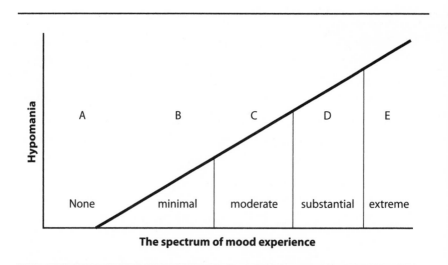

FIGURE 3.1. Hypomanic Symptoms Fall on a Continuum Between Normal and Manic

TABLE 3.1. The Spectrum of Hypomanic Symptoms

Symptom	Point A	Point B	Point C	Point D	Point E
Energy and activity	Steady, reliable, takes on projects they can finish	Productive, takes on a little more and gets it done	Multiple projects, hard to sit still	Too many projects, most don't get finished, restless motion	Endless but directionless activity, constant motion
Irritability	Able to control anger when needed	Irritable with family	Anger is starting to show up at work or in public	Irritability is causing problems at work; violent to objects	Anger is getting unsafe; physical fights with people
Distractibility	Able to focus when needed and shift tasks when necessary	Slightly unfocused	Notable difficulty staying on task	Looks like attention deficit disorder	Nonfunctional

Sleep	7 to 9 hours of restful sleep	6 hours or less, sometimes broken	4 hours or less, frequent awakenings	2 hours or less, waking too early	Nights with virtually no sleep
Confidence	Balanced, consistent view of oneself	Pleased with accomplishments, abilities, prospects	"Life of the party," charismatic	Stubborn, irritating, intrusive	Dangerously unshakeable confidence, inflexible beliefs
Thoughts	Thoughts move a little faster when alert or excited	Thoughts are quick, sharp, and clear	Highly creative, making rapid connections	Multiple unrelated ideas pass by at a high speed	Thoughts are not comprehensible to others
Speech	Normal flow and rhythm	Quick but otherwise unremarkable	Rapid speech, occasionally difficult to follow	Very rapid speech, losing most listeners	The proverbial "fire hose"
Impulsivity	We all make mistakes, but risks are at least thought out	Quick to action, a few impulsive decisions or purchases	Driving faster, saying things they wish they had not, many small purchases	Spending hundreds of dollars, sudden vacations, speeding tickets	Spending thousands of dollars or to the point of debt, illegalities, dangerous choices

SIZING IT UP: A SELF-TEST FOR HYPOMANIA

At different times in their life, everyone experiences changes or swings in energy, activity, and mood ("highs and lows" or "ups and downs"). The aim of this questionnaire, the Hypomanic Check List-32, is to assess the characteristics of the "high or hyper" periods.

1. First of all, how are you feeling today compared with your usual state: (Please mark only one of the following)

29

Much worse than usual	Worse than usual	A little worse than usual	Neither better nor worse than usual	A little better than usual	Better than usual	Much better than usual
☐	☐	☐	☐	☐	☐	☐

2. *How are you usually compared with other people?* (*Independently of how you feel today, please tell us how you are normally compared with other people, by marking the following statements that describe you best.*) *Compared with other people, my level of activity, energy, and mood . . .* (*Please mark only one of the following*)

. . . is always rather stable and even.	. . . is generally higher.	. . . is generally lower.	. . . repeatedly shows periods of ups and downs.
☐	☐	☐	☐

3. *Please try to remember a period when you were in a "high or hyper" state. How did you feel then? Check all the statements below that happen during a high or hyper state:*

In such a "high or hyper" state	Yes	No
1. I need less sleep.	☐	☐
2. I feel more energetic and more active.	☐	☐
3. I am more self-confident.	☐	☐
4. I enjoy my work more.	☐	☐
5. I am more sociable (make more phone calls, go out more).	☐	☐
6. I want to travel and/or do travel more.	☐	☐
7. I tend to drive faster or take more risks when driving.	☐	☐
8. I spend more money/too much money.	☐	☐
9. I take more risks in my daily life (in my work and/or other activities).	☐	☐

10. I am physically more active.	☐	☐
11. I plan more activities or projects.	☐	☐
12. I have more ideas; I am more creative.	☐	☐
13. I am less shy or inhibited.	☐	☐
14. I wear more colorful and more extravagant clothes/makeup.	☐	☐
15. I want to meet or actually do meet more people.	☐	☐
16. I am more interested in sex and/or have increased sexual desire.	☐	☐
17. I am more flirtatious and/or am more sexually active.	☐	☐
18. I talk more.	☐	☐
19. I think faster.	☐	☐
20. I make more jokes or puns when I am talking.	☐	☐
21. I am more easily distracted.	☐	☐
22. I engage in lots of new things.	☐	☐
23. My thoughts jump from topic to topic.	☐	☐
24. I do things more quickly and/or more easily.	☐	☐
25. I am more impatient and/or get irritable more easily.	☐	☐
26. I can be exhausting or irritating to others.	☐	☐
27. I get into more quarrels.	☐	☐
28. My mood is higher, more optimistic.	☐	☐
29. I drink more coffee.	☐	☐
30. I smoke more cigarettes.	☐	☐
31. I drink more alcohol.	☐	☐
32. I take more drugs (sedatives, anxiolytics, stimulants, etc.).	☐	☐

4. *Did the previous chart, which characterizes a "high," describe how you are? (Please mark only one of the following)*

    ☐ *Sometimes?*   If you mark this box, please answer all questions 5 to 9.

☐ *Most of the time?*   If you mark this box, please answer only questions 5 and 6.

☐ *I never experienced such a "high."*   If you mark this box, please stop here.

5. *Impact of your "highs" on various aspects of your life:*

	Positive and negative	Positive	Negative	No impact
Family life	☐	☐	☐	☐
Social life	☐	☐	☐	☐
Work	☐	☐	☐	☐
Leisure	☐	☐	☐	☐

6. *How did people close to you react to or comment on your "highs"? (Please mark one of the following)*

Positively (encouraging or supportive)	Neutral	Negatively (concerned, annoyed, irritated, critical)	Positively and negatively	No reactions
☐	☐	☐	☐	☐

7. *Length of your "highs" as a rule (on the average): (Please mark one of the following)*

☐ 1 day	☐ longer than 1 week
☐ 2–3 days	☐ longer than 1 month
☐ 4–7 days	☐ I can' t judge / don't know.

8. *Have you experienced such "highs" in the past 12 months?*

☐ Yes	☐ No

9. *If yes, please estimate how many days you spent in "highs" during the last 12 months:*

Taking all together: about _____days

10. *Scoring.*

If you circled at least 14 items in part 3, and those highs lasted at least 4 days, then it's very likely that you have had full hypomania (and possibly mania if the highs caused a major problem). The rest of this test does not count toward the score but can help you further describe those highs. If your score did not cross the threshold of full hypomania, but you think a fair amount of this test described you, then read on—you may find more answers in the tests ahead.

FOUR

The Mixed-Up Side:
When Mania and Depression Collide

Key point: *Mixed states happen when manic and depressive symptoms overlap. These are desperate states of anxiety, agitation, and irritability.*

When symptoms of mania and depression overlap it's called a mixed state. Unfortunately, the ups and downs don't cancel each other out. Instead, the overlap causes anxiety and tension as the symptoms pull in opposite directions. "I feel tired and wired; restless; driven to do something but I don't know what to do" are common complaints.

The word bipolar, which means "two poles," does not capture the experience of a mixed state. The overlap creates a third mood that is fundamentally different from either of the two poles traditionally associated with bipolar: mania and depression. We picture mixed states as a graph, with manic symptoms on one axis and depressive symptoms on the other. People can find themselves all over this graph, as in Figure 4.1.

We'll pick out a few points on that graph to give you a sense of how you might feel. At point 1, in the lower left corner, both the manic and depressed symptoms are mild. Here you might feel kind of bummed out with an edge to it. Not one of those zero-energy depressions. This one's got some push behind it. Can't really focus. Mind going a little too fast to really concentrate on the book that just last week you were enjoying. If you didn't know to connect this state to your mood disorder, you might

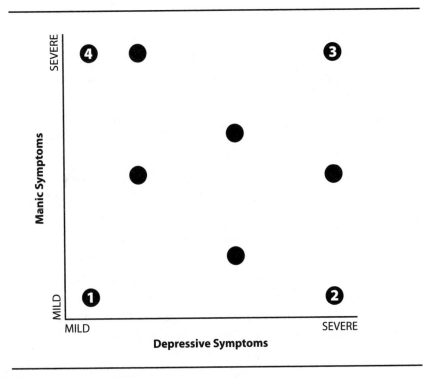

FIGURE 4.1 Mixed States

just think it was a bad day. Maybe your husband's fault. You hate when he leaves his shaving stuff out.

Now shift to the right, to point 2, where depression is severe and mania mild. Everything seems negative, and your body is slowed down, but your thoughts are racing. In that state, you may just sit and think, and think and think—and almost everything your mind comes up with is negative.

Move the manic symptoms up a notch and you get point 3. This is the worst kind of mixed state, definitely more painful than depression or mania alone. You're agitated and anxious. Can't sleep, can't think, and you're so irritable it's all you can do to keep from biting people's heads off. The tension strains muscles throughout your body, causing all sorts of physical symptoms. At this level, we hear things like "Doc, I wouldn't wish this on anyone," or "I'd do anything to make this go away." That's why the risk of suicide goes up in a mixed state, as people do desperate things to escape the anxiety (Beyer & Weisler, 2016).

Let's clear some of that depression and move to point 4, where manic symptoms spike and depression is mild. Here you could feel overenergized, wired, maybe even giddy. You might lose patience easily and come across as a bit testy and sarcastic but generally you'd think your mood was OK.

Mixed states tend to be unstable, so your mood could bounce around on this graph from day to day or even within a day. Often the depressive symptoms peak in the morning, while the manic ones are higher at night, but every pattern is possible.

The graph explains why some days can feel one way, others completely different, and yet all of these experiences can be part of one process. Mixed states fly around in the space of the graph. That's why the word bipolar does not even begin to capture how complex these variations can be. Some of that complexity is shown in Table 4.1, which contrasts a sunny hypomania (not mixed at all) with a dark hypomania (very mixed).

A telltale sign of a mixed state is unpredictable sleep. It's as though the biological clock is completely unhinged, and sleep comes at random times for varied durations, from short naps to 16 hours of oversleeping.

In a mixed state, it's usually not the individual symptoms that bother people but the overriding anxiety that the mix-up creates. Anxiety is a powerful distracter that pulls your attention away from everything else. Anxiety is never passive, it always carries the message that "something must be done, and now!"

This anxiety leads people to do all kinds of destructive things in a desperate attempt to find some relief. Drugs, alcohol, and binge eating are common. People often break things or hurt themselves: cutting their skin or banging their head. One woman would throw herself into the wall until the plaster cracked. All these destructive actions are really forms of self-medication, even if they don't involve drugs. For example, physical pain releases opioids in the brain that briefly calm the frayed nerves of a mixed state (Stanley et al., 2009). The problem with these solutions is

TABLE 4.1 Sunny and Dark Forms of Hypomania (Akiskal, Hantouche, & Allilaire, 2003)

Sunny hypomania	Dark hypomania
Greater drive and energy	Irritable, impatient
Socializing	Excess traveling, imprudent driving
Less shy, less inhibited	Unwise or impulsive decisions
More plans and ideas	Heightened sex drive
Motivated	Distracted
Happy, euphoric	Excessive spending
Physically active	High anxiety
Faster thoughts, more jokes	Urges to self-medicate
Talkative	Verbal aggression
Laughter, good humored	Disregard for authority
Less need for sleep	Careless of responsibilities
Confident	

Safe Relief from Dangerous Urges

Take a very hot or very cold shower
Squeeze an ice cube until it hurts
Go for a vigorous run or swim
Lift weights
Go outside and pull weeds
Tense your muscles for 3 seconds, then release (one muscle at a time)
Use body paint in place of self-cutting
Clean out something that needs heavy scrubbing
Put on loud music (or soothing music)
Pour school glue on your skin, let it dry, and slowly peel it off
Bite a hot pepper, lemon peel, wasabi or fresh ginger

that they only work temporarily and make things worse down the road. In the sidebar we've listed some less destructive ways to get some relief from that desperation.

Mixed states are treatable, but the treatment takes patience. Side effects to medications are much more common during mixed states than in the other phases of bipolar.

WHAT CAUSES A MIXED STATE?

Mixed states come about for different reasons. If mania goes on too long, it usually turns into impatience, anxiety, and agitation. When people cycle in and out of depression and mania, the cycling can increase in frequency to the point that the two states nearly overlap, as in Figure 4.2.

Mixed states are more common in people who've had head injuries or suffered trauma or abuse in their life (Perugi, Quaranta, & Dell'Osso, 2014). Irregular sleep and substance abuse can also cause mixed states, and there's a vicious cycle with these two, as mixed states worsen sleep and heighten the cravings for drugs.

Antidepressants are another cause. It's often said that antidepressants cause hypomania, but they are more likely to bring on a mixed state than flip people into the bright and sunny hypomania in Table 4.1. The reason is simple: They do not treat the depression, but they do cause manic symptoms. In other words, you're still just as depressed but now have manic symptoms on top of it.

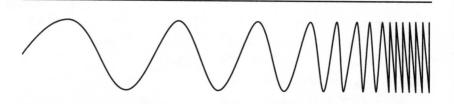

FIGURE 4.2 Cycles of Depression and Mania Increase in Frequency Until They Overlap in a Mixed State

That is why antidepressants are dangerous in bipolar. Most patients are not worried that they can cause hypomania. "Great—I could use some of that right now" is the kind of reply we hear to that warning. Unfortunately, the kind of hypomania they bring is too often this anxious, agitated mixed state.

OTHER DIAGNOSES
THAT RESEMBLE MIXED STATES

Anxiety, depression, agitation, insomnia: These may be the hallmarks of mixed states, but they are also common in many other psychiatric disorders. Posttraumatic stress disorder (PTSD), GAD, and borderline personality disorder can all resemble a mixed state. So can ADHD when it overlaps with depression.

That's why a person in a mixed state could see three different mental health providers and walk away with three different diagnoses. It's even possible that all three of those could be correct—just because you are having a mixed state doesn't mean you can't also have PTSD and borderline personality disorder.

How should this overlap be handled? We suggest keeping an open mind as to whether bipolarity is part of the problem. A lot of times it isn't. For example, many people with GAD do not have any bipolarity. Because the symptoms themselves can be misleading, we often look for other features to guide us in these situations. Which features are those? That would be a chapter in itself; let's make it the next one.

SIZING IT UP: A SELF-TEST FOR MIXED STATES

There is no official self-test for mixed states, so we created one for this book. Each of the 12 symptoms below can arise from the overlap of mania and depression, much as the color green results when yellow is mixed with blue.

Aiken Mixity Scale

Over the last week, how often have you been bothered by any of the following problems?

	Not at all	Several days	More than half the days	Nearly every day
1. Feeling tired and wired at the same time or within the same day	0	1	2	3
2. Easily irritated or impatient	0	1	2	3
3. Trouble sleeping or irregular sleep patterns (such as sleeping in the day and awake at night)	0	1	2	3
4. Driven to do something but you don't know what to do	0	1	2	3
5. Feeling nervous, anxious, or on edge	0	1	2	3
6. So restless that it is hard to sit still	0	1	2	3
7. Urges to self-medicate	0	1	2	3
8. Easily distracted, racing thoughts, or thoughts that move from topic to topic	0	1	2	3
9. Thinking that other people have bad intentions toward you	0	1	2	3
10. Rapid changes in emotions	0	1	2	3
11. Doing reckless, violent, or dangerous things	0	1	2	3
12. Thoughts that you would be better off dead or of hurting yourself in some way	0	1	2	3

If you had any of these problems, how difficult did they make it for you to do your work, take care of things at home, or get along with other people?			
Not difficult at all	Somewhat difficult	Very difficult	Extremely difficult

Scoring

This scale does not have official cutoffs because we designed it to track mixed states rather than to diagnose them. You can use the scale to measure your progress as you recover from a mixed state.

FIVE

A Little Bipolar? How Much?

Key point: *Symptoms are not the only clues to bipolarity. Other features, such as family history and treatment response, are just as informative. Bipolarity is not an either/or condition, and its features can be rated on a continuous scale from 0–100 called the Bipolarity Index.*

At this point you've learned about the symptoms of mood disorders, from depression to hypomania and mixed states. We've emphasized that those symptoms occur along a spectrum, and that diagnostic dividing lines within that spectrum are somewhat arbitrary (when, for example, does a really good day become a little too good, and thus hypomanic?). In this chapter we're going to show you how the current diagnostic system, the *DSM-5*, divides up that spectrum of symptoms. Your provider will almost certainly be using the *DSM* system, so familiarity with its terms will be helpful. Then we'll close with a new way of looking at diagnosis, which steps beyond symptoms to consider other signs that point toward bipolarity.

Over 200 different genes play a role in mood disorders. If each gene had only two forms (many have far more), there would be thousands of possible combinations, leading to thousands of different mood disorders. And that's just the genes alone. As you'll see in Chapter 7, childhood environment and adult stress directly affect how those genes are expressed. No wonder we have never seen two patients with exactly the same mood problem. Patients are like snowflakes—no two are alike. How can all that individuality fit into a handful of diagnostic labels?

Here's one way to think of it. Diagnoses are a bit like the lines between regions on a map. Here is the coast, there are the plains, then the foothills, over there the mountains. Knowing which region of the mood map you're in (i.e., your diagnosis) can predict which treatments are most likely to work. On such a map, symptoms are like the terrain. They change gradually, from the coast to the mountains. The lines between these regions may be somewhat arbitrary, but they are still very informative.

So as you look at these *DSM* diagnoses, remember that within these labeled regions there are many variations in terrain. And remember that the cutoffs between regions are like county lines on a map. Whether you are on one side of the line or the other does not in itself decide how you should be treated. Two people could live right next door to one another, yet one could live in Linn County and the other in Marion County. Likewise with mood disorders, going from major depression to major depression with mixed features could be like stepping over the county line to walk from your house to your neighbor's.

Diagnosis in *DSM-5*

For people who've had depression, the *DSM-5* offers a handful of possible diagnoses. Which one fits best depends on whether you've had manic symptoms, how long they've lasted, and how intense they've been—even if they happened many years ago.

Table 5.1 lists the major *DSM-5* mood disorders. The duration and intensity of hypomania begins at zero and increases as you move down the list from Major Depression to Bipolar I. It sounds like a mood spectrum, especially in the middle part, between the two extremes of unipolar depression and Bipolar I.

For people with unipolar depression and Bipolar I, the *DSM-5* works pretty well. Those diagnoses have been around for over 50 years, and research has clarified which treatments work best for them. For example:

TABLE 5.1 DSM-5 Mood Disorders

Mood spectrum position	DSM-5 disorder	Depression?	Hypomania?	Mania?
Unipolar	Major Depressive Disorder	Yes	No	No
Unipolar	Persistent Depressive Disorder	Yes (lasting at least 2 years)	No	No
Mood Spectrum	Depression with Mixed Features	Yes	A few hypomanic symptoms during the depression, but no full hypomanias	No
Mood Spectrum	Depression with Short-Duration Hypomania	Yes	Yes, but brief (less than 4 days)	No
Mood Spectrum	Cyclothymic Disorder	Yes, but brief and mild	Yes, can be brief (less than 4 days) or longer	No
Mood Spectrum	Bipolar II Disorder	The main problem	Yes, lasting at least 4 days	No
Bipolar	Bipolar I Disorder	Optional (very likely)	Optional	Yes

- Major depression: Psychotherapy and antidepressants often help, and the combination usually works a little better than either alone. Psychotherapy has fewer risks, but it can be hard to find therapists who are skilled in the types of therapy that treat depression.

- Bipolar I: Antidepressants are likely to make things worse, but mood stabilizers are likely to help. Adding one of several bipolar-specific psychotherapies gets even better outcomes, but these are even harder to find (see Chapter 27).

Between those two extremes lies the mood spectrum: People with bipolar, but not so much. DSM-5 breaks the spectrum up into four categories in Table 5.1, and everyone in those categories has had varying degrees of hypomania. The cutoffs between them are arbitrary, so much so that the dividing lines have actually changed with each new edition of the DSM.

Even when the cutoffs are clear, researchers have more trouble identifying these spectrum conditions than any other diagnosis in the book. That's because they all depend on that elusive state called hypomania, which you'll recall is very difficult for doctors and patients to pin down.

With all of these uncertainties, we think it's better for people in the middle categories to ask "How bipolar am I?" rather than "Do I have bipolar or not?" Even better, what if there was a way to answer that question without counting up the fuzzy symptoms of hypomania? That's what we'll aim for next, as we add some new landmarks that can tell you where you are in the spectrum.

HOW BIPOLAR AM I? A DIFFERENT WAY TO ANSWER

Up to this point we've talked about diagnoses as though they depend purely on the symptoms you've had. Yet, a good doctor doesn't just count your symptoms when you go to her for, say, chest pain. She'll likely ask about the timing and frequency of the symptoms, what makes them better or worse, and if heart disease runs in your family.

Depression requires the same kind of careful assessment. In 2004, researchers at Harvard's Massachusetts General Hospital collected all the signs of bipolarity that aren't in the DSM, and matched those with the DSM criteria to create a diagnostic tool called the *Bipolarity Index*, summarized in Table 5.2. It pulls together the spectrum map and the DSM map, allowing the most informed approach to the question "How bipolar are you?"

The Bipolarity Index has five dimensions (Table 5.2), and each is rated from 0 (no evidence of bipolarity) to 20 (strong evidence of bipo-

TABLE 5.2 The Bipolarity Index

	Dimension	Points
DSM	1. Type of symptoms (e.g., hypomania vs. mania)	20
Non-manic bipolar markers	2. Age of onset	20
	3. Course of symptoms over time	20
	4. Response to treatment	20
	5. Family history	20
	Total	100

larity). Some of the items are straight out of the *DSM-5*, such as mania, depression, and mixed states. Others are signs that we call *non-manic bipolar markers*. When they are present, they increase the chance that a depression has some degree of bipolarity along with it. Working with the Harvard group, one of us demonstrated this by testing the Bipolarity Index in practice (Aiken, Weisler, & Sachs, 2015).

The Five Dimensions of the Bipolarity Index

1. *Type of symptoms.* The Bipolarity Index includes the *DSM-5* criteria as a first step. This dimension rates how much hypomania or mania you've had, and how obvious or subtle it was.
2. *Age of onset.* Depressions that begin in adolescence or early adulthood are more likely to stem from bipolar disorder.
3. *Course of symptoms over time.* This looks at how your symptoms have changed over time and what kinds of problems came along with them. For example, frequent depression points to bipolarity because cycling of mood is part of the mechanism behind bipolar disorder.
4. *Response to treatment.* Antidepressants can trigger hypomania and mania. Though most people who have that reaction eventually

go on to develop bipolar disorder, there are some who don't, so the Bipolarity Index gives a little less weight to mood swings that were triggered by antidepressants.

Such a reaction should be enough to make everyone think long and hard before trying *another* antidepressant, but it doesn't mean a patient has to go on a mood stabilizer and stay on it—even if the brief phase was fully manic. Just think of it as a strong caution. The more manic the reaction was, the stronger the caution.

5. *Family history of bipolar disorder.* This is one of the strongest markers of bipolarity, but it is also one of the trickiest to figure out. A close relative (parent, sibling, child) with a very clear diagnosis of bipolar disorder carries a lot of weight. Even if you don't know your relative's exact diagnosis, the Bipolarity Index allows you to rate this section based on the problems you saw in them. For example, if your uncle had bouts of depression, a violent temper, and a gambling problem you could say he had depression with behaviors that look like bipolar. Any information about your family's mental health is helpful. Some research suggests that substance use or anxiety disorders in the family increases the likelihood of bipolar disorder *a little*, so listen for any problems, not just bipolar disorders.

SIZING IT UP: A SELF-TEST FOR BIPOLAR SPECTRUM

Now you can take the Bipolarity Index yourself. Beside each item is a number in brackets from 0–20 that tells you how strongly that item is associated with bipolar. Circle all the numbers in brackets that apply to you. You'll score each of the five dimensions by picking the highest number you circled within that dimension (you don't add the numbers up within a dimension).

Dimension 1: Types of Symptoms

A. *Have you ever had at least one of these episodes, where it wasn't directly caused by a drug, medication, or medical problem?*
  - A sunny or euphoric mania (one that mostly felt good). [20]
  - A dark or irritable mania or a severe mixed state (one that *did not* feel good). [15]
  - A hypomania that lasted at least 4 days. [10]

B. *Have you gone into one of these states within three months of starting an antidepressant?*
  - A mania or a severe mixed state. [10]
  - A hypomania that lasted at least 4 days. [5]

C. *Have you ever had any of these in your life?*
  - A hypomania that lasted *less than* 4 days, or a phase that you think was a hypomania but you can't recall more than three hypomanic symptoms during it. [5]
  - A depression with at least two of the following symptoms: oversleeping, overeating, or heavy feelings in your arms or legs. [5]
  - A time when you heard or saw things that weren't there, had strong paranoid feelings that other people were out to get you, or held unshakeable beliefs that you now realize weren't true (if that happened when you were depressed, circle [5], otherwise circle [2]).
  - More than three episodes of depression in your life. [2]
  - *For women:* A depression that came on within 6 months of childbirth. [5]

Score for Dimension 1: Enter the highest number that you circled among all of the items A–C (0–20): _____

Dimension 2: Age of Onset

How old were you when you first had significant symptoms of depression, mania, or mood swings? Think about when it all began, not just when you started treatment. This may be hard to recall; your best guess will do fine.

- It started before age 15. [15]
- Age 15–19. [20]
- Age 20–29. [15]
- Age 30–45. [10]
- After age 45. [5]
- I've never had mood problems. [0]

Score for Dimension 2: Enter the number in brackets that you circled (0–20): _____

Dimension 3: Course of Symptoms over Time

A *clear episode* is a distinct period of time where you were manic, hypo-manic, or depressed. By *distinct* we mean it had a clear beginning and end. A *blurry episode* is one that didn't have a clear beginning or end. For example, if you always feel a little manic or depressed, and it gets more intense now and then, it would be a blurry one.

A. *How many clear episodes have you experienced, if any:*
- At least two clear manic episodes. [20]
- At least two clear hypomanic episodes. [15]
- At least three clear depressed episodes. [5]

B. *How many blurry episodes have you had, if any:*
- At least two blurry manic episodes. [15]
- At least two blurry hypomanic episodes. [5]

C. *During any of those mood episodes, did you ever hear or see things that weren't there, have strong paranoid feelings that other people were out to get you, or have unshakeable beliefs that you now realize weren't true?* [10]

D. *Circle if you were ever diagnosed with, or are pretty sure you had:*
- Problems with drugs or alcohol (except nicotine/caffeine). [10]

- PTSD. [5]
- Panic, phobia, or other anxiety disorders. [5]
- Obsessive compulsive disorder (OCD). [5]
- ADD or ADHD. [5]
- Eating disorders (bulimia, anorexia, or binge eating disorder). [5]
- Borderline personality disorder. [5]

E. *(For women) Did your mood ever have a strong tendency to worsen in the 2 weeks before menstruation? [5]*

F. *Are you the kind of person who always tends to be a little manic, but in a good way? For example, do at least four of these traits describe you: charming, talkative, very outgoing, confident, "the life of the party," active, a short-sleeper, quick-tempered, a natural leader? [2]*

G. *Below are life events that are common in bipolar disorder; circle if you had any:*

- Have you ever been incarcerated? Or, have you had more than one legal charge for problems related to impulsivity (such as shoplifting, reckless driving, bankruptcy, or violence)? [10]
- Have you ever done risky things that could have posed a problem for you or your family (such as gambling, overspending, or affairs)? [5]
- Have you been married three or more times? [2]
- Have you changed jobs quickly (after less than a year on the job) at least twice in your life? [2]
- Do you have more than two graduate or other post-college degrees? [2]

Score for Dimension 3: Enter the highest number that you circled among all the items A–G (0–20): _____

Dimension 4: Response to Treatment

A. If you've ever taken an antidepressant (see Appendix B), how did you respond? If you've tried more than one, circle any answers that apply:
- It worked completely. [0]
- It helped some, but I didn't recover fully. [0]
- I've tried at least three antidepressants, and took each of them for at least a month, but never responded to any of them. [5]
- An antidepressant made me feel agitated, irritable, anxious, or more depressed, but I wasn't clearly manic or hypomanic on it. [10]
- I had a mania or mixed state within 3 months of starting an antidepressant; it was a big problem. [15]
- I'm pretty sure my mood episodes became more frequent or more intense while I was on an antidepressant. [10]
- My mood got much better within a week of coming off an antidepressant. [2]
- Abruptly stopping an antidepressant actually sent me into a mania or hypomania. [5]

B. If you've ever taken a mood stabilizer (see Appendix B; atypical antipsychotics can also be counted as mood stabilizers here), how did you respond? If you've tried more than one, circle any answers that apply:
- I recovered fully within a month of starting a mood stabilizer. [20]
- I recovered fully within 3 months of starting a mood stabilizer. [15]
- A mood stabilizer helped some, but not all the way. [10]
- I felt worse within 3 months of stopping a mood stabilizer. [15]

Score for Dimension 4: Enter the highest number that you circled among the items in A and B (0–20): _____

Dimension 5: Family History

This section rates mental health problems that may run in your family. You'll score different points depending on whether it was first-degree relatives or second-degree ones (see sidebar for definitions).

THREE DEGREES OF FAMILY RELATIONS

- *First-degree relative:* parent, brother, sister, or child. A first-degree relative shares about half of their genes with you.
- *Second-degree relative:* uncle, aunt, nephew, niece, grandparent, grandchild, or half sibling. A second-degree relative shares about a quarter of their genes with you.
- *Third-degree relative:* first cousin, great grandparent, or great grandchild. A third-degree relative shares about one-eighth of their genes with you.

A. *Have any of your first-degree relatives had:*
  - Bipolar disorder? [20]
  - Multiple episodes of depression (at least three) and behaviors that make you think they had bipolar (such as spending sprees, impulsivity, or significant irritability)? [15]
  - Multiple episodes of depression (at least three)? [10]
  - Possible multiple episodes of depression, but you're not sure how many they had. [2]
  - Problems with drugs or alcohol (except nicotine/caffeine). [5]
  - PTSD, OCD, eating disorder (bulimia, anorexia, or binge-eating), ADD or ADHD, or an anxiety disorder. [2]

B. *Have any of your second-degree relatives had:*
  - Bipolar disorder? [15]

C. *Have any of your second- or third-degree relatives had:*
  - Bipolar disorder? [10]

- Multiple episodes of depression (at least three) and behaviors that make you think they had bipolar (such as spending sprees, impulsivity, or significant irritability), even though they weren't diagnosed with bipolar? [10]
- Possible bipolar disorder (meaning the details are hazy but you think it's a possibility)? [5]

Score for Dimension 5: Enter the highest number that you circled among all the items A–C (0–20): _____

Final score: You should have a score (from 0–20) for each of the five sections above. Now add those up to get your final score (0–100): _____

Interpreting Your Bipolarity Index Score

A score of more than 50 points on the Bipolarity Index is strongly associated with a *DSM* diagnosis of bipolar disorder (e.g., Bipolar II or Bipolar I).

For scores *less* than 50, the main value of the Bipolarity Index is to bring attention to the possibility of bipolar disorder. If you're in that boat, you'd want to keep a close eye and an open mind about your diagnosis. Usually things become more clear over time.

A high score on this test does not mean you have a more severe case. It just means you have a more classic form of bipolar disorder, which can be a good thing. Higher scores actually predict a better response to treatment. In general, the higher your score:

a. The more you should learn about bipolarity,
b. The more caution you should take with antidepressants, and
c. The higher the chances that a mood stabilizer will help you.

To home in even more on your diagnosis, you should interpret this test in consultation with your provider and along with the other tests in this book. The next chapter gives you examples to help you do that.

SIX

About Your Diagnosis

Key point: *Diagnoses point the way toward better treatment and prevention. The more mood episodes you've had, the more likely they are to come back, particularly if there's a degree of bipolarity.*

Diagnoses are not made by reading a book or taking a paper-and-pencil test. If it was that simple, people would just take questionnaires and match them up with treatments. The self-tests in this book are designed to give you and your provider a rough guide to your coordinates on the mood map.

In this chapter we'll show you the types of stories that go along with different scores on those tests. You'll see how the two diagnostic systems—the *DSM* and the mood spectrum—would view the same patient.

FIVE LIVES ON THE SPECTRUM

The stories below are based on real patients, but the details have been chopped up and mixed around so that even they would not recognize themselves.

Rachel: The Unipolar Side

Rachel is a 22-year-old college student working on her master's thesis. She always loved big ideas but is wondering what she'll do with a degree in philosophy. She worries about her student loans. She's become more socially isolated since moving out of the college dormitory. Her parents think she should have kept her job at the shoe store. Her boyfriend of several years, with whom she's had an on-off relationship, recently found someone else, and the breakup was very rough.

Her mood has been spiraling down for about 6 months, and it's becoming harder to work on her thesis. This is the first time she's ever been depressed, and she knows something is wrong. She doesn't want to get out of bed, and sleeps in when she doesn't have class, averaging about 14 hours of sleep per night.

Depression does not run in her family, but her brother has ADHD and her father had struggled with alcoholism before she was born.

Test Results

Patient Health Questionnaire for Depression (page 12): 18 (moderately severe)
Hypomanic Check List (page 29): 6 (low)
Aiken Mixity Scale (page 40): 8 (low)
Bipolarity Index (page 46): 20 (low)

Diagnoses

DSM *diagnostic group:* Major Depression.
Spectrum position: Unipolar side of depression.
Main treatment options: Increase physical activity and social engagement, depression-focused psychotherapy, antidepressant medication.

Hideo: Bipolar II Depression

Hideo is a 35-year-old man. He's had severe, repeated episodes of depression and has been on an antidepressant for several years. He's also had "up" phases with great ideas and big plans but never thought these were part of his mood problem. Those were the relief from the terrible depressions he would struggle to get out of. He would whip himself into extreme physical workouts to prevent slipping into dark thoughts and total-body fatigue. The first time he came for help was after a foot injury left him unable to manage his mood through exercise.

Lately, his depressions have been less severe than they once were, but they are much more frequent (a *rapid cycling* pattern). He was astounded to learn that the antidepressant he's been taking might be causing that cycling.

During his up phases, Hideo was more social and spent a little more, but he usually kept that within his budget. He also took in more alcohol and became more sexually active during those times.

Hideo's depressions began when he moved from his native Japan to the United States to start college. It was a difficult transition, as he had been very close to his mother growing up—"she was my rock"—and he had no family in the United States. His father has been in treatment for depression a few times, but Hideo added "his depressions are nothing like mine. I take it out on myself, but my dad had a violent temper—you never knew when he would erupt." His parents are married but had separated in the past due to his father's affairs.

Test Results

Patient Health Questionnaire for Depression (page 12): 20 (severe)
Hypomanic Check List (page 29): 20 (high)
Aiken Mixity Scale (page 40): 11 (low)
Bipolarity Index (page 46): 70 (high)

Diagnoses

DSM diagnostic group: Bipolar II.
Spectrum position: Bipolar side of depression.
Main treatment options: A mood-lifting stabilizer, such as lamotrigine (see Chapter 18), while gradually reducing the antidepressant to reduce the frequent cycling in his mood. And lots of learning about Bipolar II in the process.

Jelani: Trauma, Depression, and
Anxiety in the Middle of the Spectrum

Jelani is a 36 year old man who has struggled with depression for 20 years. He has long phases of complete inactivity, but sometimes in the midst of this depression he'll get a boost of energy and catch up on all work he'd procrastinated on. His boss has figured this out and tolerates it because Jelani is so smart (when he's functional). He has read about social anxiety disorder and thinks that describes him pretty well. He avoids social events, thinking he is so boring that no one would want to talk to him. However, during his more energized phases, he is able to go to a party and talk with other people. He is far from "the life of the party," but he does enjoy himself during those times and can socialize without much struggle. He did not know that social anxiety disorder usually doesn't come and go like that and that another diagnosis might explain that pattern.

Jelani had a complicated childhood. He was raised by his grandparents whom he calls mom and dad. His real father left when he was two, and he has rarely seen him since. When he was five, his mother had a "nervous breakdown" after his half brother was born, and she was in and out of his life since then. "She was diagnosed with bipolar once and took lithium, but I think she's just a classic narcissist—she was always more absorbed with whatever man she was with than with us kids—people like that should never be allowed to have children."

A therapist had diagnosed PTSD, based on Jelani's unstable childhood (which included an incident of sexual abuse by a neighbor). He attributed Jelani's depression and social avoidance to this long period of trauma.

Jelani has tried three antidepressants without success. The first made him feel worse: "I felt more anxious on it. There was a pressure inside my head like it was going to explode. I even started thinking about suicide on it—and I *never* have those kinds of thoughts." The next two antidepressants "did nothing—it was like I was taking a sugar pill."

Even though he has not had a full hypomanic episode, he does have a few hypomanic symptoms during his depression (increased energy and activity). His Bipolarity Index score, which is just on the cutoff of 50, suggests that his anxiety could be rooted in bipolarity as well as trauma.

Test Results

Patient Health Questionnaire for Depression (page 12): 14 (moderate)
Hypomanic Check List (page 29): 11 (medium-low)
Aiken Mixity Scale (page 40): 19 (moderate)
Bipolarity Index (page 46): 50 (medium)

Diagnoses

DSM diagnostic group: Persistent depressive disorder (a long-standing depression without hypomania).
Spectrum position: Middle, neither purely unipolar nor bipolar.
Main treatment options: Try psychotherapy again, this time requesting cognitive-behavioral therapy for anxiety. In the process, monitor those cycles of mood and anxiety to see if other hypomanic symptoms show up that he may have missed. If hypomania does become clear, consider adding a mood-lifting stabilizer to the psychotherapy (Chapter 18).

Anne: Bipolar? Or Not so Much?

Anne is a 30-year-old mother of two with depression and anxiety. Her therapist diagnosed her with GAD, but cognitive-behavioral therapy had not helped much, even though she worked hard at it. She is also taking an antidepressant, the third in a row (each of them would work for a while and then wear off).

She first started treatment for depression 5 years ago, shortly after her second child was born. The depressions became more severe after that birth, but she also had two brief ones in her teens. Those early ones lasted about 3 months and then suddenly went away, leaving her puzzled as to what had happened (she was stressed about college admissions before the first one, but not *that* stressed, as her grades were still good).

When she first started an antidepressant 5 years ago, the depression went away for a few months but then returned. She changed to a different antidepressant, but that one wore off even faster. She is now on her third antidepressant and has had no relief from it. The depression is constant, though variable in intensity and quality (sometimes crippling, sometimes just dulling everything).

Although she's depressed, anxiety is her main concern. The anxiety also started 5 years ago—before that she was pretty easy going. Now she gets flooded with fearful ideas that dominate her thinking for hours. She'll see images of her children falling out of a window or getting run over by a car, though she knows these tragedies aren't likely to happen.

She loves her children but gets easily irritated with them and feels guilty about this. She would never hit them, but she knows she could handle them better.

Anne was adopted at birth and knows nothing about her biological family. We'll give her a zero on the family history section of the Bipolarity Index (but we'll keep in mind that bipolar disorder is actually more common among adoptees. Sadly, many young adults with bipolar have to resort to adoption, either because mania led to an unplanned pregnancy, or a post-partum depression left the mother unable to raise the child).

Test Results

Patient Health Questionnaire for Depression (page 12): 21 (moderate)
Hypomanic Check List (page 29): 12 (medium-low)
Aiken Mixity Scale (page 40): 28 (severe)
Bipolarity Index (page 46): 40 (medium-low)

Diagnoses

DSM diagnostic group: Major depressive disorder, recurrent with mixed features.
Spectrum position: Middle, neither purely unipolar nor bipolar.

Main treatment options: Though the antidepressants were helpful at first, they haven't worked lately and may even be contributing to the problem. Before taking antidepressants, she had no evidence of bipolar disorder, but lately she is showing signs of rapid cycling and a mixed state. Slowly lowering them off may help her in the long term, but in the meanwhile, she may need a mood-lifting stabilizer that can help more rapidly with her symptoms (Chapter 18).

THE IMPORTANCE OF REPEATED EPISODES

The number of mood episodes you've had is just as important as the symptoms they come with. The word *cyclicity* refers to the frequency of your episodes, while *polarity* describes the nature of the symptoms (manic, depressed, or mixed).

Some experts, including the past director of the National Institute of Mental Health (Frederick Goodwin), think the cyclicity of mood disorders is as important as their polarity. If Rachel was in her sixth episode of depression, instead of her first, her treatment options would change. Treatment needs to prevent further episodes while still getting her out of the current one. Depending on where she is on the bipolar spectrum, prevention might involve an antidepressant or a mood stabilizer, or even psychotherapy (which has good evidence to prevent depression, but only in very active forms that coach people to keep up with positive changes in their lives outside the therapy room).

The main reason to think about prevention after repeated episodes is that *the more episodes you have, the more likely they are to come back.* Fortunately, the opposite may be true as well. By preventing episodes, you may lower the likelihood of having more of them, even if you were to let your guard down for a short while.

What might surprise you is how few episodes it takes before you need to think about prevention. Consider these numbers, which are for unipolar depression (Gotlib & Hammen, 2010):

TABLE 6.1 The More Depressions You've Had, the Higher the Chance that They'll Return

Number of unipolar depressions	Chance of depression returning
1	50%
2	80%
3	90%

For bipolar disorder, the risks of relapse are even higher. In the first 5 years after just one episode, the chance of a new one (on either the manic or depressive side) is 90% (Yildiz et al., 2015). That's true for both Bipolar I and Bipolar II disorders. For people with bipolarity who don't have full Bipolar I or II, we don't have exact figures but imagine the risks are somewhere between those for unipolar and bipolar.

Of course, this also means that 10% of people with bipolar disorder won't have a new episode within the first 5 years of their recovery. That's why we don't generally tell people that they'll have to take medication for the rest of their life after only one episode. (Fortunately, prevention of future episodes does not rely entirely on pills. Part 2 of this book describes nonmedication approaches that can help you lower your chance of relapse whether you're taking medication or not). But because the rate of recurrence is nine out of ten, people should continue for at least several years before thinking about the pros and cons of coming off medication. The longer you stay well, the longer your brain has to build up strength (and in brain-time, a few months is not very long).

It is tempting to think these risks only apply to people whose depressions are biological, driven by genetics or a chemical imbalance. We share that temptation, but it's not exactly true. Nearly all the depressions counted above were caused by stress. For most people, the first three mood episodes are caused by a clear stress, like job loss or grief. This is true for hypomania as well as depression, and applies to both the unipolar and bipolar sides of the spectrum. The story gets more interesting after those first three episodes. At that point, they start to develop a life of their own; they come on both with and without stress. What is going on here?

Stress appears to change the brain in ways that make future episodes more likely. This is similar to what happens with skin cancer. A single sunburn isn't likely to turn into cancer. But after five sunburns the risk of skin cancer doubles. Once cancer comes on, it has a chance of coming back even if one avoids the sun entirely. A threshold has been crossed.

This pattern is so common in medicine that it has its own name, the *diathesis–stress model*. *Diathesis* refers to a person's biological or genetic vulnerability to the problem, and *stress* is the psychological or environmental trigger that tips the balance. If the balance is tipped too much, the stress can actually alter a person's genes so that the problem starts happening even without any stress.

Stress alters genes in many ways, and the details are a little beyond this book. In the case of skin cancer, ultraviolet rays from the sun directly damage genes in the skin. Psychological stress does not damage genes, but it can change the way they are expressed by turning them on or off. For example, some genes may lie dormant, doing nothing, until they get activated by stress, at which point they start to cause trouble.

If you have the genetics for a mood disorder, the kind of trouble those genes cause is likely to be some version of depression, mania, or a mixed state. Once those genes get activated it's hard to turn them off. If we could do so, we might have a cure for mood disorders. Until that time, most people with mood disorders need some form of prevention to keep those activated genes in check.

Measuring Cycles

There's one type of episode-repetition that warrants special consideration: *rapid cycling*. Rapid cycling is actually not very rapid. It means that you go in and out of mood episodes at least four times a year. Those episodes can include any polarity: hypomania, depression, mixed states, or even a single pole such as pure depression cycling by itself.

There are other words to describe episodes that swing faster than that. *Ultra-rapid cycling* means there are at least two episodes a month, and *ultradian cycling* means the symptoms cycle up and down within a day (some mood experts would call that last one a mixed state).

The frequency of cycling is important to recognize because it reveals a lot about what to do with your treatment. For example, antidepressants can make the frequency worse in bipolar, as can street drugs and thyroid problems. Mood stabilizers, on the other hand, help settle those waves. It is hard to see these cycles at an office visit, so we recommend keeping a daily mood chart to identify the frequency of your swings (see Chapters 16 and 17).

SEVEN

Is It All in the Genes?

Key point: *Depression has a genetic basis, but there's no such thing as a gene for depression. Genes interact with each other and the environment in complex ways that can result in mood disorders. Genetic tests have recently become available, and while their usefulness is currently limited, it's expected to grow.*

The earth is not flat. Neither are children born on a level playing field. Some kids have genes that make them more susceptible to depression and bipolarity. This issue used to be in doubt, but 50 years of research has proven it true, from following identical twins who were separated at birth to looking at actual genes in large groups of families. Parenting matters a lot, as do head injuries, drug use, infections, and other factors in the environment. Genes and environment interact in ways that are just beginning to be understood.

Which genes increase the risk for mood problems? In 1993, a single gene was found to cause a devastating mental illness called Huntington's disease. That accelerated the search for genes that might cause depression, bipolar disorder, and schizophrenia. But it slowly became clear that these illnesses were not caused by a single gene or even a handful of genes. Unlike Huntington's, these more common mental illnesses are caused by many genes that interact with each other as well as with the environment. For example, a recent review identified as many as 225 different genes that were associated with bipolar disorder (Nurnberger et al., 2014).

In this chapter we'll introduce you to a few genes that can increase the risk of depression. There is a puzzle behind a gene like that. If it can increase the chance of depression, it wouldn't be very useful evolutionarily. People with depression withdraw, avoid dating, and give up easily. Tragically, they can even take their own lives. You would think a gene that raises those kinds of risks would gradually disappear from the gene pool. And yet here they are.

One explanation for this puzzle is that there just might be something good about those genes, as well as something risky. That seems to be the case for the genes associated with depression and bipolar disorders. In small doses, in the right environment, and with the right mix of other genes, they can lead to creative, accomplished lives. But too big a dose or a wrong combination can tip that balance from functional traits to dysfunctional moods.

Evidence is starting to point toward that story. If it proves true, then getting your genes tested might allow you to know whether you're one of those people with too high a dose or a bad combination. Maybe that would explain why you've had such troubles with your mood. It could even give you a glimpse of what kind of trouble your children are at risk for, and maybe that could guide you toward some form of prevention for them.

This turns out to be an oversimplification. It's true that the same genes that cause depression can also be associated with great abilities. But thinking of these genes as directly conferring risk or advantage, and hoping that a genetic test might tell you about your risk, or your children's risk, or their possible advantages, does not work out. We'll show you a bigger picture of the relationship between genes and mood in this chapter. We'll then finish with a look at how genetic testing is coming closer to helping us figure out which medications are the best fit.

COMPLEX GENES, SIMPLE CONCLUSIONS

This story begins with an important research finding that has held up over and over again since it first came out in 2003 (which is good, that's how we gain confidence that a finding is really true). The finding involves serotonin, which you may have heard is at the center of the action in depression. Serotonin is one of the ways that brain cells communicate with each other. Always economical, these cells recycle their serotonin by bringing it back in after it's been released and done its job. This recycling is done by a protein transporter that's buried in the tip of the brain cell. Instructions for making that transporter reside in your chromosomes, which are tightly coiled strings of DNA: your genetic code.

You have the same DNA in the cells of your cheek as you do in your brain cells, so a saliva sample can tell you which version of this serotonin transporter gene you have. Why should you care? Because one version of this gene leaves people more vulnerable to depression when they are faced with stress. The other version seems to make people stress-resistant.

The version of the serotonin transporter gene (SRT) that's vulnerable to stress and depression is shorter than the stress-resilient version, so we'll call them the short and long genes here. Everyone has two versions of this gene: one from your mother and one from your father. That means you may have two shorts, two longs, or one of each.

Each version, long or short, is called an allele. This story has been called "getting the short end of the allele," because getting two shorts sounds like a bad deal. But there's another factor involved in the vulnerability to depression that is seen with shorts. That vulnerability depends a lot on the environment you grow up in. A handful of studies have revealed that these short genes only turn into liabilities in people who've been through rough childhoods or other major stress. In the first study, people with two short SRT genes who were raised in safe, supportive homes had no more trouble with depression than did the people with two long SRT genes (Caspi et al., 2003). That could be useful information to know. For parents, it means you could wipe out any genetic risk a short gene carries by providing a safe, supportive home for your kids. We'll go into more specifics on the types of parenting that can prevent depression in Chapter 30. A good childhood can vaccinate kids against the depressive effects of the short gene. But it turns out that there's far more to the story than this, which includes good news for short carriers. Research is beginning to show that the short gene can actually leave you better off than the long one, depending on your environment.

This has been called the "Orchids and Dandelions" story. If you inherit two longs, you're a dandelion. You are resilient and can grow just about anywhere, even in the cracks of the sidewalk. No water, little sunlight, you'll still do okay. But if you inherit two shorts, you are an orchid. You'll turn into something really spectacular if you grow up in the right environment. But if you end up in a dry pot in a window, it's going to be tough. You might make it, but you're not likely to bloom full. On the other hand, your offspring could still turn into spectacular orchids if you give them a good place to grow.

The moral of this story: short SRT genes are not bad genes. They do more than just make people vulnerable to depression. They help people adapt very closely to the environment they are raised in. If a baby with two short genes is repeatedly left alone, or repeatedly punished, the environment is teaching him "it's dangerous out there. Better mature fast and have sex early because you'll probably die young. Take risks, because you can't count on a long, protected childhood. You're going to be on your own, so better go for it now." Kids with two short SRT genes respond strongly when their environment gives them this message. In a different household, with safe and nurturing adults close by, the message is "take your time, this is going to be really good, you can afford to bring out your most creative self and find your talents." Kids with two short SRT genes can respond strongly to that message as well (Belsky et al., 2009; Benedetti et al., 2014).

One more twist: Whether a short SRT gene turns out to be helpful or hurtful also depends on the other genes it's interacting with. Take the case of two short genes, the combination that makes people more vulnerable to depression under stress. Now let's look at how two short genes interact with a second gene, one that affects sleep. The sleep-related gene also has two different versions, A and B, so a person can have an A/A, A/B, or B/B. These sleep genes can pair up with the two versions of the

SRT gene in nine different combinations (e.g. A/A + short-short, A/B + short-long, etc.).

Now for the twist. It turns out that the short SRT allele confers risk when combined with the A/A pair of the sleep gene, but is neutral, or even beneficial, when combined with the B/B pair. For example, there's a behavioral treatment for depression called *chronotherapy* which involves altering sleep schedules and exposure to bright lights. Chronotherapy doesn't work very well for people with the short genes. It works much better for people with the long SRT. But that's only half of the story. The short gene only gets in the way of chronotherapy when it's paired with the A version of the sleep gene. When paired with the B version of the sleep gene, people with the short gene respond even better to chronotherapy than those with the long one.

The story that emerges from all this is a lot more complicated than a tale of good and bad genes. The short SRT gene can be an asset or a liability depending on how it interacts with the environment as well as with other genes. What we saw above with the sleep gene is just an interaction between two genes. Think of how that plays out when the hundreds of genes that are associated with mood problems interact with each other and the environment. We lost count of how many different versions can come out of those interactions, but it may explain why there are never two patients with exactly the same problem.

This means that knowing your SRT genotype (two shorts, two longs, or one of each) doesn't tell you the whole story. With all those interactions, there is simply no way to infer a definite meaning from your SRT gene. Psychiatric genetics tells us more about large populations than individual people. In other words, if we looked at 1,000 children, as the original study did, we'd see a shift toward depression in the group that had the short gene and a stressful life. It would be a shift, but not an absolute one. Not everyone in that group would have depression, and some may have even had advantages because of their two short genes. You have to look at 1,000 children before the shift is even noticeable. When we zoom in on any one person, as when someone gets their DNA tested, it's hard to tell what the SRT gene is doing.

SRT GENES AND TREATMENT RESPONSE

Genetic research starts to get very practical when we look at how genes can influence a person's response to treatment. As with the story above, this is a complex area, and not enough is yet known to guide treatment very well. One of those genes that can influence treatment response will be familiar to you: the short and long SRT.

In general, people with two shorts are more likely to have insomnia and agitation on a serotonin-based antidepressant like fluoxetine (Prozac) or citalopram (Celexa) (see Appendix B). Although that's true statistically, the difference is not big enough to consistently predict how any particular patient will respond to a selective serotonin reuptake inhibitor (SSRI) (Porcelli, Fabbri, & Serretti, 2012). Other factors matter a lot more when it comes to choosing an SSRI, such as bipolarity (SSRIs can make that worse), and whether sexual side effects, which are very common on SSRIs, are a concern. There are other genes that have been linked to lithium response, and they seem to have a stronger influence than the SRT does for antidepressants (Hou et al., 2016). That's not surprising: Lithium is one medication where family history has always been a useful guide. If anyone in your family responded well to lithium, you're likely to have a good response as well, regardless of where you are on the mood spectrum. So, until those genes become available for routine testing, take a careful poll of your family members who've tried psychiatric-medications.

Even better, you could try a little lithium for a month or two and see how it works. There's little to lose with that strategy, and, as we'll see in Chapters 18 and 19, a lot to gain.

CAN GENETIC TESTING
FIND THE RIGHT MEDICATION?

Several companies offer genetic tests for the short and long SRT gene as well as other genes that have weaker associations with treatment response.

You can find links to those companies on our website (moodtreatment-center.com/bipolarnotsomuch).

There is skepticism about using tests routinely to predict how people will respond to medication. The brain is just too complicated for that to be useful right now (check back, science is likely to change). However, there's a more simple organ in the body where genetic testing can play an important role: the liver.

About 20% of people have genetic differences in their liver that can lead to unusually high or low levels of certain medications. Armed with that information, your doctor could avoid those medications, or adjust the dosage if they had to be used. That information would help with both psychiatric and nonpsychiatric drugs (Lanni, Racchi, & Govoni, 2013).

Not all drugs are sensitive to these genetic differences in the liver, but many antidepressants are. So if you've not responded well to antidepressants, but you're pretty sure you don't have much bipolarity, this kind of genetic testing might be a good idea before jumping into treatments for bipolar disorder.

On the other hand, the available genetic tests don't reveal much about what to do with medications for bipolar disorder. Genetic differences in the liver rarely affect mood stabilizers, and most bipolar medications are dosed by checking the blood level so that any unusual levels would be dealt with directly. All that may change soon, as new genes relevant to bipolar treatments are rapidly being discovered.

A third area where genetics can help guide treatment is in predicting side effects. Here's a place where we're starting to see progress on the bipolar side. One gene called HLA-B*1502 predicts whether someone will have an allergic reaction to the mood stabilizer carbamazepine (Equetro). This gene is so rare that it's not worthwhile to routinely test, except in people of Asian descent where it's more common (Hamilton, 2015). Other genes have been discovered that influence the risk of weight gain on atypical antipsychotics (Hamilton, 2015).

The International Society for Psychiatric Genetics released a position statement saying that we're not ready for genetic testing to guide treatment except in the cases of unusual liver genetics and the HLA-B*1502 gene with carbamazepine. We agree with that, but we're aware that may change by the time you read this book (International Society for Psychiatric Genetics, 2014).

EIGHT

The Living Side:
Finding Normal

Key point: *If your sleep and energy are stable, and your thinking is flexible, then you're probably "normal enough."*

I wouldn't trade it all in
How high how low I've been
Broken bones aside, I miss the edge sometimes, I miss the edge . . .
But I promise to stay on the living side.
—MEG HUTHINSON, *At First It Was Fun*

"What is normal?" It's a question people often grapple with during recovery. Looking back, they wonder how much of what they did in the past was really just a sign of a mood disorder. Looking ahead, they know they have to keep a close eye on their symptoms to prevent another episode.

That kind of self-monitoring is important, but it's no easy task. To start with, all the symptoms of bipolar—anger, rash decisions, sleepless nights—are also found in normal people. Trying to figure out what's a mood disorder and what's you is difficult at first, but as you get the hang of it you'll start to feel more confident and more in control of your moods. To start with, it's easier and more accurate to monitor energy instead of emotions.

Emotions are not the same as moods. Emotions are temporary reactions to life, and we hope you'll experience their full range while in recovery. In fact, cultivating an attitude of emotional acceptance rather than trying to control or judge your emotions can help prevent depression (psychologists call this *mindfulness*).

As one physician with Bipolar II put it, "Normal is a place I visit" (Fiala, 2004). If there is such a thing as a normal mood, there are many versions of it. There is good reason for that, for moods need to be flexible enough to help you adapt to new situations. That point is well illustrated by a study that looked at what type of mental outlook helped people stay well after recovering from a depression. Those who had extremely positive or extremely negative outlooks did not fare so well. Those who were flexible stayed well the longest, perhaps because their ability to shift perspective helped them deal with stress more effectively (Teasdale et al., 2001).

Allen Frances, the psychiatrist who chaired the 1994 edition of the *DSM*, uses the word *homeostasis* to describe this flexible way of adapting to stress:

> We can feel sadness, grief, worry, anger, disgust and terror because these are all adaptive. At times, our emotions may temporarily get out of hand and cause considerable distress or impairment. But homeostasis and time are great natural healers, and most people resiliently right themselves and regain their normal balance. Psychiatric disorder consists of symptoms and behaviors that are not self-correcting— a breakdown in the normal homeostatic healing process (Frances, 2013).

WHO AM I NOW?

Finding yourself is not the same as finding normal. Life is not always well in the aftermath of an episode. Relationships may have been broken, careers derailed, and spiritual life put to the test.

Even without those losses, bipolar takes a major toll on self-confidence. Before the illness, you probably took for granted that your mind would always work well. In recovery, people wonder if their mind is working all the way. They tread lightly through the world, once bit and twice shy. They may back away from opportunities, such as starting school, stepping into positions of leadership, dating, or making new friends.

That is a real loss for the rest of us, because people with bipolar have many gifts that the world needs. Studies suggest that the genes for bipolar are connected to genes for personal strengths. For example, positive traits like creativity and leadership occur more often in bipolar individuals as well as in their nonbipolar relatives (Kyaga, Lichtenstein, Boman, & Landén, 2015; Simeonova, Chang, Strong, & Ketter, 2005). That's good news: It means that you may have inherited some strengths along with the illness, and it is even possible to pass down the good genes without passing on the bad ones. Let's look closer at the positive traits that can ride along with bipolarity (Galvez, Thommi, & Ghaemi, 2011).

Openness

This strength includes artistic sensitivity, intellectual curiosity, creativity, love of variety, flexible thinking, and a nonjudgmental attitude. People with these qualities can find new solutions by thinking outside the box. They accept their own emotions and are open to those of others. If you have this strength, don't be swayed by the stereotype that being emotional or artistic can cause mood problems. It's only a stereotype. Research has found that these traits actually help people recover from depression (Bagby et al., 2008).

Extroversion

People with bipolarity have a broad range of personality traits, perhaps because of all the different moods they have to adapt to. Sometimes these strengths can seem contradictory. They may possess both spontaneity and caution, confidence and humility, and extroversion with introversion. On average though, people with bipolarity have a higher dose of strengths that psychologists call *extroversion*. For example, they express their emotions easily, exuding a warmth that makes others feel more con-nected to them. They are lively, assertive, and seek out excitement and activity. These qualities can help people with bipolarity build the kinds of social supports that protect against depression. Indeed, bipolar indi-viduals tend to have more friends than those on the unipolar side (Pora-dowska-Trzos, Dudek, Rogoz, & Zieba, 2007).

Intelligence

Although mood disorders can impair concentration, bipolarity is slightly more common among people with high IQs (Meyer et al., 2015). Those with bipolarity are often more creative and skilled with language (Kyaga et al., 2011; MacCabe et al., 2010). They tend to know more words and use them more expressively than others.

Resilience

Resilience is the ability to handle stress and recover from setbacks. No strangers to crises themselves, people with bipolarity often rise to the occasion when a crisis hits. They seem to build up a resilience to trau-matic events, and recover faster than the rest of us when faced with repeated traumas (Galvez et al., 2011).

Empathy and Realism

While the prior strengths are unique to bipolar disorder, these final qualities—empathy and realism—are found in both bipolar and unipolar depression.

Those who've been through depression often see the world more accurately, including themselves. It turns out that most people have an inflated sense of their own talents and importance. Those rose-colored glasses can be blinding in moments of crisis.

The psychiatrist Nassir Ghaemi noticed that leaders who excelled in times of crisis, such as Abraham Lincoln and Winston Churchill, also had significant depression. He credits their success in part to their realistic sensibilities (Ghaemi, 2010).

Though depression makes people withdraw from the world, recovery from depression can bring greater empathy for others. It's not always easy to live with this sensitivity to other people's pain, but it can be a great asset. The ability to sense when others are uncomfortable or dissatisfied can go a long way in jobs that depend on relationships with clients, customers, and coworkers.

It may be a coincidence, but it's a striking fact that three leaders whose compassion helped change the world also had periods of suicidality in their early adulthood: Abraham Lincoln, Martin Luther King, Jr., and Mahatma Gandhi. Those visionaries did not work alone; it took legions of people with a similar sensitivity to bring about the revolutions they led.

PART TWO

A HEALING LIFESTYLE

Now that you've seen the many symptoms within the mood spectrum, let's look at how you can improve them. We'll start with things you can do on your own before delving into medication. Lifestyle and medication work together. It usually takes both to reach full recovery, and they both work in complementary ways by causing changes in the brain.

Consider this telling story from the world of mouse research. Mice get depressed, but antidepressants did little for them when they were kept in isolation or weren't able to exercise. Simply allowing them to run on a wheel or play with other mice didn't help either. It was only when both changes happened together—an active, social lifestyle along with an antidepressant—that these mice perked up (Berchtold, Kesslak, Pike, Adlard, & Cotman, 2001; Dankoski, Agster, Fox, Moy, & Wightman, 2014; Leasure & Decker, 2009; Rief et al., 2016; Stranahan, Khalil, & Gould, 2006).

Just as we saw with genetics, there is a complex interaction between the brain, the environment, and medications. Once you've found the right mix, things start to change. As you read about the lifestyle factors that can help in your recovery, keep in mind that each one helps lay the foundations in your brain that medications will need to do their work.

For example, moderate exercise raises levels of *brain derived neurotrophic factor* (BDNF), a chemical messenger involved in the growth and repair of brain cells. Having more of that around helps medications work better (Hashimoto, 2010).

Regular sleep is another key to treating depression. Darkness at night, sunlight in the morning, and regular activity throughout the day all help stabilize the neurohormones that keep sleep on track. Medications work better when those hormones are running smoothly.

The ideas in this section were discovered through careful scientific research and have all been tested in the real-world of practice. Well, that's how we arrived at them. As we were writing this book, though, we learned that patients had already figured out most of these things on their own. A survey by the Google company 23andme asked people with bipolar which treatments they found most helpful. Surprisingly, nearly all the "treatments" at the top of their list were lifestyle changes, not medications. These were, in order:

1. Regimented sleep
2. Reducing alcohol
3. Exercise
4. Sunlight
5. Yoga
6. Psychotherapy
7. Mindfulness meditation
8. Small, frequent snacks
9. Self-tracking
10. Journaling
11. Reducing caffeine

Source: CureTogether, from 23andme.com

Noticeably absent from the list were the following:

1. Television in the bedroom
2. Fast food
3. Irregular sleep
4. Lack of daily rituals and meaningful activity
5. Bright lights, big city
6. A desk-job in a windowless cubicle
7. Social isolation
8. Long commutes to work
9. Family conflict
10. Increasing caffeine
11. International flights

That second list could be our top mood destabilizers (in no particular order). Unlike the first list, most of these destabilizers are inventions of modern life, which may explain why problems like bipolar are more common in modern, industrialized countries. That theme crops up as we review the lifestyle changes that help bipolar. Many of them take us back to a simpler, more natural way of life.

NINE

Daily Rhythms

Key point: *The biological clock drives your neurohormones, and for most people with bipolarity, it doesn't run on time. You can set this clock—and improve your mood—by keeping your sleep and daily routines on a regular schedule.*

You've probably realized by now that the word *bipolar disorder* does not capture the many faces of this condition. A better term might be "fragile circadian rhythm disorder." That lengthy title gets closer to the root of the problem and guides you toward the best way to control it.

Each of us has a biological clock that changes how the body works throughout the day. These changes are called the *circadian rhythm* because they run on a 24-hour cycle (*circa* means "around"; *dian* means "a day"). They include alterations of energy, temperature, appetite, and hormone levels. In bipolar disorders, the clock does not set right, which leads to the symptoms it is known for: irregular energy, sleep, concentration, and mood. It's like living in perpetual jet lag. In fact, the genes that run the biological clock are tightly linked to bipolarity, and one of the main medications for bipolar—lithium—helps restore the functioning of that clock.

If the only clock you owned ran slow, you'd probably have to set it every day. The same principle applies to your internal clock. Certain events help set that biological clock, and the Germans have a name for these events: *zeitgebers* (in English, *time-givers*). The most important among them are light and darkness.

Time Flies Fast and Slow

The perception of time can shrink and expand as moods shift. During hypomania, people feel it flies by faster, and during depression, it grinds to a painfully slow pace (Ghaemi, 2007). It's not known if these changes are due to the biological clock, but it would not be surprising if they are. The biological clock tends to get unhinged in mood disorders, and grounding it in regular daily rituals can help.

The ideal lifestyle for a person with bipolarity might be that of an eighteenth-century farmer. You would rise with the sun at the same time each day, work outdoors with plenty of exercise, eat at regular times, and gradually drift off to sleep after sunset. Research has indeed found that rural cultures have lower rates of bipolar than urban ones, with their clock-disrupting lights in cities that never sleep.

At the University of Pittsburgh, the psychologist Ellen Frank looked at dozens of daily events to see which had the most significant effect on mood. She narrowed it down to these four:

- The time you get out of bed each morning
- The time you start work or chores
- The time you first have engaging social contact with other people
- The time you eat dinner

When people with bipolar did those things at the same time each day (within half an hour), their mood became significantly more stable (Frank, 2007). While those four events are the most important on average, everyone's clock is also sensitive to time-givers that are unique to them. We recommend starting with these top four, while paying close attention to activities that add a sense of structure or ritual to your day. Examples might include exercise, walking the dog, bathing, going outside, reading, and watching a favorite TV show. All of these activities share one thing in common: They impact *neurohormones*.

Neurohormones circulate between the brain and body to help the two communicate. In a literal sense, they are the mind-body connection. They have names that may be familiar like adrenaline, cortisol, oxytocin, steroids, and melatonin.

Neurohormones are one of the few things that actually pass from the body to the brain, and for good reason. The brain is the most important organ in the body, and that's not just our opinion. It's the only organ protected on two levels. On the inside, it's surrounded by a tight barrier (called the *blood-brain barrier*), which keeps all but the essential chemicals from passing through. On the outside, it's the only organ that's completely surrounded by a thick bone (the skull).

As an aside, the blood-brain barrier is the reason it took so long for medical science to develop psychiatric medications. Very few chemicals could pass through it. But neurohormones do, and several of them are directly involved in setting the rhythms of the mind and body. Not surprisingly, these hormones themselves are affected by how you spend each 24-hour period.

Social interactions have a big effect on neurohormones. Just think of the flush of love, tinge of embarrassment, or surge of excitement that you've felt around other people. You felt it in your body, right? That's those neurohormones.

Now think about a time you had a more hum-drum interaction with other people. An example might be waiting in line to make a bank deposit. You probably didn't feel that in your body (unless you have anxiety about being in public) because it didn't alter your neurohormones.

Interactions with others that are intense or engaging can alter the biological clock, while those that are dull do very little to change it. Common engaging activities include having breakfast with your spouse, driving your children to school, and planning a project with colleagues at work.

There is an entire therapy for bipolar disorder that's based on these ideas, called *interpersonal social rhythm therapy*. In this work, the therapist has people keep track of the times they do major activities and rate the intensity of their social engagement while doing them:

0 = I was alone
1 = Others were present but not involved
2 = Others were actively involved
3 = Others were very stimulating

That last item, where other people are very stimulating, is one to watch for, as too much of it can disrupt mood. People with bipolar often understand this intuitively, and tell us that they feel "overstimulated" when they are around too many people or the interactions are too intense. That word captures it well, for there is often something exciting, or even pleasurable, about the interaction, but at the same time, it grates on the nerves like too much caffeine on any empty stomach.

Speaking of caffeine, one of the best ways to tell if something is a helpful time-giver or a harmful mood-disruptor is how it affects your sleep. Caffeine is a common mood disrupter, as are intense discussions, big projects, family arguments, noise, crowds, and bright lights—especially if they happen in the evening.

The best time-givers are those that help you settle into bed and rise from sleep at regular times. Regular sleep seems to improve mood even for people without bipolarity. For example, sleep scientists were recently studying a therapy for insomnia that involves strict regular wake times. To their surprise, they found this method not only helped insomnia, it also doubled the rate of recovery from depression (Carey, 2013).

Regular wake times are helpful, but what about bedtime? Should that be regular too? Ideally, yes. But you can't make yourself fall asleep the way you can make yourself wake up. Trying to force yourself asleep can lead to a vicious cycle, as any effortful work like that tends to keep people more alert and awake. Chapter 11 looks at more indirect ways to establish a regular bedtime, and setting up rituals throughout the day is one of them. The things you do in the last few hours of the day, from dinner time on, are particularly critical here.

The next chapter introduces you to two of the most powerful time-givers we know of: light and darkness.

Up in the Air: Jet Lag and Mood

The earth has 24 time zones, and a commercial jet can fly through half of them in a single day. Before air travel, it would take an ocean-liner a month or two to travel half way around the globe. That slower pace gave the biological clock plenty of time to adjust, so jet lag was not a big problem. Today, jet lag is considered a medical illness (called *circadian dysrhythmia*), and bipolar experts rank it among the most potent mood disruptors.

Mood can get particularly unstable after flying across two or more time zones. Depression is more common after a West-bound flight, and mania is more common with East-bound travel. You can prevent these problems by slowly shifting your sleep schedule toward the new time zone a few days before departing. For example, if you're traveling West over three time zones, you'd set your clock one hour earlier each day in the 3 days before departure. That means you'd go to bed later, and wake up later, while preparing for the Westbound trip. You would do the opposite in the 3 days before returning on an Eastbound flight.

You can read more about preventing jet lab in the supplementary materials for this chapter we've placed online (moodtreatmentcenter.com/bipolarnotsomuch).

TEN

Light and Dark

Key point: *Light can either cause or treat depression, depending on the time of day and even the color of the light. Darkness has an equally important role in keeping mood stable.*

Now that you understand how time-givers impact mood, let's focus in on the most important two of all: darkness and light. Well, maybe sleep should take top place, but that one's harder to control; we'll save it for the next chapter. For now, sit back and get ready for the easy part. This chapter will cover one of the few healthy changes that can make a big difference with very little effort.

Sunrise and sunset help set the biological clock. This clock is a little broken in bipolar disorder—in fact it's a little broken in all of us. The average person's clock runs a little slow, taking 24 hours and 15 minutes to cycle through a day instead of an exact 24 hours. The sun smoothes over this error, correcting our clocks as it rises and falls every 24 hours on the dot. If an average person lived in a cave for a few weeks (this experiment has been done), the lag in her internal clock would cause her whole schedule of sleep and activity to shift a bit later each day—about 15 minutes later (Terman & McMahan, 2013). After a month like that she'd be upside down, sleeping during what had been her day, and awake during what had been her night. So we all depend on cues in nature to keep our clocks set right. People with bipolarity just need those cues a little more.

This biological clock is tightly linked to the hormone melatonin.

Light shuts down melatonin, and darkness turns it on. The sun, then, is a pretty good mood stabilizer; it sets the clock every day and helps maintain your daily rhythm. But there are a few ways that this can go wrong, and if you're on the bipolar spectrum, you might feel these problems more intensely:

- *Gray winter days.* When the morning sun is dim and rises late, your biological clock may not pick up on its weak signal. This can lead to winter depression, also called seasonal affective disorder.
- *Sudden changes in sunlight.* The amount of daylight falls rapidly in September and rises with equal intensity in March. These shifts, called the *equinox,* can destabilize your clock, leading to all kinds of mood swings. Typically, it causes manic symptoms in the spring and depressive ones in the fall, but we tend to see a lot of mixed states on both sides of the change. This may be why the rates of suicide and violence peak during spring. Those who live where the seasonal changes are more drastic are at greater risk for this effect (Bauer et al., 2012).

So nature is not always friendly to mood disorders, but the next two disruptors are inventions of the civilized world:

- *Daylight savings time.* In the United States, the official clocks "spring forward" an hour every spring and "fall behind" in the fall. These sudden shifts have an interesting effect on people with seasonal depression. In the winter, the shift brings an extra dose of morning sunlight, which helps winter depression a little. In the spring, it does the opposite, making people wake up in darkness for a few weeks until the sun catches up with the time change. That can make winter depression extend a bit into the spring. This problem is more pronounced in places like Indiana where the time change is particularly out of sync with the sun (White, Terman, Musa, & Avery, 2005). A simple way to adjust to these changes is to spread them out over a week before the official time shift (e.g., adjust your wake time by 10 minutes a day over 6 days instead of a full hour all at once).

- *Electric light.* Light is often thought of as a good antidepressant, so this part may come as a surprise: Evening light can cause depression (Bedrosian & Nelson, 2013). Remember, it's all about the timing. We have a lot more to say about this one, but first let's go back to the beginning and look at how light can improve depression in the early morning.

MORNING LIGHT

Morning light is one of the best natural antidepressants. It treats all kinds of depression—from unipolar to bipolar—even depression in people with dementia. Indoor living, shift work, and dark winters can deprive people of this needed light, and in this case, technology actually offers a solution. It's called a *dawn simulator,* a device that creates a sunrise in your room.

This sunrise effect is exactly what your biological clock needs to reset each morning. The gradual increase in light pulls you from deep sleep to wakefulness. In contrast, a buzzing alarm clock can yank you straight out of deep sleep, leaving you with the hazy impression that something is very wrong with the world to make you wake up just then. Your impression is right: The brain was not designed to wake up to sound. Waking gradually with the sunrise helps people feel more alert and energized throughout the day.

A dawn simulator can treat depression as well, particularly winter depression (Terman & Terman, 2006). For many years, people have sat under light boxes in the morning to treat the winter blues. These boxes are powerful devices, as bright as a summer beach, but they can also trigger mania and mixed states so they aren't right for everyone.

The dawn simulator is a milder, gentler light, and we've never seen it trigger mood swings. Instead, it seems to stabilize mood by helping people wake up at regular times. It won't make them get out of bed though, so if that's the difficultly you have, there are a few lively alarm clocks that may get you moving (see sidebar).

There are many dawn simulators to choose from. Some work on their own while others plug into an existing lamp. Smart bulbs, which are controlled through a smartphone, can be programmed to work as dawn simulators. There are also apps that can make the flashlight on a smartphone turn on gradually like a sunrise in the morning; this option won't be as bright as a dawn simulator but it's great for portability. Our website lists specific products and apps (moodtreatmentcenter.com/bipolarnotsomuch). They key is to find one that turns on gradually (e.g., over 30 minutes) and reaches a level that's bright enough to actually wake you (around 300 lumens is ideal).

As you use the dawn simulator, you may need to adjust the positioning of the light to get the best effect. If the light is aimed directly at your head it may jolt you up like a spotlight in your eyes instead of waking you gently. If it's too far away, it may not wake you at all.

Lively Alarm Clocks

Depression can make it very hard to get out of bed, and while a dawn simulator can help, it may not be enough. Even the noisiest alarms fall short, especially when the snooze button is hit.

This problem is probably not unique to depression, which may explain why there is a large market for alarm clocks that force people to get out of bed. Some make you do mental arithmetic, or physical exercises, to turn off the alarm. Others run or fly around the room so you have to get up and chase them down. There's *Clocky* who wheels itself away; *Tocky* who plays MP3s as it rolls around the floor (load some 1980s hair-metal in there and just try to stay in bed); *Blowfly* which launches a small helicopter for you to chase down.

There are also beds that slowly raise their temperature in the morning (a rise in temperature signals the brain to wake up).

For those on a budget, there are smartphone apps with creative tricks to get you out of bed. One won't turn off until you scan the barcodes on items in your kitchen. We have mixed feelings about the ones that send embarrassing posts or tweets to your social media accounts when you sleep in.

We've highlighted a few of these funny alarms on our website (moodtreatmentcenter.com/bipolarnotsomuch).

DARK THERAPY

If morning light can treat depression, could evening darkness have mood benefits as well? The answer is a tentative yes. This is a newer science, and there's a lot less research to guide us than there is on the light side. We'll present one story of dramatic improvement in a man with severe bipolar disorder who recovered without medications, using just darkness as the treatment. Usually we would not hinge an idea on a single case, but this one is quite instructive.

A patient at the National Institute of Mental Health consented to experimental use of darkness as a treatment. He had been experiencing years of rapid cycling bipolar disorder: first a manic phase, then a depressed phase, then manic again, never a well interval. He was placed in a dark room at 6 p.m. every night and stayed there until 8 a.m. the following morning: 14 hours of enforced darkness. No phone, no radio, no lights. There was a bed but he was not required to sleep the entire time. With this dark therapy, he improved so quickly that they lowered the enforced darkness from 14 hours to 10 hours each night (10 p.m. to 8 a.m.). That regimen kept him well, with no further cycling, for over a year thereafter.

His sleep had been extremely erratic prior to the dark therapy: never more than a few hours at a time, and never at a regular time. With the regimen of darkness, he rapidly settled into a regular pattern of about 8 hours of sleep, all at night. Indeed, the improvement in his sleep preceded the improvement in his mood (Wehr et al., 1998).

The moral of this story: Darkness does indeed appear to act as a mood stabilizer. Of course this is just one case. There is another, similar case report, and a small trial that looked at the effects of adding dark therapy to medication in people who had been hospitalized for bipolar mania. In that study, most of those who got the dark therapy were able to leave the hospital sooner and on fewer medications.

Dark therapy works better in the early phases of mania (e.g., the first 2 weeks). It's a great tool to use when manic symptoms first appear. In that early phase, a good dose of nocturnal darkness could keep things from getting out of hand and potentially avoid the need for a medication change.

As with light therapy, this remarkable story usually sparks some interest but quickly gets shelved when people think about the time commitment. Fortunately we've found a workaround that costs close to nothing and has no known risks. To understand it, you'll need to learn about one more feature of the biological clock.

ALL LIGHT IS NOT CREATED EQUAL

Red, orange, green, blue: These are all colors within white light, as can be seen by shining it through a prism. But all light is not created equal when it comes to your daily rhythms. Only one color of light sets your biological clock. When that color is gone, your body thinks you are in the dark. Which color is it?

It's the same color that can penetrate through 30 feet of water, where our original ancestors evolved: blue. Humans have a special relationship with this one particular color. Your retina inside your eye processes light into images. But there's another receptor in your retina that's not involved in vision at all; it simply senses the presence of blue light. This receptor allowed our early ancestors to sense the blue light that filtered into the ocean, and it remains with us today, where it works to set the biological clock (Foster, 2005).

Okay, interesting. But what does this have to do with mood problems? This blue light story is what is going to allow you to cheat, to have your darkness and eat it too. Because the biological clock relies on this one color to recognize daylight, if you block that color, *your clock will think it is night.*

And night is what we lack. Edison's light bulb has allowed us to stretch the day far beyond the limits of sunlight. The problem has doubled up in the past decade as large-screen televisions, laptops, and smartphones have been added to the mix. What is the main color these devices emit? You got it, blue. The shift away from incandescent bulbs has also added to the problem beacuse LEDs and compact fluorescents tend to emit more blue waves. It's everywhere, and often at close-range. You'll get the same dose of blue light from a smartphone at reading distance as you would from a large TV across the room.

HOW CAN YOU HAVE YOUR DARKNESS AND EAT IT TOO?

You've figured it out? You just need a blue-light filter. You can have all the other wavelengths of light. A pair of amber-tinted safety glasses will do. These lenses work so well that when you wear them at night, your body will make melatonin (the sleep-related hormone that's only made in the dark) even with the lights on. They filter out all the blue and let the other colors pass through.

True, things look kind of funny through these lenses. Blue objects appear gray or black. Television may look off, but you can read, study, write letters, crochet, and play games. If these lenses really worked, you could do the dark therapy treatment that the National Institute of Mental Health patient received. Call it "virtual darkness." Put them on around 8 p.m. and take them off after you've settled into bed with the lights off.

You don't need to wear them while you're sleep, but you may need to take other measures to block out any light that leaks into your bedroom. Hang black-out curtains or dark towels. People with a streetlight outside have even covered their window in tin foil.

Dr. Phelps was involved in the clinical tests for these amber lenses, along with a group of very kind and intelligent physicists who deserve the credit for getting this idea going (Doctors Hansler, Carome, and Kubulins). Of the first 20 patients to use them, half came back and said they saw no difference. But the other half said "when I wear these for an hour or two before bed, I can fall asleep much more quickly." That result has been published, as well as a small controlled trial initiated by the physicists above (Henriksen et al., 2014). A full scale trial is currently underway, and the initial results look very positive. So this appealing idea is going from theory to practice quickly, and so far appears to be effective. There are no known risks to these lenses, and with other research linking blue light to cancer, diabetes, obesity, and heart disease, amber glasses may be good for your physical health as well. Just don't wear them while driving your car.

Amber lenses come in several styles, including models that fit over prescription glasses. Prices range from less than $10 to over $100, and we've gathered a list of good products on our website (moodtreatment-center.com/bipolarnotsomuch for options). There are also low-blue lamps and bulbs for nocturnal use, as well as options that will filter the blue out of your computer, smartphone, or e-reader at night.

ELEVEN

Managing Insomnia

Key point: *Nothing keeps people awake like trying to fall asleep. Instead, we recommend indirect ways to improve sleep. The most important are to rise at regular times, stay awake during the day, and only go to bed when tired.*

There's a paradox to sleep: the more you try to get it, the less you're likely to get. Sleep improves when you give up that struggle. There are physical things you can do to improve sleep, but you can't fall asleep by force of will. The more you try, the more you'll stay awake.

Sleep and mood are connected. Disruptions of sleep are often one of the first signs of an oncoming mood episode, and restoring sleep patterns can help prevent them. But sleep can be so elusive. How frustrating, when you know you need to sleep, you're ready to sleep, you're *trying* to sleep, and you can't. In this chapter we'll look at natural ways to break that cycle, including a behavioral program that's been proven to work better than sleep medicine (Jacobs, 2004).

WHAT MAKES YOU SLEEP?

So many people have difficulty sleeping that insomnia seems almost a normal part of life, particularly as we age. About 20% of the general population has frequent insomnia, and among our patients, the percentage is far higher. Given that you're reading this book, you're very likely to have had difficulty sleeping at times. Knowing how sleep works will help you understand the nonmedication strategies that can improve it.

Sleep is brought on by two forces: *sleep drive* and *circadian rhythm*. We reviewed circadian rhythm in Chapter 9. This is the body's biological clock that is set by light, dark, and major events throughout the day. Sleep drive simply refers to how sleep deprived you are. The longer you go without sleep, the more your sleep drive increases.

Ideally, your sleep drive would kick in around the time your internal clock recognizes that it's bedtime. Because bipolar disorder disrupts the biological clock, it's not unusual for this process to go awry.

The way to improve sleep is to focus on the parts of the cycle that you have control over. Most people with insomnia focus on falling asleep, which is where you have the least control. Stressing over that, and *trying* to fall asleep, will only activate your fight-or-flight system and make you more alert and awake. Instead, good sleep stew has two ingredients: first, the things to do (and not do) before getting in bed; and second, things to do if you find yourself awake.

Some of these steps may seem too basic. You may think "oh, I've tried that, and it didn't work." And for some people, at least some of the time, these steps won't work. But doing them as part of a regular routine will improve your *chances* of falling sleeping at night. These steps have been called *sleep hygiene* (Edinger & Carney, 2014). Careful now, don't dismiss them right away, because if you've done them all and you're still having difficulty sleeping, you'll face a more difficult step called *sleep restriction*. Better to maximize the hygiene steps first.

SLEEP HYGIENE IN TEN STEPS

1. A *dark, cool bedroom.* You've already heard our sermon about darkness in the previous chapter: Light, particularly blue-light, prevents sleep while darkness helps bring it on. Sleep in a cave. And here's one more tip: Make it a cool cave (meaning lower temperature, ideally 60-65 degrees). Your body cools at night, and warms just before you wake. If you don't let

it cool slightly, you are dampening one of the sleep signals. To enhance that cooling effect, take a hot bath (as hot as you can touch—around 105°F—and not just a shower) before entering the cool cave. The hot bath should last 20–30 minutes and take place 1–2 hours before you go to bed. The bath will alter neurohormones in ways that deepen sleep quality, and the 1–2 hours gives it time to do that.

2. Beds are for sleep and sex. The idea here is to train your body to expect great sex; wait, sorry . . . train your body to expect *sleep* when in the bed. The two go together. The sex part is just in here because sleep hygiene doesn't have to be so extreme as to interfere with your sex life, if you're fortunate to have one, in which case you understand that sex is difficult enough to maintain without prohibiting use of the bedroom. The point of this recommendation is simply to create an unconscious association between the bed and sleep.

Unfortunately, this means you can't do things in bed that could interfere with this association. No food, no reading, no computers or phones, and no television.

3. Avoid stimulating activity before bedtime. Anything you do in the hour before bedtime will influence how deeply you sleep. You want to turn on the slow brain waves in that time. Meditation, relaxation, and even imagination (such as visualizing fantasy scenes) can all bring you there. Avoid problem solving, goal-oriented thought. Avoid worry, intense discussion, and angry e-mails. Steer clear of the television, especially those frightening news shows, comedy that energizes with laughter, and political rants that induce righteous indignation. If you feel better with something on, try music or audio programs—not only will you avoid the blue light of the TV, but these can activate your imagination as you picture what you're listening to. Vigorous exercise before bed is also a problem, though exercise in the late afternoon can deepen sleep.

You don't need us to remind you about caffeine, but: have you figured out the latest hour in the day that you can get away with it? For many people that's around noon. And did you know that chocolate has caffeine in it? It does, and the dose goes up as the chocolate darkens (white chocolate has almost none; milk chocolate, some; dark chocolate, quite a bit).

4. *Daytime napping.* Sleeping during the day reduces your sleep drive and confuses your circadian rhythm, both of which will worsen insomnia. A possible exception is for people over age 60. As you age, sleep tends to become more fragmented. Older people fall asleep earlier, wake up more often, and may effectively sleep in two shifts. A few studies have found that a brief (20–60 minute) afternoon nap improves concentration without any negative effects in older individuals. If you use this approach, try to nap at regular times and avoid napping too long.

5. *Alcohol's double effect.* Alcohol can briefly energize you (wee) then make you sleepy. Thus, many people think "just a little shot at bedtime" will help them sleep. And it can indeed help you fall asleep. But after about 2–5 hours, depending on your metabolism and other factors, that alcohol wears off and when it does, *zing*, your brain rebounds awake. It's like pressing down on the bedsprings and then suddenly letting go. So while alcohol may help with initial insomnia (difficulty falling asleep), it tends to create middle insomnia (waking up after a few hours and having difficulty getting back to sleep).

6. *Regular rise time.* Waking at a regular time is one of the keys to maintaining your circadian rhythm. That rhythm is one of the two forces that create sleep. Lose rhythm, lose sleep. But this is really difficult sometimes. You lay awake much of the night and finally fall asleep around 4 A.M., and then you're supposed to *get up* at 7 A.M. just because some guys who don't have sleep problems tell you to? No. You get up because you understand that if you don't, you are inviting your clock to rotate. You'll have even more difficulty falling asleep that night and have more difficulty getting up the following morning. So you leave your alarm clocks on and allow them to push and drag you out of bed even if you don't have to get up for kids or the other job.

7. *The anxiety download.* A colleague of ours says that "Planning, after dark, becomes worry." If you take worries to bed, they'll keep you awake (same fight-or-flight physiology problem) or make it difficult to get back to sleep in the middle of the night. Of course no one worries for fun; what are you supposed to do with it?

Try what another colleague calls an anxiety download. Before you get in bed, take a pad of paper and write down, fast and furious, all the thoughts you're going to have 10 minutes later while you're lying there hoping to fall asleep. Or the ones that will keep you from getting back to sleep at 3 a.m. For some people, simply writing them down seems to decrease the energy behind them. Once you're in bed, you can remind yourself that there's no point in going over that stuff again, you already did that.

Finally—though be careful with this one, it can turn into planning that should have been done at 4 p.m.—some people like to make two columns on the paper. One is for worries they can do something about and when they plan to do it. The other is for worries that are beyond their control. You may recognize this distinction from the Serenity Prayer:

> God grant me the serenity to accept the things I cannot change; the courage to change the things I can; and the wisdom to know the difference.

Whether in two columns or just writing free, the idea is to put some of your anxious energy onto the page before you get in bed.

8. *Basic relaxation technique.* This is not woo-woo, not meditation; this is simple stuff, something to focus your mind on besides worry. You can do this in bed in the middle of the night (for up to 20 minutes; more on that in a moment). It beats lying there *thinking*! That's very unlikely to help you get back to sleep.

The most basic relaxation technique is simply breathing, but breathing in a deliberate way. Try this simple method:

A. Breathe in slowly, counting to yourself, "in–2–3."
B. Hold briefly.

C. Breathe out slowly, counting again, "out–2–3."

D. Notice the quiet space before deciding to take the next breath, in–2–3. Slow the whole thing down but breathe again whenever you're ready.

While you're doing this in bed, you can place one hand on your belly, noticing it rise and fall with each breath. Now, here's the key. After you take two or three such breaths, your mind will wander back in with some juicy thought, probably an anxious or angry one. Before you know it, you'll be thinking again. But the simple beauty of this technique is: Just notice that this has happened, that you're *thinking* instead of counting. Let go of the thought and turn your attention back to your breathing. You might end up doing this for the next 20 minutes, repeatedly letting go of an intruding thought and returning your focus to each breath. You might have to let go of a thought every few seconds, but you'll still be more likely to fall back to sleep than if you lie there *thinking*. And you'll be better off physiologically. These breathing exercises move you toward physical relaxation. You'll find an app to guide you further on our website (mood-treatmentcenter.com/bipolarnotsomuch).

9. *If you don't fall asleep after 20 minutes, get up.* This is another standard sleep hygiene recommendation. Have a comfy chair near your bed with a dim light and a dull book (even better, use a low-blue light like the ones from Chapter 10). One of our patients is an accountant, and she reads her tax books. Read until you're tired and feel like falling asleep, then climb back into bed. If you're not asleep in 20 minutes (but don't watch the clock!), it's back to the chair again.

Two reasons for this seemingly harsh requirement:

A. This helps maintain an association between bed and sleep, not bed and a struggle to sleep.

B. You should only get in bed when tired; doing otherwise is to force sleep, which means back to the struggle.

10. *How to think about not sleeping.* It's easy to lie awake and worry about insomnia, especially with all the emphasis we've placed on the relationship between good sleep and stable moods. And of course that worry does not help you get back to sleep.

Granted, if steps 1–8 haven't worked and you're in a mixed state or irritable hypomania where sleep is essential, you should consider taking a sleep medicine in addition to this approach.

But if your mood is okay, and you're just having difficulty sleeping; or if you're depressed, and are averaging 10 or 12 or 14 hours of sleep every 24 hours, then not sleeping *is not a problem unto itself.* Your body *will* sleep, because the longer you go without it, the stronger your sleep drive will become.

Thus arises one last simple step, before the hard one: Just notice what kind of thoughts your mind is offering you about sleep. Or rather, about not getting it. If your mind comes up with all sorts of terrible things about how bad it is to not be sleeping, well obviously that won't help you sleep. Granted, it's understandable that your mind would come up with them at 3 a.m. "I have to go to work in three hours." "I have to give a presentation today." "The kids will be awake, and I'll be dog tired." Let those worries pass, and invite another thought: "Not sleeping is not a problem unto itself. I'll go read until I'm more ready to sleep. I'll have more sleep drive tomorrow night."

WHEN ALL ELSE FAILS: SLEEP RESTRICTION

This is the hard step we've been hinting at. It may be difficult to pull off without someone to help guide and encourage you.

Count the hours of sleep you've gotten per night, on average, over the past week. Don't fudge now, it will come back to bite you in a moment. Say you're getting a total of 5.5 hours. Okay, here's the deal: You can only spend 6 hours in bed (average sleep time plus 30 minutes). And you have to keep your previous regular rise time. So if you're getting out of bed at 7 a.m., you can't go to bed until 1 a.m. During this sleep window from

1 a.m. to 7 a.m., if you're awake in bed for more than 20 minutes, follow step #9 above.

This technique is part of cognitive behavioral therapy for insomnia (CBT-I). CBT-I has a very good track record for treating insomnia. It works better than medications for most people, though it takes a few weeks to fully kick in. The sleep restriction component we're looking at here is the hardest part, but also one of the most powerful parts.

After several nights of the narrow sleep window (your average time asleep plus 30 minutes), you can add back 15 minutes of time in bed, per night. But your sleep efficiency must stay high. Most of the time you're in bed, you need to be asleep. If that falls off, back up a step (in other words, make your "sleep window" narrower again, to make sure that you're likely to stay asleep most of the time).

You might wonder if it's safe to limit your time in bed so severely, especially with the link between sleep deprivation and mania. Good point. If you are prone to manic symptoms or have Bipolar I, we recommend restricting your time in bed to no fewer than 6.5 hours when using these methods.

The goal of adding sleep restriction to sleep hygiene is to reestablish a strong circadian rhythm and a set of sleep habits to maintain it. In research trials, the majority of patients who go through all these steps see a dramatic improvement in their quality of sleep, without the risks that come with medications (Edinger & Carney, 2014). It can be difficult to find a therapist who's familiar with these techniques, so we've listed a few apps, online programs and old-fashioned workbooks that can guide you further with this on our website (moodtreatmentcenter.com/bipolarnotsomuch).

There are times when sleep medications are needed, as too much insomnia can lead to major mood problems. For people with bipolarity, that risk is often greater than the risks that sleep medications bring. There are several options that have very low risks of dependence, and using sleep medicine along with the behavioral strategies in this chapter reduces that risk even further.

We'll cover specific sleep medicines in Chapter 22. Next, let's shift from the nighttime and look at how daily activity can help depression.

TWELVE

Getting Active

Key point: *Depression causes avoidance, which then causes more depression. Purposeful action can reverse that cycle. Consistency is key: Taking small daily steps does more good than making giant leaps every now and then.*

You've seen how doing things at regular times helps stabilize mood and sleep. Timing matters, but so does quantity and variety. Low activity levels, and monotonous, directionless days can cause depression.

This chapter shows you ways to break the vicious cycle between motivation and activity that fuels depression. Low motivation leads to low activity. The vicious part is that low activity levels cause depression, which then lowers motivation further, and on and on. It doesn't have to be that way, however. Imagine a scenario where your motivation drops and you hide out in your room for a few days. Eventually you feel so stir-crazy that you call a friend and go out for dinner. Instead of feeding more depression, those few days of loafing triggered you to get active.

Taking action like that is a great way to prevent low moods, but it's difficult to do it consistently if you're already in a deep depression. If that last paragraph left you thinking, "Yea, I should call someone," but you feel light-years away from actually doing it, then you may need to pause and reorient before stepping into action.

There are some mental steps to take first, before you try to change your daily life. This is best done with the help of a therapist, and there is a form of therapy that focuses on this called *behavioral activation* (Martell,

101

Dimidjian, & Herman-Dunn, 2013). We'll introduce you to the basics here, with the understanding that reading it on your own may not be enough to get you moving. As long as you're clear on that—there's no expectation that reading this chapter will get you to change your life— read on.

Good, you've made the first step. Letting go of expectations can actu-ally help you step out of that depressive stagnation. Expectations can help you along when your mood is good, but face it, depression doesn't inspire people with very positive expectations. Most possibilities get buried in fears of rejection, failure, or sometimes just a nameless dread. You can't block out those fears, but you can practice recognizing them for what they are: It's depression talking, not the truth. Picture yourself stepping back from those thoughts, as though you're seeing them through a foggy window.

Next, notice what you do at each moment in the day. When we ask people with depression what they did last week, the number one answer is "nothing." That amazes us, because it's physically impossible to do noth-ing. If you're sitting in an arm chair flipping channels, then you're *chan-nel surfing*. If you're worrying about the class work that you're behind on, then you're *worrying about school*.

Once you're able to observe what you're doing, try to get in touch with the effect that each activity has on you. How did you feel afterward? How did it compare with the expectations you had beforehand (the ones you let go of, remember?). Did you enjoy it? Did it give you a sense of accomplishment? Would you do it again?

Likewise, start to think about why you do what you do. Depression makes people feel like they have no choices and make no choices. It's a powerless, helpless state, but it's not the truth. "Everything feels like a punishment. All I think about is escape—if I had any choice I'd run away from it all, but I don't know how to do that except to sleep and numb myself out." It can feel that way, but in reality, your life has some freedom and some limits, much like anyone else's. You are not powerless, and you do make real choices even if it feels like you have no say in them.

There is a reason behind everything you do. If you're depressed, the most common reason is probably *avoidance*. For example, you stay in your room because you don't want to risk seeing your neighbors or anyone you'd have to talk to. You're staying in to *avoid* the unpleasant, anxious, or negative emotions that would come up if you went outside. Notice: you're not really trying to avoid people. You are avoiding the feelings that come up when you run into them.

There is nothing wrong with avoidance. We all do our share of it, Aiken and Phelps too. We just want you to come clean and admit that you're no different from us when you do it. Like us, you *choose* to avoid. Sometimes we cover ourselves up in a blanket or zone out in front of mindless TV as well. Avoidance can be a guilty pleasure, we just ask that you recognize that you have the power to make that choice. Nobody is forcing you to avoid.

Avoidance is not always the wrong choice, but too much of it can slow your recovery from depression. Like any guilty pleasure, it's best in small quantities. Now that you're able to recognize the reasons behind what you do, start to look for other reasons besides avoidance. Here are some that people often have when they're not depressed:

1. "I enjoy it."
2. "It's a responsibility I have to take care of."
3. "It's a step toward something better in my future."
4. "It's part of my beliefs and values."

Give yourself credit whenever you do something with those motivations in mind. Write it down and pay attention to the outcome and how it affected you. These kinds of things can shake up the system that's keeping you down.

A mix of pleasurable, constructive, social, and value-driven activities will help you step out of depression. You may not feel it at first because depression has a way of smothering the goodness that comes with those.

Pleasure? How's that possible, when a key symptom of depression is the inability to experience pleasure? Constructive things? You might be able to do them, but it's not likely you'll give yourself credit for the accomplishment when depression has your confidence locked up. Social? Not an easy one. Values? Depression can make everything seem meaningless, which keeps people from the higher callings that inspired them in the past.

That's a pretty bleak picture, but fortunately it's rare that depression has a 100% hold in all those areas. This is hard work. You've got to look for areas in life where you can still feel pleasure, connect with people, and find meaning and reward in the things you do. While you're searching, you've got to start trying new things, even if only out of blind faith that it might help. If you can't think of anything, try Appendix C. We've listed dozens of simple ideas that patients found helpful in their depression. Pick one at random and see what comes of it.

Congratulations—you made it through all the steps. Let's summarize:

1. Step back from your expectations.
2. Become aware of what you do each day.
3. Get in touch with how each activity affects you.
4. Recognize that you're making choices every day, and think about the reasons behind them.
5. Let go of your judgments. There are no bad reasons or bad actions. Focus on the results of your actions rather than the judgments or expectations you have about them.
6. Look for times when you're doing something for a positive reason, rather than to avoid anxious or unpleasant feelings.
7. Slowly add new activities into your day, even if they don't help or feel good at first.

This takes a lot of patience. You may not feel that great after trying it for a week. You may even feel worse at first, as you'll be taking on the things you've been dreading and avoiding, but it may not be as bad as you anticipated. Give it time—it takes a few weeks before the hard work you're doing pays off and the depression starts to lift.

Most people do some journaling to help make a habit of those seven steps. You could keep a calendar or list of what you do, why you did it, the expectations you had going into it, and the actual effect it had on you. On our website you'll find smartphone apps and workbooks that can guide you further in this work (moodtreatmentcenter.com/bipolarnotso-much).

Once you get the hang of these steps, they'll start to come more naturally. Any new activity will help you fight depression. Depression doesn't like novelty, change, risk, or creativity, and it won't stick around long if it realizes that's the game you're playing.

THIRTEEN

Exercise? How About Just Walking

Key point: *Brisk walking three times a week, 45 minutes per day, treats depression as well as an antidepressant, but has a more lasting benefit.*

You've heard it before, exercise is great for your health, everyone should do it, so on, and so on. So let's face it, there must be something very difficult about getting exercise (in the U.S. culture, anyway) because even though everybody knows it's a good thing, so few people actually do it.

We don't expect depression to make this any easier, so aim for a simple plan here. No gym. No trainer. Let's look at the evidence.

THE BEST EVIDENCE YOU EVER HEARD

Tara scheduled a visit because her depression was slowly coming back. Her mind was sluggish, her energy low, "I just don't care much about anything." She had been doing well for over a year and was as puzzled by this change as her doctor. Her life was going well, and she hadn't experienced any recent stresses or physical illnesses. "What about exercise—you'd been so diligent about that—have you kept it up?" "No, my walking buddy has a new job and hasn't been able to meet me, so I kinda let that slip. Come to think of it, I started to get depressed a few weeks after I stopped."

We hear stories like that every week. One time, Aiken spent a long session trying to figure out why his patient had fallen back into depression, until he looked down and saw the man had a medical boot on his leg and clearly hadn't been able to keep his routine of riding a bike to work. People don't always make the connection between their movement and their mood. We didn't either, until we saw the research and started asking the right questions (and looking at patient's feet!).

That story began in 1999 when psychiatrists at Duke proved that exercise could work as well as the popular antidepressant sertraline (Zoloft). That's great, or maybe it's a good reason to sit back and take some sertraline. Those researchers took it one step further when they checked up on their patients 6 months later. By that time, depression had started to creep up on the ones who had taken sertraline. Specifically, 38% of those on medication fell back into depression compared with only 8% of those who had recovered through exercise (Babyak et al., 2000).

Since then, over 50 other studies have come up with similar findings. Exercise doesn't just help depression, it improves anxiety, sleep, energy, concentration, memory, and decision making (Cooney et al., 2013; Kelly et al., 2014; Pedersen & Saltin, 2015). It even has benefits for two of the hardest brain illnesses to treat: schizophrenia and dementia (de Souto Barreto, Demougeot, Pillard, Lapeyre-Mestre, & Rolland, 2015; Rosenbaum, Tiedemann, Sherrington, Curtis, & Ward, 2014).

How does exercise achieve all this? Brain studies suggest that untreated depression can eventually lead to brain shrinkage, particularly in regions associated with decision-making (frontal lobes) and memory (hippocampus). Effective antidepressants all seem to increase the brain's growth factors and reverse this shrinkage. In 2003 we learned that exercise can do the same thing in a study titled "Aerobic Fitness Reduces Brain Tissue Loss." The authors began by reminding us that "the human brain gradually loses tissue from the third decade of life onward" (Colcombe et al., 2003). That means age 30. That's in people without depression. In mood disorders, the problem is bigger, and the solution is the same. Around 20 studies, involving over a thousand people, have taught us that exercise helps the brain repair itself in people with depression (Schuch et al., 2016). What type of exercise are we talking about?

The answer is one of the most important aspects of their study. The exercise program was . . . brisk walking. That's it. Brisk walking, three times a week, 30 to 45 minutes per day, produced these changes. Around 30 minutes might work, but 45 minutes seems to be the best dose.

Brisk walking means slower than a jog, but faster than a walk. Enough to raise your heart rate by 10 beats per minute and get you breathing a little faster. If you want to be exact, that means walking three miles, or 6,000 steps, in 45 minutes. If you're using a pedometer, those 6,000 steps need to be brisk ones, and above and beyond your usual daily stride.

Just like with medication, you can turn up the dose if that doesn't get you there. About 1 in 8 people respond better to more intense exercise (Rethorst & Trivedi, 2013)—just a little more intense, such as changing the walk to a jog or adding resistance training (weight lifting) to the routine. But as with medication there's also a max dose. Going beyond that does not bring additional brain benefits. In the words of one research group, "too high-intensity exercise may create hatred toward it and have negative consequences" (Ranjbar et al., 2015).

If walking isn't right for you, any light aerobic exercise at the same frequency could also work. Swimming, dancing, basketball, cycling, and rapid house cleaning are all aerobic, as long as it raises your heart rate and breathing. You could even break it up into 10- to 15-minute chunks instead of doing it all at once. Breaking it up like that can have better effects for weight loss, as it raises your metabolic rate throughout the day.

There's also good evidence that tai chi, yoga, and resistance training (weight lifting) can treat depression, but these require equipment or training. Stretching and walking slowly don't have the same benefits, but stretching is great to add to the routine. If a slow walk is all you can muster, start there. Remember: slow, weak muscles are a symptom of depression, and that's what you are trying to treat. It will get better with time. We take the same approach with medication when we start at a low dose and raise it gradually.

We'll stick with brisk walking for the rest of this chapter. It's the easiest and most accessible, and it's where most of the research points us. It's safe for nearly everyone. If you've had recent pains in your chest or arm, dizzy spells, or problems with your heart, lungs, or bones, you should talk to your primary care doctor first.

As amazing as these findings are, we suspect you may have heard something like them before. So why isn't everybody out there moving?

WHAT KEEPS PEOPLE FROM EXERCISING?

Let's face it: it is much easier to focus on what is right in front of us than to think about the long-term. There are plenty of other matters that require immediate attention. Your children's needs, your boss's expectations, paying the bills. The list goes on and on.

So it's clear: Exercise is not going to start happening regularly just by reading that it will help you feel better in a couple months. Actually, the benefits come on a little quicker than that, in about 4 weeks, and they continue to build in the months thereafter. But that's still a ways away compared to more immediate priorities. For mothers, this will be meeting someone else's needs. For good responsible workers, it will be pleasing the boss or the customer. For students, it will be the upcoming exam. Benefits tomorrow, or preventing a dam-burst today: guess which one wins? So to overcome this pattern, you've got to have a system that can put exercise in front of almost everything, or it won't happen. That means lowering the barriers or raising the benefits, or both. Let's start with the barriers, as they tend to be more of a problem.

LOWERING THE BARRIERS

Remember these three T's: time, tools, and traditions. Lack any one of them, and your walking routine is in trouble.

1. *Time*. Most people in the United States have tight schedules that would need adjusting in order to make room for regular walks. If you believe it's important, you'll have to find a time for it.

2. *Tools*. All you'll need is comfortable shoes. You don't need a gym membership; if you prefer walking indoors, a shopping mall will do. A treadmill is optional, but you may prefer their softer terrain if joint pain is an issue. A flat treadmill doesn't require as much exertion as the sidewalk, but that can be overcome by setting it on a slight incline.

3. *Traditions*. We needed a T-word for routines and habits. You don't decide to brush your teeth at night. You don't think, oh, I'm looking forward to brushing my teeth tonight. You just do it because you always do it. You will need to turn walking into the same kind of routine. If this is a decision you have to make every day, rather than a habit, there are just too many chances that you'll decide on something else.

Walking Toward Health

Brisk walking doesn't just help the brain. It's among the top things you can do to improve your physical health and increase your life span (by about 3.5 years; Moore et al., 2012). Here's just a few areas in your body that will improve with walking:

Strengthens bones
Slows aging
Lowers stroke risk
Improves heart and lung health
Relieves arthritis and joint inflammation
Builds muscles
Weight loss
Deepens sleep quality
Reduces pain by lowering endorphins
Improves memory and prevents dementia
Lowers cancer risk

Lowers blood pressure, cholesterol, and lipids
Prevents diabetes
(Pedersen & Saltin, 2015).

RAISING THE BENEFITS

What if this was actually fun? That is how kids do it, right? When did adults stop using that approach, and why? When you look at what many adults do for exercise, you'd think they weren't interested in fun anymore. Are they really that short on ideas on how to have fun while moving around?

If you can't find something fun, better raise the benefits some other way. Here are two more: First, you can try charting your progress. Lots of people are motivated by seeing themselves make gains. Pick an outcome that is very likely to change. Don't use weight loss; that tends to happen slowly with exercise (diet is three times faster). Try speed, endurance, strength, skill, or heart rate at a given level of exertion. You can even track exercise itself: what you did and how long you did it, because that in itself will be an achievement for many people. Chart your mood as you take on this routine, or add exercise to your mood chart (see Chapters 16 and 17).

Finally, if there are some significant others around who will benefit from your exercise program (because *your* mood will be better), you can measure their benefit as well as your own, and use that as an additional incentive. Are they acting nicer toward you? Are they less angry, or crying less?

Playful Aerobics

Swimming

Hike in nature

Put on audio books or music

Dance

Place the treadmill in front of the TV: you can only watch that show
    if you're on it. Or strap a tablet to your treadmill.

Join a kickball or softball league

Turn business meetings into walking meetings

Jumping jacks

Play a very active video game (Wii tennis, Wii fit, Just Dance)

Shoot hoops

Roughhouse with your kids

Roughhouse with your dog

Roller or ice skating

Wash the car

Belly dancing

Sign up for an adult gymnastics class

Use a standing desk

Park far away

Play tag with kids

Rowing

Do your shopping and errands by foot

Choose an active volunteer job, like Habitat for Humanity

Explore a new area

Jump rope or hula hoop

Walk the dog, or someone else's dog, or volunteer at an animal shelter
    to walk a dog

Join a martial arts class

Aerobic cleaning (scrub, vacuum, sweep, mop, rake)

Bike to work

ARE YOU READY FOR A SIMPLE PROGRAM?

If you just heard "no" to that question, then the limiting factor may be motivation. Of course motivation is not a depressed person's strength, right? If you have depression, you know this: Cooking dinner is hard enough. And look, even people who aren't depressed don't exercise regularly. Most surveys indicate that at least half of all Americans get no regular physical activity. So if *they* don't, why should you expect that you can? After all, you're the one with the mood problem, right?

Ah, but there's an irony here, one that you might be able to use to your advantage. Motivation may not really be necessary. Motivation is a feeling, right? An inclination, a state of energy, and willingness. Yet people act differently than they feel, all the time, right? They may feel like yelling at their kids, but they choose to wait, calm down a little, and speak softly but firmly. So, maybe you don't need to be motivated.

For those of you who are very depressed, you might be thinking that the depression itself is holding you back. You might think this whole exercise idea will have to wait until you're feeling better. But that doesn't have to be the case. One depressed patient said, "I agree it is very difficult to walk when one is suffering depression, but I have forced myself out the door many times, knowing from experience I will feel better when I return home."

SHOULD YOU WALK ALONE?

When Dr. Aiken first heard about the benefits of walking, he suggested it to all his patients. Months went by, and no one took it on, until finally a man with depression said he had started walking regularly. "Wow! How do you keep that up?" His answer: "I really don't want to do it, but I don't want to let my friend down. I told Dave I'd meet him every morning, and we walk together."

We've seen the same pattern again and again when people connect their routines to a friend or—just as reliable—a pet. Lately that motivation has become virtual, as people connect with friends through their pedometer and encourage each others' progress. Your sense of obligation is a powerful motivator. Depression usually doesn't take that motivation away, and can even raise it. Guilt, after all, is a symptom of depression, and people with depression tend to take care of others before they take care of themselves.

Still, that's a delicate balance, and we wouldn't want the potential of guilt or shame to keep people from walking. You may feel greater ease about taking these steps if you don't tell anyone except that walking buddy. You probably don't need all the added pressure that brings on. So, try staying mum: Say you're going to go for a little walk and be back in about 15 minutes. That will do for today.

PAY YOURSELF FIRST

There's a book series out there on how to build wealth, called *Rich Dad, Poor Dad*. There is a striking idea in these books: Pay yourself first. The author says that you shouldn't put your money in savings *after* you've paid the electric bill, the gas bill, the insurance bill, and so on, but put the money in first. Wait a minute, you say, what if you're out of money at the end of the month and can't pay those basic bills? Ah, he says, doing it his way will show you: Either you need to reduce your expenses, or make more money—but either way, the most important step for your future has already been taken (Kiyosaki, 1997).

This is the opposite of the usual, responsible approach to money. Note that the key idea is: Make your future such a priority that it gets top position. Assume that otherwise, the daily stuff will be so much more obvious to you—after all, there's that bill from the gas company right there on the table—that you will risk, every month, not being able to invest in your own future.

If exercise is an investment in your future, you can see how this idea can apply to your walking routine. If everybody else's needs get taken care of first, before you can invest in your own future, then every day your long-term needs will be pushed to the bottom of the list. Isn't that pretty close to your experience? What would happen if you paid yourself first? After all, you can't really help other people very well if your end of the boat is sinking.

FOURTEEN

Diet

——

Key point: *Our top three dietary changes for depression: lower calories, reduce saturated fats and simple sugars, and increase fish (particularly salmon). If your goal is weight loss, caloric reduction works better than exercise, but exercise beats diet in its antidepressant effects.*

The food you eat plays a role in the brain's health just as it does for the body. Changing your diet is not going to cure depression, but it can improve mood and concentration. These changes aren't easy to make, particularly if you're depressed, so you might save this chapter for a day when your motivation isn't buried in 6 feet of quicksand. Better to prioritize. If you can only make one lifestyle change when you're depressed, we'd recommend the walking routines in the previous chapter.

Many of the dietary changes that doctors recommend for physical health are also good for the brain, so you'll get two birds with one stone here. Let's look closer at these, and then we'll focus in on foods that have specific brain benefits.

CALORIC INTAKE

Lowering your daily intake of calories will help you lose weight, and this alone can make your medications work better. This isn't just because self-image improves when people shed pounds. Obesity increases inflammation in the body in ways that cause depression and interfere with the benefits of medications (Woo, Seo, McIntyre, & Bahk, 2016).

Yet calorie counting is stressful (there are even studies showing that the stress of calorie counting interferes with weight loss; Tomiyama et al., 2010). We recommend an easier route. It turns out you can lower your appetite by spreading your meals out and increasing your intake of protein and fiber. Remember all those times your mother told you not to spoil your appetite before dinner? Well, breaking that rule is at the heart of this diet. Below are the basic steps in order of importance—start with the ones that are easiest to do.

- *Eat five meals a day* by adding a high-protein or high-fiber snack before lunch and dinner. Good options include nuts (a handful of nuts a day actually extends the life-span; low-salt nuts are best), raw fruits or vegetables (try a little peanut butter on carrots), and protein bars (Bao et al., 2013).
- *Eat a high-protein breakfast* within 30 minutes of waking. This will lower your appetite throughout the day. Good options include eggs, Greek yogurt, cottage cheese, nuts, and smoked salmon (Leidy, Bossingham, Mattes, & Campbell, 2009).
- *Cut sodas.* Sodas contribute more to weight gain and other health risks than almost any other popular food. Changing to diet sodas is a good first-step, but keep in mind those can actually increase your appetite in ways that prevent successful weight loss (Suez et al., 2014; Yang, 2010).
- *Increase fiber.* Fiber helps you feel full, relieves constipation and hemorrhoids, lowers cholesterol, and prevents cancer (Slavin, 2013). Good sources include fresh fruits and vegetables, beans, whole wheat breads and pastas, brown rice, bran cereal or oatmeal, popcorn, and fiber supplements.

BAD FATS AND SIMPLE SUGARS

Reducing these two ingredients will not only lower your risk of diabetes, heart disease, and high cholesterol, it will help brain growth in ways that can prevent depression (Jacka et al., 2010; Opie et al., 2015).

The main fats to avoid are saturated and trans fats. Those come from fast food, fried food, non-lean and processed meats (e.g., bacon, ham, salami, hot dogs), milk, margarine, lard, and some snack foods. Try substituting these with healthy alternatives:

- *Dairy:* plain or vanilla yogurt (add fruit/honey yourself), low-fat milk or cheese. Milk made from tofu, soy, almond, or rice (without added sugar).
- *Snacks:* for the absolute healthiest options, try nuts, seeds, fresh fruit, vegetables (carrot, celery), edamame, and seaweed. Second best: popcorn without butter (it's a whole grain), dried fruits (in small quantities, they have lots of sugar in them), hummus, guacamole, almond or peanut butter, and raisins covered in yogurt or chocolate.
- *Packaged snacks:* look for those that are high in fiber and low in corn syrup, saturated and trans fats. Consider low-salt pretzels, veggie or tortilla chips.
- *Meat:* grilled lean meats (fish, chicken, turkey, pork, bison, roast beef, lamb). Choose cuts that are graded "choice" or "select" instead of "prime."
- *Oils and butter:* healthy oils (olive, walnut, canola, safflower, sunflower oil).

Simple sugars are found in sweets, white bread (pizza, rolls, sandwich bread), and high fructose corn syrup. Healthier substitutions include:

- *Sweeteners:* honey, agave nectar, maple syrup, rice syrup (made from brown rice), stevia, xylitol, Whey Low. Reduce sugar by eating whole fruit instead of fruit juice. Or, for a drink, make your own smoothie by blending whole or frozen fruit in a food processor with water or yogurt.

- *Healthy grains*: whole grain breads, cereals, crackers, and crispbreads. Oatmeal, brown rice, bulgur, wheat berries, whole wheat pasta.

Next we'll look at foods that have specific benefits for the brain.

OMEGA-3 FATTY ACIDS

Omega-3 fatty acids coat brain cells and help make them more flexible. Around 30% of the brain is made up of these essential ingredients, and people who don't get enough in their diet have higher rates of depression and bipolar (Opie et al., 2015). Omega-3s are also called fish oil, as fish is the most common source for them. The two omega-3s that are critical for the brain are ethyl eicosapentaenoic acid (EPA) and docosahexanoic acid (DHA). In pill form, omega-3s are almost as powerful as an antidepressant, and unlike antidepressants, they also help stabilize mood and prevent bipolar disorder.

A regular diet of fish could actually provide enough omega-3s to treat depression, though some fish (e.g., salmon) have much greater amounts than others (e.g., catfish). Table 14.1 lists the amount of each type of fish you would need to eat to treat depression, ranked by cost. The daily amounts could be converted to weekly (multiply by 7) and eaten in a single meal.

Among the options above, salmon rises to the top, and you don't need to buy expensive salmon. In 2013, the *Washington Post* conducted a blinded salmon taste test with professional chefs. To their surprise, Costco's frozen salmon (farmed Atlantic from Norway, frozen in 4% salt solution) was the favorite—by a wide margin. Another low-budget option, Trader Joe's farmed Atlantic, came in second (Haspel, 2013). By our calculations, the Costco frozen steaks are more cost-effective than most pill forms of omega-3s.

TABLE 14.1 Omega-3s from Fish: Daily Amounts You'd Need to Treat Depression*

Food	Ounces/day	Price/day
Salmon, farmed	1.3 oz	$0.49
Herring, Atlantic	1.8 oz	$0.68
Mussels	4.5 oz	$1.13
Trout	3.8 oz	$1.90
Caviar	0.5 oz	$2.10
Albacore (white) tuna	4.1 oz	$2.31
Anchovy	1.7 oz	$2.41
Atlantic mackerel	2.9 oz	$2.54
Oysters	5.1 oz	$2.55
Sardines	3.6 oz	$3.15
Salmon, wild	3.4 oz	$3.83
Swordfish	4.3 oz	$4.03
Golden bass (tilefish)	3.9 oz	$5.61
Shark	5.1 oz	$6.38
King mackerel	8.7 oz	$7.61
Halibut	7.6 oz	$9.50
Snapper	11 oz	$10.31

The fish we didn't list above have significantly less omega-3s and would require 2 to 3 servings a day to get a decent dose. They are, in order from most omega-3s per serving to least: crab, scallops, Atlantic cod, Atlantic pollock, shrimp, farmed catfish, clams, light tuna, mahimahi, and lobster.

There is controversy about pollutants such as mercury in fish, but most experts believe the benefits of fish outweighs those risks, and rec-

*Omega-3s in tables 14.1 and 14.2 were calculated from the USDA National Nutrient Database. For nonfish sources, the necessary daily amounts were multiplied by a factor of 10 to account for limited uptake by the brain.

ommend eating at least 1 to 2 servings of fish per week. The concern about mercury may be greater if you are pregnant, but even there, the harm of not eating omega-3s is also greater if you are pregnant. Fish with high mercury content are shark, swordfish, tile-fish, and king mackerel.

What about nonfish options? There are plenty of vegetarian sources of omega-3s, but they don't have the type of omega-3s the brain needs (they contain alpha linolenic acid (ALA), rather than EPA and DHA). Only 10% of the omega-3s in vegetarian sources are converted into forms the brain can use. However, with a little determination, you might be able to make it work. Table 14.2 shows what we found when we did the math on the best vegetarian sources of omega-3s (admittedly, most options are not realistic as a treatment for depression).

TABLE 14.2 Omega-3s from Vegetarian Sources: Daily Amounts You'd Need to Treat Depression

Food	Daily dose
Nuts and seeds:	
Flax seeds	0.25 cup
Chia seeds	0.35 cup
Hemp seeds	0.75 cup
Walnuts	1 cup
Pecans	10 cups
Oils:	
Flaxseed oil	0.7 oz
Canola oil	5 oz
Soybean oil	5 oz
Mustard oil	6 oz

As you see there, it's possible to get enough omega-3s through flax seeds, chia seeds, walnuts, edamame beans, and spirulina seaweed. Flax seed oil, which can be mixed into salads or smoothies, could also get you there. After that, the amounts you'd need to ingest get a little unrealistic if your goal is to treat depression. Don't let this turn you away from these foods though. Vegetables, beans, fruit, and nuts have

Beans:	
Edamame	1 lb
Soy beans	4 lb
Mungo beans	7 lb
French beans	8 lb
Navy beans	13 lb
Kidney beans	13 lb
Lentils	60 lb
Vegetables:	
Kale	12 lb
Brussels sprouts	13 lb
Cauliflower	13 lb
Spinach	16 lb
Broccoli	19 lb
Collards	24 lb
Acorn squash	60 lb
Butternut squash	85 lb
Cabbage	160 lb
Fruit:	
Raspberries	18 lb
Blackberries	24 lb
Strawberries	34 lb
Blueberries	39 lb
Cantaloupe	48 lb
Kiwi	53 lb
Mango	60 lb
Honeydew melon	68 lb
Bananas	82 lb
Cherries	86 lb
Pineapple	130 lb

Other:	
Wheat germ	3 lb
Seaweed, spirulina	0.7 lb
Seaweed, agar	25 lb

so many other benefits for the brain and the body that we'd recommend them for anyone's diet.

FLAVONOIDS

Flavonoids are nutrients found in fruits and vegetables (especially in the skin). Good sources include berries, black and green tea, parsley, citrus fruits, almonds, peanuts, quinoa, and most fruits and vegetables. Their antioxidant prosperities enhance brain-growth and improve mood and memory (Letenneur, Proust-Lima, Le Gouge, Dartigues, & Barberger-Gateau, 2007). Berries seem to slow the cognitive decline that comes with age. The amount of berries you would need to eat to get that benefit is about 0.5 cups of blueberries or 1 cup of strawberries a week (Devore, Kang, Breteler, & Grodstein, 2012).

Another example of the flavonoid effect comes from tea. Drinking three cups of tea lowers the risk of depression by 37%, and the benefit doubles when you go to 6 cups a day (Dong et al., 2015). The benefit is strongest with black and green teas. Though not a flavonoid, coffee has similar benefits. People who drink coffee have lower rates of depression, but unlike with tea, that antidepressant effect does a reversal when you drink too much. The antidepressant effects of coffee level out around 1 to 2 mugs per day (2.5 metric cups); beyond that it seems to cause depression (Grosso, Micek, Castellano, Pajak, & Galvano, 2016). Drinking any caffeine after 2 p.m. can worsen mood by disrupting sleep, but with tea the flavonoid effect we're describing here holds up for decaffeinated options as well.

Two other sources of flavonoids are best taken in limited amounts: dark chocolate and red wine (once the dose of wine goes beyond 5 ounces per day, the toxic effects start to outweigh any brain benefits).

CASHEWS

Word that two handfuls of cashews a day can treat depression has gone viral on the Internet. It's an unproven claim, based on the amount of tryptophan in cashews, not on studies of people who ate those cashews. Tryptophan is involved in the production of serotonin, and it has a mild antidepressant effect when taken over the counter. However, it seems to have the opposite effect in people with bipolarity, so we recommend moderation with the cashew idea (Applebaum, Bersudsky, & Klein, 2007; Sobczak, Honig, Nicholson, & Riedel, 2002). That seems to be the underlying message in this chapter: All things in moderation, except tea.

CURCUMIN

This ingredient of turmeric helps prevent dementia and has benefits in depression and anxiety. The main food source is curry, but if that's not to your liking, it can be taken in a capsule. The dose used for depression is 1 gram per day, and the curcumin BCM-95 form is preferred (Al-Karawi, Al-Mamoori, & Tayyar, 2016).

GLUTEN-FREE DIET

This is complicated territory. Even in patients with celiac disease (the full immune-based reaction to wheat gluten), evidence for mood improvement on gluten-free diets is limited. Patients who stuck to the diet did better, in terms of mood. But was their mood improvement due to the diet, or due to some other factor associated with being the kind of person who can stick with a somewhat difficult diet for a prolonged period of time? Maybe such motivated people were also doing more physical activity, for example.

Nevertheless, gluten can clearly generate gut inflammation, even in people who don't have celiac disease. And gut inflammation has been linked to a body-wide inflammatory response that itself is linked to depression. So the possibility that one can treat or prevent depression by changing gluten intake is still an active area of research.

FIFTEEN

Managing Substances

Key point: *Recreational drugs are a two-edged sword, and some are sharper on the harmful side than others. The risks are different for people with mood disorders, and there are ways to minimize them.*

Medication, or recreational drugs? Marijuana, alcohol—or worse, methamphetamine, heroin, and the like: In the long run, a thoughtful approach with preventative medicine has to be better than chasing the tail with self-medication. For some street drugs, that should be easy to figure out. Meth does not work as well as a mood stabilizer, for example. People use methamphetamine when they've given up on other ways to get out of feeling awful. The good news, then: Perhaps there is hope for some other way out of that awful place. Maybe you have a mood problem, as well as a meth problem. When people can see that, meth is easier to give up. Not easy, but easier than when there is no hope of things changing.

On the other end of the spectrum, marijuana seems to help some mood symptoms and worsen others. You can say the same thing about some medications. Biases abound on all sides here, so we'll do our best to step back and look at this subject with a fresh set of eyes. There are some surprises here.

CAFFEINE

No question you can cause trouble for yourself with this stuff. At a minimum, it can interfere with sleep if used after, say, 2 p.m. Everyone metabolizes it differently, so for some folks that's more like noon. Large amounts can add to anxiety, which is already a problem for many of our readers, and even worsen the side effects of some medications (like tremor and dry mouth).

On the other hand, if those things aren't issues for you, then caffeine itself probably isn't a problem. However, if you are drinking large amounts, you could wonder what problem you're trying to fix with caffeine. Sleep deprivation, sleep apnea, ADHD, and a host of things that impair concentration or energy may be going on under the surface. Some of those can be dangerous if they go on too long, particularly sleep apnea (see Chapter 25).

If you're starting to question your caffeine, please don't stop it all at once (the withdrawal headaches are terrible). Lower it slowly, perhaps by gradually mixing in some decaf. How slow? That varies—if you get headaches you need to go slower.

ALCOHOL

Fear not: We're not going to imply moral failure or insist on abstinence here. On the other hand, just a few drinks a day can cause depression in some people (Jaffe et al., 2009). Then there are people who can get away with small binges once in a while and stay okay (we don't recommend trying to find out if that's you; it's a dangerous wager).

The key here is to keep track of your results (do good science, in other words). Approach alcohol just as you approach medications. What outcomes are you getting? Are they dose related? If you can't figure out what it's doing, one of the easiest ways to get a clean slate is to take it out entirely for a while and then start over. If things are going smoothly, you could try putting it back in, but do so in small amounts, when nothing else in your life is changing much.

Pardon, did we say "When nothing else is changing?" Life doesn't really stand still for these experiments, does it? But at least try to change one thing that you can control at a time. If you're adding a medication, for example, don't add back your alcohol at the same time. You might think the medication is messing you up when it was really the alcohol. Pretty basic, huh?

How much alcohol is okay for most people? This is highly variable, and the answer depends on how alcohol affects your mind as well as your body. Let's start with the body. New recommendations came out while we were writing this book. Pay attention, as they are stricter than the old ones:

- No more than one standard drink* per day (on average), and no more than 3 drinks on any given day.
- People should have 2 to 3 drink-free days each week to allow their liver to recover.
- Drink alcohol slowly, and drink it along with plenty of water.

The old guidelines allowed men to drink double those amounts, as they metabolize alcohol quicker than women. However, a host of new research prompted England's chief medical officer, Sally Davies, to lower the safe limits in 2016. The main reason for the cut is cancer risk. She pointed out that staying below these new guidelines would save 20 in 1,000 people from cancer (Weaver, 2016). High blood pressure, heart disease, stroke, and liver disease are among the other reasons to keep within the new limits. For some people, the safe amount may be even less than these limits (for example, people of Asian descent, those over age 65, and those with health problems that alcohol can worsen).

Now for the effects of alcohol on mind and mood. You can figure out

---

*A standard drink is 12 ounces of beer, 5 ounces of wine, or 1.5 ounces of 80-proof spirits.

your own quota by going without alcohol for a week, or two, or preferably a month or so to get a better baseline, and then adding back a little bit at a time. Of course in the interim, hopefully your mood is becoming quite stable, either from taking out alcohol, or from adding some mood stabilizer treatment (nonmedication or medication approach, hopefully both). Once things are going pretty well, then if you're willing to risk it, you can add back a little alcohol and see how that goes.

In our experience, an acceptable amount of alcohol is like what is healthy for most people: Rarely more than one drink per night, and at least several nights per week with none so your body doesn't get used to having it around.

METHAMPHETAMINE, HEROIN, PCP, SPICE, AND COCAINE

If you've ever used any of these harder drugs we're guessing that you found it slightly useful in the short term but pretty disastrous in the long run. Yet even those negative effects can fuel an addictive cycle, giving more reason to use again—why not, life's a wreck anyway.

If that's where things are for you, get help so you can figure out what's wrong and start over. On the other hand, for those of you who have been through several treatment programs (or for your loved one who may be reading this for you): Is it possible that you have a mood disorder driving your substance use? In some ways, that doesn't matter. You still have to get clean to have much chance at all in the long term. But if you keep getting nowhere with treatment, and especially if there's been a hint somewhere that you have a mid-spectrum mood problem, then you could try treating the mood problem *while you are still using*. Not our preferred approach, of course, but frankly it often happens that way. And it works, sometimes. If only it was every time.

Methamphetamine and cocaine can take a toll on mood and concentration. There is a natural supplement that may help repair some of that damage. Citicoline has unique benefits in people with bipolar who've abused these drugs. It helps them stay sober, and also improves concentration and mood (see Chapter 22).

MARIJUANA

Here the balance of benefit and harm is much more complicated. Patients figured this out a long time ago. In the free clinics where Dr. Phelps has volunteered, people often had no access to medications for bipolar. They found that "just a puff or two of marijuana before I go to bed helps turn my mind off so that I can sleep." On the other hand, marijuana can cause depression to drag on or even trigger paranoia and psychosis in people with bipolar. It's a two-edged sword.

Marijuana's effects are hard to pin down because it's really a mixture of many drugs. There are over 85 active cannabinoids, and their ratio varies greatly by the plant. The high from marijuana comes from tetrahydrocannabinol (THC), and the amount of THC in commonly available marijuana has increased dramatically in the past few decades. It's a much more potent drug than it was in the 1970s.

Marijuana's calming effects likely come from a different chemical called cannabidiol (CBD). The spread of medical marijuana in recent years has led some growers to produce strains with more CBD and less THC. One of these, called *Charlotte's Web*, has become rather famous after speculation that it may have antiseizure effects. *Charlotte's Web* has 15% CBD and very little THC (less than 0.3%). Not much is known about CBD's mental effects, but over 15 studies are currently underway as of the time of this writing, so stay tuned (Devinsky et al., 2015).

Marijuana's effects depend so much on what's in the plant that blanket condemnations of this drug don't make much sense. Actually, thinking critically about the risks and benefits is a good idea for any drug—including prescription ones. The risks to watch out for with marijuana are:

- Paranoia and psychosis
- Decline in IQ level

- Depression and low motivation
- Anxiety
- Altered brain development
- Heart and lung disease
  (Volkow, Baler, Compton, & Weiss, 2014).

Among these, psychosis is the one we'd be most concerned for in our readers, as you'll recall from Chapter 5 that people with mood disorders are already at risk for this problem. So if you're using marijuana, pay close attention to this next paragraph—it may be the most important one in the book. If you're young and plan to continue using marijuana despite the risks, which could be a very bad idea, you might be able to tilt those risks a little back in your favor with a natural supplement called fish oil. Fish oil?

Yes, fish oil. The same brain food we talked about in Chapter 14. A remarkable study found that it dramatically reduced the development of psychosis in adolescents and young adults. The researchers gave fish oil or a sugar pill to 81 people who were at high risk for psychosis. Six years later, 40% of those who took the sugar pill had gone on to develop psychosis while only 10% of the ones who got the fish oil had that fate (Amminger et al., 2010). Remember, that was 6 years after they took the fish oil, and they only took it for 3 months (some may have continued it on their own for longer). We were floored by these results, as we know how hard it is to prevent psychosis. Even antipsychotics have failed to protect vulnerable people from this devastating disorder (though they can treat psychosis after it develops).

You'll find more about how to use fish oil in Chapter 23, as it's also one of the best supplements for bipolar and depression. The dose they used to prevent psychosis was similar to what we recommend for mood disorders (in this case, 700 mg of EPA omega-3s and 480 mg of DHA omega-3s per day).

The pros and cons of substances could fill a whole book, and we've only highlighted the ones that are most relevant to readers with mood disorders. We'll get back to this subject in Chapter 22, where we'll roll out a few medications and natural approaches that can help both mood and addictions. But that approach rarely works alone, just as reading that a drug is harmful is not likely to shock people out of addiction. Most people need something more—a therapist or a 12-step group—to make that kind of change.

That's not much different from the rest of the ideas in this lifestyle section. They are a lot easier to stick to when you've got other people supporting you.

SIXTEEN

Coming Soon: Bipolar and Technology

Key point: *Apps and devices are helping people take control of their physical and mental health and see the connection between them. Everybody's doing it, which is a good thing when it comes to reducing stigma.*

Bipolar disorder is more common in modernized, urban cultures than in their rural counterparts. We've looked at some of the reasons behind that in this book, including electric lights, lack of exercise, and poor diet. This chapter turns the tables and looks at ways that technology can help people manage mood disorders. This is a rapidly evolving field, so we'll keep the links and apps updated on our website (moodtreatmentcenter.com/bipolarnotsomuch) in case they've changed by the time you're reading this.

ELECTRONIC MOOD CHARTING

Mood charts are a great example of how paper and pencil can outperform high-tech solutions. A few months of data on a mood chart would tell more about what to do with your medications than modern brain imaging. Mood charts are starting to enter the digital age, as numerous apps are available to help you track all that data.

Most apps only track emotions, which is not as accurate as tracking moods, so we looked for one that would track both manic and depressive symptoms. We also wanted one that allowed back-dating of entries—

you may not remember to enter your mood every day, but back-dating is nearly as good. Last, it had to be free and easy to use.

These apps all fit the bill:

Moodlog: The simplest option. Tracks depression, mania, and, if desired, sleep and medications.

DBSA WellnessTracker: This app was developed the Depression and Bipolar Support Alliance (a national support group), and tracks depression, mania, and everything else you could imagine. This includes lifestyle factors, physical health, medications, and labs. Fortunately, many of these are optional so you can keep it simple, and it has good definitions for all the symptoms, which makes it a great place to start if you're just learning how to recognize them.

ThriveSync: Almost as comprehensive as the DBSA WellnessTracker, this app tracks depression, mania, anxiety, irritability, self-care, and allows free-entry journals.

Triggers: This one is not specifically for bipolar, but is great if you like to customize things. You can create your own names for the symptoms you track, as well as lifestyle factors that might influence those symptoms.

The bottom line: We recommend *MoodLog* for simplicity, and DBSA *WellnessTracker* for those who like to follow a lot more than just depression and mania.

AUTOMATIC MOOD MONITORS

When you think about it, many symptoms of bipolarity could be measured by a smartphone. The phone's accelerometer knows if you're moving fast or slow, and the GPS tracks whether you are depressed and homebound or traveling in a manic frenzy. Social and shopping apps light up during mania, and the phone itself could measure your rate of speech.

Actually, someone has thought of that, and the results are just becoming available. One of these, *Ginger.io*, is ready for use and allows free access if you sign up for one of their research programs (www.mood-matters.org). Others, such as *PRIORI*, *CrossCheck*, and *Companion*, are not yet publicly available.

Some may find this approach too invasive, and we sympathize with that, but this is also the direction that physical health is going. More and more people are wearing activity trackers like FitBit and Jaw Bone, which monitor their steps and heart rate. Devices that give you feedback on your sugar levels while you eat are also underway. These devices encourage people to be involved in their own health, and to consider both their mental and physical health as they strive for wellness. We hope that kind of integration can help reduce the stigma of mood disorders.

SLEEP MONITORS

An overnight sleep study can measure your quality of sleep by analyzing the pattern of brain waves during sleep (a *polysomnogram*). These waves reveal phases of sleep, such as REM and slow-wave sleep, which make up your *sleep architecture*. This kind of information could be useful for someone with bipolarity. For example, you could monitor your sleep architecture before and after starting a new medication or lifestyle change to see if it is affecting your sleep quality.

New devices are coming out that can estimate sleep quality at home by measuring your movements, heart rate, breathing, and temperature. The best of these products, the ResMed S+, does all those things without requiring you to wear any awkward devices in bed.

We can't vouch for the accuracy of the S+, but the manufacturer has a long history of making medical-grade sleep devices and claims their S+ monitor has been tested against standard polysomnograms.

Just as with mood charting, the accuracy of any given sleep rating may be off, but over time, the pattern can give you some confirmation that changes you're making in your life are improving the quality of your sleep. The S+ also gives you personalized tips based on your reading, such as adjusting the lighting or temperature in your room (both of which it measures). The device is small (8 inches tall), pairs with a smartphone, and costs around $130.

Two other options that don't require you to wear a device are Beddit and Withings Aura. These use a motion-sensing pad that goes under your mattress. These devices are more expensive, but they were less reliable than the ResMed in a comparative test by the *Wall Street Journal* (Stern, 2014).

Cheaper versions (from free to $3) are available as smartphone apps that use the phone's accelerometer to estimate sleep quality. The problem with these are that body movements only roughly correspond to stage of sleep, though they may give a reasonable estimate of your total sleep length. Examples include *Sleep Cycle*, *SleepBot*, and *Sleep Time*, which uses an algorithm designed at Stanford University, for iPhone or Android. Some of these also monitor for sounds (such as snoring or getting out of bed), and all require you to sleep with your phone next to the pillow. Many activity monitors, such as FitBit and Jaw Bone, can also measure sleep when worn at night, and these have the same limitation of relying on body movements.

Home sleep measurement is a new field, and it's not exactly clear how to use it with mood disorders. Mood charts usually record sleep duration, so a measure of sleep quality would fit right in with that and could help you and your doctor fine tune your treatment. If your mood chart suggested that changes in sleep quality were causing new episodes, that information could help guide your medication options or lifestyle choices.

Besides the potential for inaccurate readings, there is another downside to using a sleep monitor. Sleep experts have found that people with insomnia tend to overthink their sleep. It's possible that all this new data could worsen sleep by fueling that kind of obsessive worry. On the other hand, having a machine do the tracking could relieve an insomniac from staring at the clock. Others (perhaps those who've read this far in this book) find their anxiety goes down when they have more information.

APPS FOR MENTAL HEALTH

The following programs are just some examples among many apps and websites available. These are some of the best that we know of at this writing, but these sites can change quickly. You'll find a few more in Appendix D.

We're interested in high-quality programs that are free and likely to stick around. As with self-help workbooks, these programs work best when used with a real, person-to-person therapist. Remember, you're doing this stuff to change your brain, and human interaction changes it faster than paper or digital.

Two great programs from Australia offer cognitive-behavioral therapy (CBT) for depression and anxiety:

- Mood gym (for depression, moodgym.anu.edu.au)
- E-couch (for anxiety, ecouch.anu.edu.au)

Another therapy that helps depression and anxiety is mindfulness. It's defined as "the basic human capacity to pay attention on purpose, with intention, in the present moment, in a friendly and nonjudging way." Mindfulness is meant to be practiced daily, and there are many audio guides that take you step by step through the process. The Mindful Awareness Research Center at UCLA has free audio guides for download (marc.ucla.edu/body.cfm?id=22). There are many mindfulness apps for the smartphone. Among the most popular are *Headspace, Smiling Mind, iMindfulness,* and *Mindfulness Daily*.

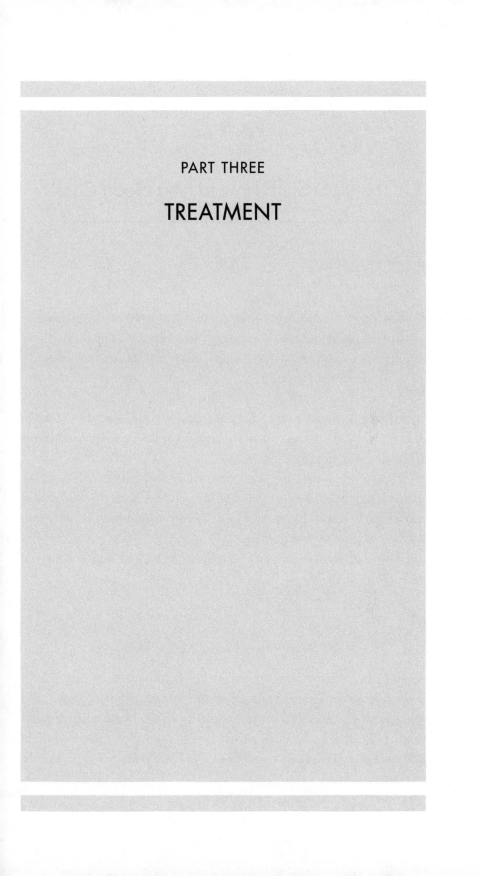

PART THREE

TREATMENT

The Right Stuff: How to Find Good Care

Key point: *Specialists in bipolar are in short supply, as are psychiatrists in general. Other professionals have stepped in to fill that gap. Regardless of whom you see, there are things you can do to maximize your success in treatment.*

Your doctor may have a lot of medical training, but you are the expert on one thing: *you.* Your expertise in this area is the key to accurate diagnosis and effective treatment.

However, you may not want to walk in and tell your doctor how to diagnose you because the relationship you have with this doctor also matters. It matters a lot. So you have to be prepared to work with your doctor and their style of practice.

This chapter gives you tips on finding a doctor and helps you prepare for your first visit.

FINDING A GOOD DOCTOR

Finding a psychiatrist who understands bipolar disorder is no easy task. In many parts of the United States, there are shortages of psychiatrists, and other providers have stepped in to fill this gap. There are psychiatric nurse practitioners (NPs) who are as knowledgeable as some psychiatrists and do much of the same work. In some states, these NPs practice independently, and in others under the supervision of a psychiatrist. There are also physician assistants who've undertaken advanced training in the field and can prescribe medications under the supervision of a psychiatrist. Primary care doctors are also stepping in, and in many places, psychiatrists are available to them as consultants, so lately they've been learning much more about bipolarity—how to spot it and how to handle it.

Psychiatrists have more training than other providers, but we don't have a strong opinion about what type of provider you should see. We're more concerned that they are knowledgeable about bipolar and flexible enough to adapt to your needs. We'll use the word "provider" instead of "doctor" to honor these shifts in psychiatric care.

You may need to try a few methods to home in on a good provider, and there's more than one way to do that:

(1) *Support groups.* Most communities have local support groups for bipolar and depression that are run by people who've been through treatment themselves (see Appendix E). These leaders hear from dozens of patients each month about their experience with local providers. They often list their cell or e-mail online because they are committed to helping people like you find good care.

(2) *Other doctors and therapists.* While the support groups have more direct experience with providers, your primary care physician can guide you toward a provider whose skill and professionalism commands their respect. Therapists may have even more in-depth knowledge, and if the therapist is sensitive to the needs of bipolarity, their opinion should hold great weight.

(3) *Professional groups.* You can also call professional groups to see if they know of physicians in your area who specialize in bipolar. The American Psychiatric Association and the International Society for Bipolar Disorders are good starts (see Appendix D).

Some professional groups bestow specific titles on the providers they designate. For psychiatrists, the most important professional designation is *Board Certified Diplomat,* from the American Board of Psychiatry and Neurology. This means the psychiatrist has not only completed their training but also passed the exams that doctors take every 10 years. For NPs, the most advanced designation is psychiatric nurse practitioner (PMH-NP). Physician assistants can complete advanced psychiatric training but currently don't have specific credentials to designate that.

(4) *Specialty centers.* Some cities have mood or bipolar clinics where therapists and physicians work together. These are often at academic hospitals that are part of a medical school. Academic physicians often take a very scientific approach to their work (a good thing in bipolar) and stay up-to-date on the latest research.

In an ideal world, you would get medication, therapy, and family therapy from the same person. That's a rare thing today, for each of those fields has become too specialized for one person to stay on top of all of them. This is not always a bad thing, as two providers can offer a greater perspective on the complex problems that bipolar brings. Your therapist and medication provider see you with different eyes, and hopefully, they can help each other see past their blind spots.

WHAT IF YOU CAN'T FIND/AFFORD/GET TO A SPECIALIST?

Many people do not have good health insurance or can't find a psychiatrist who is taking new patients. How are all these people supposed to get help for depression with bipolarity?

Here is where the psychiatric consultation may help. If you can get to a primary care provider, and if he has access to a psychiatric consultant, you may still be able to get specialty services right there in your general doctors office. This is the model Phelps is working on in Oregon. If you're stuck in this position, first finish reading this book. You'll learn a lot about bipolarity, possibly more than your primary care provider knows. That will put you in a better position to help your primary care provider help you.

You'll need to use the "Strategies for Working with Your Provider," coming up shortly in this chapter. And if you're lucky, there may be a psychiatrist working in the background as a consultant to your primary care provider. We're going to see a lot more of those partnerships in the U.S. because the Affordable Care Act has created new revenue streams to encourage them.

PREPARING FOR YOUR FIRST VISIT

Gathering key information before your first visit can save valuable time, allowing more room for discussion with your provider. This can be a daunting task (as if you're not already overwhelmed from depression), so we've divided it into the essential and the optional. You'll find a printable template with this information on this book's website (moodtreatment-center.com/bipolarnotsomuch). However, simply getting to the first appointment is an achievement for many people, so if that's what you can do at this point, just do that. Essential for the first visit:

- Current medications
- Past psychiatric treatments
- Family history

Optional for the first visit:

- History of current episode
- Past medical history
- Alcohol and substance use

Use a "just the facts" approach as you organize this information. The goal is not to overwhelm your new provider with a full biography. Anything longer than two typed, double-spaced pages is likely to distract from rather than enhance your first meeting. The longer it is, the more organized it should be so they can quickly find the information they need.

Current Medications

List the medications you take, including nonpsychiatric, over-the-counter, birth control, and supplements. Include the tablet size (usually in mg) and number you take every day if it's a psychiatric treatment.

Past Psychiatric Treatments

Make a list of the medications you've tried in the past, along with the approximate date and duration you took them for, and the maximum daily dosage you took. Briefly mention any benefits or side effects they brought.

Approximations are fine here, but you can get more exact details by asking your pharmacist or past providers for records. Your new provider will surely appreciate your efforts in getting those records before your visit.

Also list past therapists and a little about your experience with them.

Family History

As you've probably gathered from this book, this part is critical. You may not know your relative's diagnosis, but any details you can provide about unusual kin will help. Did anyone have legal problems, a short fuse, bankruptcy, addictions, or impulsive behavior? Talk with your family to clarify if you can. Ask if they had any strong reactions to psychiatric medications—either good or bad ones—as those kinds of reactions tend to run in families.

History of Current Episode

Your present symptoms will get the most time and attention at your meeting, so writing this part down is optional. Think about when the problem started and what has made it better or worse. Bring any rating scales you've done from this book but present them as something you hope your provider can help you interpret (you want to let them make the diagnosis).

Past Medical History

Name any medical conditions you have and those from your past. Women should mention their menstrual status and the date of their last menstrual period if it is active (that will help reassure your provider that you're not pregnant now). Men as well as women should explain how they are handling birth control and safe sex. If you can dig up any lab tests from the past 1 to 2 years (especially thyroid), do so.

Alcohol and Other Substance Use

More than half of people with bipolar disorder use alcohol or other drugs, so your provider is unlikely to be shocked if you come really clean here. Don't fudge. Don't underestimate. Just put it out there. Hiding it doesn't make any sense: After all, you're seeing this provider for help, right? He needs to know what you're doing in order to be able to help you.

STRATEGIES FOR WORKING WITH YOUR PROVIDER

You may have a great provider already, with whom you feel communication is going very well. If so, that's great (you can skip this last section). However, if there's room for improvement, then here are some ways to improve things. You may be in for a challenge if you're trying to convince your provider to take a new approach, such as:

- Asking her to consider a different diagnosis
- Telling him you don't want to take lithium
- Asking her if your wife can sit in on the session to help make sure you understand everything

Fortunately, not all providers resist input from patients about diagnosis or treatment. If they are really open-minded, you may be able to walk right in and say what's on your mind. But if that's not the case, here are some thoughts:

- *Start small.* If you're unsure how they'll respond to your ideas, start with something small. For example, you could ask for more information about an aspect of your illness. "I'm sorry, but I think I missed the reason we're checking my blood count while I'm taking this medication. Can you help me understand that?"
- *Providers need to feel valued.* So, start by making them feel valued. But, as you do this, you've *got to be sincere.* Find something he has done that you do truly appreciate. Then tell him, "Doc, I really appreciate the way you've . . ."
- *Assure them that your questions won't take much time.* Providers often have very busy schedules that can make them seem rushed. Try an opener like, "I have a few quick questions, and if I need to make another appointment to address it, that would be fine."
- *Providers need to feel in charge.* There are some good reasons for this, such as being responsible for their actions and vulnerable to lawsuits. Be understanding of their needs, but don't shortchange yours in the process. Instead, help them feel in charge by wondering what they think about something, and sounding like you don't know much about it.
- *If you are rebuffed, keep proceeding as best you can.* If it didn't go well, you might say something such as, "Oh, I understand what you mean. Treating me surely isn't easy, I know that." Hopefully, this is just a first exchange along these lines, and you're going to come back and try again. Start with something smaller next time, perhaps?

These steps are even harder for family members who want to be involved with the treatment. Relatives usually don't have a relationship, however strained, with the provider. In that case, all these steps are even more crucial. Perhaps the most important thing to remember is that this provider is human too, and there are probably some really good reasons she is the way she is. You may be able to make some headway by trying to understand those reasons as you push forward.

WORKING WITH YOUR PROVIDER OVER TIME

You can ask your provider what information would be most useful to bring to your follow-up visits. It can be particularly helpful to rate your symptoms, and your provider may be able to suggest a rating scale for that. Many are available for free online (see Appendix D), or you could create your own by rating the symptoms that are most important to you from 0 to 10 (e.g., depression, irritability, anxiety). Other ideas to bring to follow-up visits include:

- *Medication list.* If using as-needed medicines, include how often you take them.
- *Current symptoms.* Rate their intensity from 0 to 10.
- *Side effects.* List any you think you may be having.
- *Weight.* For consistency, it's best to measure weight in the morning, naked, after using the bathroom and before eating.
- *Important life changes and current events.* List any that might be impacting your mood. Examples include travel, shift work, people moving in or out of your house, relationship or sexual changes (including planning pregnancy), exercise, diet and substance use, and anything that impacts your sleep.

Mood Charting

If you went to a top research institute, like the National Institutes of Mental Health, they would probably teach you to track your symptoms with a mood chart. In fact, they may find that more helpful in understanding your treatment than an MRI of your brain.

Mood charts were used by early physicians to identify different types of mood disorders, and were further developed by Robert Post to assess medication response. All you need to do is check how manic or depressed you are each day (or check both sides if you're in a mixed state). Consistency matters more than accuracy here. As long as you are consistent in how you rate it, the daily marks will form a pattern over time that reads like a weather map of your moods. There is no better way to decipher the long- and short-term effects of medications (and lifestyle changes).

A few tips on mood charting:

- You don't need to list your medications every day; just indicate when important changes were made.
- You can add other information, such as irritability, anxiety, sleep, and life events, but remember that it's easier to see patterns when the data is simpler.
- Make it a routine. That means the chart itself has to live in a location where you'll pass it every night. For example, hang it in the bathroom on a clipboard and fill it out every night after brushing your teeth.
- If you can't do it every day, back-track the data and enter it weekly.
- Try a smartphone version (see Chapter 16 or our online resources at moodtreatmentcenter.com/bipolarnotsomuch).

EIGHTEEN

Medications: Our Top Choices

Key point: *Medicines work like a lock and key, and the best choice is one that fits well with the receptors in your brain. The standard keys (antidepressants) often aren't a good fit for people on the bipolar spectrum so we'll present options here that tend to fit better with those depressions.*

If anticipating a brief medication visit provokes anxiety, you are not alone. The pressure to make use of that time can make your mind go blank—not the best state for making decisions about your health. We're going to try to make that easier in this chapter by sharing our top choices for people on the mood spectrum.

We set out to find two treatments that are worth consideration for nearly everyone with bipolarity. This was not easy. Remember, no two patients on the spectrum are alike. Even the goals they bring to treatment can vary widely. Some patients would rather suffer depression than risk gaining weight, while others actually request a medication that will help them put on a few pounds.

Despite this variety, most people on the mood spectrum will want a medicine that meets these basic goals:

1. Treat depression now.
2. Prevent episodes of depression later.
3. Do so with the fewest side effects and risks.

These are surprisingly tough goals to meet. Mood stabilizers can prevent depression, but most of them were designed for mania, and their benefits on the depressed side are much weaker. Antidepressants treat some depressions, but in people with bipolarity, they can destabilize mood, making depression worse. How about combining the two? That's been a popular strategy for decades, but recent studies have found that those combinations usually don't work (Pacchiarotti et al., 2013).

What we need is a *mood-lifting stabilizer*. Unfortunately, we had to make up that name, as the category doesn't yet exist. But there is one medicine that fits the bill and meets all three of our goals. Our second choice didn't do quite as well but still beat the rest of the options by a clear margin. And the winners are:

1. Lamotrigine (Lamictal)

This is the one that nearly satisfies all three wishes. Unfortunately, it carries a risk of an allergic reaction that for less than 1 person in 3,000 can be very severe (Mockenhaupt, Messenheimer, Tennis, & Schlingmann, 2005). After the first 3 months, the risk of this reaction goes almost all the way to zero. Otherwise, it's just about perfect for people in the bipolar spectrum.

2. Low-dose lithium

This is *not* the lithium most people associate with severe mental illness. Low-dose lithium also meets all three main goals: it treats depression, prevents later depressions, and *has few side effects for most people*. Unfortunately, it can cause weight gain (not as much as many of the options in the next chapter, but we have to tell you straight, it's not weight-neutral like lamotrigine). Though grogginess is rare with lithium, about 1 person in 10 will feel flat, dull, "like a zombie." That feeling usually doesn't get better with time though it can improve by lowering the dose. Outside of that, most people tolerate lithium very well, and it has minimal risks at low doses if it's handled properly.

And the third place goes too . . . Well, we couldn't decide. Phelps suggested tapering antidepressants, though that's not really a new medicine. Aiken suggested taking lamotrigine and lithium together. There are no interactions between the two, and the combination often works better than either alone (van der Loos et al., 2009). But alas, that's not really a new offering either.

Just as we were about to despair over the third-place contender, we realized patients had given us the answer all along. Remember that Internet survey where people with bipolar ranked the treatments they found most helpful? Their top 10 list only included two medications: lamotrigine and lithium. The rest of their favorites were all lifestyle changes. When we realized the wisdom in that ranking we moved the lifestyle chapters toward the front of the book, ahead of medications. Those lifestyle ideas bring about changes in the brain just as medicine does, so we think they belong in the top three choices.

We did think of a few other medicines that could work as mood-lifting stabilizers. These next choices aren't bad. Sometimes they are the best fit, and our top choices turn out to be awful. Medications work a lot like a lock and key. There's no such thing as a "strong key" or a "safe key"—the best key is always the one that fits your lock.

With that in mind, we'll scrap the top-choice idea at this point—the list that follows is in no particular order.

Atypical Antipsychotics

There are a dozen medicines in this broad family, but we're only going to focus here on the ones that treat bipolar depression. They are:

1. Quetiapine (Seroquel)
2. Lurasidone (Latuda)
3. Olanzapine (Zyprexa)
4. Olanzapine-fluoxetine-combination (Symbyax)

Atypical antipsychotics are among the most effective and fast-acting options for bipolar depression, so they almost made it to the top of our list. Several of them treat unipolar depression as well. That should be use-ful to a lot of readers who are right near the center of the mood spectrum. The trouble is that they have too many side effects, and too many medi-cal risks to recommend them whole-heartedly.

Weight gain, grogginess, zombie-like feelings, intolerable restlessness, muscle stiffness, uncontrollable movements (which can be permanent), sexual side effects, diabetes, high cholesterol, must we go on? We will in Chapter 20. For now, just know that these may be the right choice if you can tolerate them.

Carbamazepine (Equetro) and Valproate (Depakote)

These two mood stabilizers are very effective against manic-side symp-toms and mixed states. They can also prevent depression, but they aren't as good at treating depression, which is why they didn't rise to the top of our list. Still, mixed states are the main problem for some people on the mood spectrum, and for them, these may be the best choice. Both also carry medical risks and side effects that may be deal breakers for some.

These are not the only options for bipolar depression; they are just the ones that offer long-term prevention. In Chapter 21 we'll show you a host of options that treat bipolar depression but aren't known to prevent it.

The reason we focus first on prevention is that depressions tend to be frequent in the mood spectrum, so preventing the next one is often just as important as treating the one you're in. Because depression tends to be a long-term undertaking, it's critical to find a preventative strategy that's easy to live with day-to-day.

We have one more preventative strategy in mind that's free of side effects, doesn't involve new medications, and won't require you to change your lifestyle. It turns out you can stabilize mood by removing mood destabilizers, and the most common type of medicine prescribed for bipo-lar depression is one of these: antidepressants. We'll delve into that idea more in Chapter 20, but first let's look at the major mood-lifting stabiliz-ers in full detail.

NINETEEN

Mood-Lifting Stabilizers: The Full Details

Key point: *People on the bipolar spectrum need a medication to lift depression and prevent future mood problems, and there are a handful that can do the job.*

LAMOTRIGINE

Lamotrigine is the only mood stabilizer that calms mood swings by lifting the depression rather than suppressing the mania. That makes it a great choice for the bipolar spectrum, where the depressive symptoms usually outweigh the manic ones. Its greatest benefit is in prevention. It can prevent both the depressive and manic side, but its benefits are much stronger for depression and it does not treat active mania or hypomania.

Part of the reason patients prefer lamotrigine is that it's generally free of side effects. In fact, in the original research studies people reported more side effects on the placebo than on lamotrigine (that may sound impossible, but it's likely that lamotrigine helped them feel better physically by treating their depression). Lamotrigine is also largely free of the "medicated" feelings that people dislike with mood stabilizers. People don't tend to feel dull, flat, or groggy on it.

A remarkable fact about lamotrigine illustrates this. In the research studies, patients aren't supposed to know whether they are taking the placebo or the medicine, but most patients are pretty good at guessing which one they're on. *Lamotrigine is the only medicine we know of where patients were unable to tell they were taking the medication.* That means it didn't make them feel medicated, and its benefits built up very gradually. Its greatest benefits actually occur over the long haul. After 2 years, people taking lamotrigine had half as many days of depression as those who did not take it.

This does not mean lamotrigine has zero side effects—it's just that on average, nothing stands out as a major problem. In our practice we've certainly seen headaches, vivid dreams, and word finding problems on it. A few people have worse mood symptoms on lamotrigine, particularly agitation. This is a rare, and tricky, problem. It seems to happen when lamotrigine is started during a mixed state, though lamotrigine can also be very helpful for mixed states.

The biggest risk with lamotrigine is a rare allergic reaction called Stevens Johnson Syndrome, which can be fatal if left untreated. Many medications can cause this reaction, including antibiotics like Bactrim and penicillin and over-the-counter medications like Tylenol and Motrin. What's unique about lamotrigine is that there are things you can do to prevent it:

1. Lamotrigine has to be raised very slowly.
2. It should be stopped if any new rash or skin change happens while you're starting it (after the first 3 months the risk of Stevens Johnson Syndrome goes down to almost zero).
3. Avoid false-alarm rashes in the first 3 months of starting it (e.g. new soaps, sunburn, poison ivy, new medications).

With those steps, the risk of this severe rash is about 1 in 3,000; without them it's more like 1 in 100. Unfortunately, there is still a high risk of non-serious, benign rashes (10% chance), so many people have to stop lamotrigine to be on the safe side. If you responded to lamotrigine but had to stop it because of a rash, it may be possible to restart at a lower dose (Aiken & Orr, 2010). Details on that strategy are in the online supplementary materials (moodtreatmentcenter.com/bipolarnotsomuch).

When people respond to lamotrigine, they often say they can see

Quick facts: Lamotrigine

Brand name	Lamictal (generic is available)
Forms	Lamotrigine Lamotrigine ODT (dissolves in mouth) Lamotrigine XR (extended release version, not necessary for mood disorders but used for seizures)
Psychiatric benefits	Bipolar depression, rapid cycling, cyclothymia, borderline personality disorder
FDA-approval	Prevention of new episodes in bipolar disorder Epilepsy
Dose range	50–200 mg daily For women on birth control: 75–400 mg daily For people taking valproate: 25–100 mg daily For people taking carbamazepine: 100–400 mg daily
Tolerability	Very tolerable. No weight gain, fatigue, or sexual side effects. Vivid dreams and sleep disruption can occur. Although it improves concentration in low dosages, cognitive problems (such as difficulty finding words) can occur in the higher dose range.
Health risks	The main risk is a rare but potentially life-threatening allergic reaction called Stevens Johnson Syndrome.
Useful tips	Lamotrigine can lighten sleep quality so it's best to take in the morning. If you run out for more than 1 week, do not restart without contacting your provider (you may need to restart at a lower dose to prevent an allergic rash). Lamotrigine can make your skin more sensitive to sunburn, so wear protective clothing and sunblock (look for broad spectrum products with an SPF rating of at least 30). There is a version that dissolves in your mouth if the pills are hard to swallow.
Release date	12/27/1994

things in perspective better and are less reactive under stress. They usually still have days of depression, but these tend to be shorter and less frequent.

A surprising update just came in about lamotrigine as this book went to press. A British study found that folic acid supplements can cancel out lamotrigine's benefits (Geddes et al., 2016). No one expected that result, as folic acid usually helps depression, and other medications, like valproate and antidepressants, work better when taken with folic acid. More research is needed before we can fully trust this result, but until then, we recommend taking lamotrigine without any folic acid supplements, including those found in multivitamins (this warning doesn't apply to folate or methylfolate, which are different molecules). Once you're doing well on lamotrigine, if you decide to add folic acid, watch out for a potential loss of benefits.

LOW-DOSE LITHIUM

More misinformation surrounds lithium than any medication in psychiatry. Actually lithium is not a medication but a natural salt that's found in the earth and, in trace amounts, in the human body. Keep that fact in mind, as it will help you understand why this poor mineral is so misunderstood in a little bit. First let's highlight the reasons why we placed it near the top of our list:

- It treats both bipolar and unipolar depression, so is a natural choice for people in the middle of the spectrum. It also helps manic-side symptoms.
- When it works, its benefits can be lifelong. Lithium provides excellent prevention against depression. These properties led psychiatrist Nassir Ghaemi to call it "the closest thing to a cure for bipolar" (Ghaemi, 2006).
- It enhances brain growth more than any other medicine, a property that helps it prevent dementia (Salvadore, Machado-Vieira, & Manji, 2010).
- While all other mood mediations have a warning that they can cause suicidal thinking, lithium actually prevents suicide (Goodwin & Jamison, 2007).

How can one drug do all that? Actually, lithium is best thought of as three drugs, as it works very differently depending on the level in your blood (Table 19.1).

TABLE 19.1 Lithium Acts Very Differently Depending on Its Blood Level

Level	Benefits	Side effects
Very low dose (0.2–0.6)	Enhances brain health, promotes immunity and partially prevents depression, bipolar, suicide, and dementia.	Rare
Low dose (0.6–0.8)	Treats and prevents depression.	Few
Full dose (0.8–1.2)	Treats and prevents depression and mania.	Common

Because low-dose lithium has so many benefits and so few side effects, anyone with a recurrent mood disorder should consider it. Higher doses can be helpful in Bipolar I but are usually not necessary for people on the spectrum.

It's hard to know exactly who will benefit from lithium, though there are a few hints. Lithium works best if your manic and depressive symptoms don't overlap much (in other words, you don't have a lot of mixed states). Suicidal thoughts and a family history of response to lithium are also signs that point towards lithium. Lithium does not work as well if you have a lot of other psychiatric problems in addition to a mood disorder, such as anxiety disorders or substance abuse. If lithium works for you, it is likely to keep working, and it may allow you to reduce the number of other medications you take.

How Lithium Lost Its Shine

Few medications inspire as much fear as lithium, but things weren't always this way. To understand why, here is a little history. Lithium is almost as old as time (it was the third element to enter the universe), but we'll fast-forward to its more recent history.

Lithium's healing properties were known to the ancient Romans and Native Americans. By the early twentieth century, Americans were flocking to health spas to drink lithium water, which relieved headaches, physical pains, and nerve problems. Two U.S. presidents were so impressed with this very low-dose lithium that they had it shipped to the White House.

Lithium was so well thought of in those days that sodas like 7-Up and a version of Coca Cola were advertised as "lithiated beverages." Up to this point, lithium was beloved by the public, but doctors and scientists took little interest in it. All that changed in 1949, when an Australian physician named John Cade discovered that full-dose lithium treated depression and bipolar disorder.

Soon after this, lithium became regulated as a medication. That meant it was no longer legal to put it in sodas or sell the water that flowed in lithium mineral springs. A few years ago a company tried to revive the market for lithium water, but the FDA shut them down for distributing a medicine without a proper license (U.S. Food and Drug Administration, 2012).

Classifying lithium as a drug created a big problem for the little mineral. As a natural element, it can't be copyrighted, and this kept pharmaceutical companies from earning enough profit from it to support a promotional campaign. Promoting a drug involves more than TV and magazine ads. The industry sponsors educational conferences and books for doctors, support groups for patients, and press-releases for journalists. The goal of all this is to shift public opinion so that people feel more comfortable taking the medicine and doctors feel more confident prescribing it.

None of that happened for lithium. Although scientists consider it the most effective treatment available for bipolar, doctors in the United States rarely prescribe it (tellingly, it's used much more often in countries where heavy pharmaceutical advertising is not allowed).

Lithium and Suicide

It's a strange fact that nearly every psychiatric medicine has a warning that it can cause suicidal thoughts. In reality, there is extensive research showing that many of these warnings are overstated. What's really shocking is that most medications for depression don't have strong evidence that they *reduce* the suicide rate.

Lithium is the main exception to that. The rate of suicide in bipolar disorder is 20 times higher than in the general population. When people with bipolar take lithium, their rate of a suicide falls very close to that for the general population (based on data from 100,000 patients; Goodwin & Jamison, 2007). We have seen people who struggled with suicidal thoughts their whole lives find that those thoughts vanish after taking lithium.

Patients often tell us that this benefit won't apply to them, as they would never make that fatal choice. Our view is a little different. We don't see suicide as a choice but as a tragic outcome of a serious illness. Suicide is not the only cause of death in medicine, it's just the only one that has a lot of stigma surrounding it. Sadly, one of the best ways to prevent it—lithium—is also shrouded by stigma.

When we say that suicide is caused by an illness, we're not just speaking in analogies. There is an unnamed illness behind suicide, and it's not the same as bipolar or depression, though it's closely linked to them. This unnamed illness has more in common with impulsivity and violence than it does with mood disorders. Both the brain changes that lead to suicide and the genetic risks behind it are similar to those for impulsivity and violence. Amazingly, lithium lowers the risks of all three of these problems, regardless of whether someone has a mood disorder (Bauer & Grof, 2006).

There is a catch to all this good news though. Lithium is one of the easiest medicines to overdose on. Simply taking triple your usual dose can be toxic. For those contemplating suicide with lithium, we'll warn you that an overdose is unlikely to be lethal, but could leave you disabled by impairing your kidneys or your ability to walk.

This overdose risk means that many providers are reluctant to prescribe lithium to people who are suicidal, despite the evidence that it can prevent suicide. This is where a trusting relationship is essential; you don't want your provider to think you might take too much lithium whether intentionally or not. If you are having strong thoughts of suicide and want to consider lithium, have a family member lock up the pills and dispense one day's worth at a time. Bring that person to your appointment to help reassure your provider that you can take lithium responsibly.

Taking Lithium Safely

Lithium is generally safe in the normal dosage, but can be toxic if your blood level goes too high. There are a few things that can cause high lithium levels:

- Severe dehydration (e.g., from heat, alcohol intoxication, vomiting, or diarrhea)
- Accidentally taking too much
- Drug interactions

Many medications can raise lithium levels, especially blood pressure medicines, so make sure your medical doctors know you are taking lithium before prescribing something new. Talk with your pharmacist or check online for drug interactions (moodtreatmentcenter.com/bipolarnotsomuch). The only over-the-counter medicines that interact significantly with lithium are the nonsteroidal anti-inflammatory pain medicines (or NSAIDs). These include ibuprofen (Advil, Motrin) and naproxen (Aleve). Sometimes these medicines are hidden in other products so check the ingredient list. Aspirin and acetaminophen (Tylenol) will not affect lithium.

A toxic overdose can cause confusion, imbalance while walking, slurred speech, nausea, vomiting, diarrhea, and tremor. If you think your level is too high, stop lithium, call your doctor, and hydrate with fluids (Gatorade can flush out lithium, as can normal saline, which can be made by dissolving 1/4 teaspoon of salt in 1 cup of warm water).

Side Effects

We are genuinely surprised by how many people tolerate lithium, especially given its daunting list of side effects. Nearly all lithium's side effects occur at the higher dose range, which is used for full mania. For depression, a lower level is all that is needed, and side effects are rare. Those that do occur are usually manageable, with the most common being thirst, tremor, and nausea. Here are the side effects along with strategies to manage them:

Thirst: Drink water, reduce caffeine, use sugarless gum for dry mouth (e.g., Spry, SmartMouth). If all that water makes you wake up to urinate, avoid drinking in the 2 to 3 hours before bed.

Stomach problems: Nausea and diarrhea are common reasons for stopping lithium, but they are also among the easiest to help. Nausea improves with one of the extended-released forms (e.g., Lithobid or Eskalith), while diarrhea tends to get better with immediate-release lithium (when both problems occur, we've even found success by mixing extended-release with immediate-release tablets). Diarrhea can also improve with over-the-counter remedies like loperamide. Most nausea medications can be taken with lithium, but try a home remedy first: Take it with milk, ginger products, or even ginger capsules (1,000–2,000 mg daily).

Tremor: Lithium can cause a fine tremor that isn't dangerous or permanent. To improve tremor, first reduce caffeine. Propranolol is a well-tolerated medication that helps lithium (and other) tremors. Other options include primidone, gabapentin, and even high-dose vitamin B6 (900–1,200 mg daily; Goldberg & Ernst, 2012). All of these carry some risks, even the vitamin.

Fatigue: This is very rare on lithium (about 1 in 28 people have problematic fatigue on it, compared with 1 in 5 for many other mood stabilizers; Ketter, 2009). It can improve by taking the full dose at night (ask your doctor if that's safe, as higher doses may need to be divided throughout the day).

Concentration: Sometimes people feel flat, slowed down, or "like a zombie" on lithium, and this can improve with lowering the dose.

Poor coordination and muscle weakness: These side effects usually improve by lowering the dose.

Acne: If it does not improve with over-the-counter remedies, consider an antibiotic (e.g., doxycycline) or consult with a dermatologist.

Psoriasis: These are thick, dry patches of skin. Lithium may need to be stopped if they occur, or consult with a dermatologist. Two natural treatments for bipolar depression, omega-3 fatty acids and inositol, actually improve psoriasis.

Hair loss: Try the vitamin biotin (10 mg daily).

Weight gain: In the short-term, lithium can cause a little weight loss (Srivastava & Ketter, 2011), but there is a mild risk of weight gain with lithium over the long haul. Some of this weight gain comes from lithium's most common side effect: thirst. You can control that by avoiding caloric beverages and sticking with water.

Headaches: Lithium treats cluster-type headaches, but can also cause headaches as a side effect. This side effect usually improves with aspirin or acetaminophen (Tylenol) (you should avoid other over-the-counter pain meds as they interact with lithium).

Sexual dysfunction: A recent study found that this affected one third of patients taking full-dose lithium, and we've often wondered whether this was truly a side effect or if it had to do with the fact that full-dose lithium was restoring manic hyper-sexuality to normal levels. In this study, sexual problems were more common with the full-dose lithium that's used for Bipolar I. In our experience, sexual dysfunction is much rarer with low-dose lithium. One study found a surprisingly simple solution for it: Aspirin (240 mg daily) helped men who had erectile dysfunction on lithium (Saroukhani et al., 2013).

Medical Risks

Lithium has a few important medical risks. Some of these can be prevented by stopping lithium if warning signs appear in your labs. Unlike lithium's side effects, which tend to improve over time, its medical risks are more likely to occur the longer lithium is taken, and they may persist after it is stopped.

Lithium can lower thyroid levels. This is a common, but not very serious, risk because it is readily correctable with a thyroid supplement. More serious is the risk that your kidneys will slow down with long-term lithium use. Recent studies provide some reassurance here. This risk is lower than once thought, it can be managed by lowering the lithium dose, and it does not seem to progress to kidney failure (Kessing L.V., et al., 2015; Clos S., et al., 2015). The kidneys tolerate lithium better if it is given in a single dose of the regular release form. Another risk is mainly relevant to people with heart disease: Lithium can cause irregular heart rhythms.

Lithium also has a number of health benefits. It raises the white blood cell count, which helps fight infection. People who take lithium are less prone to colds and the flu. It is even used to treat some viral infections, such as HIV and herpes. It also reduces menstrual cramps (Bauer & Grof, 2006).

Stopping Lithium

It's usually best to come off psychiatric medicines slowly, but this is especially true for lithium. Stopping lithium abruptly can lead to worse mood swings, so it's best to come off over at least a 3 month period. There's another concern in coming off lithium. There have been people who responded very well to lithium and then tried to come off it. When their mood worsened, they thought again and decided to restart the medicine, only to find it didn't work like it used to.

If you've had a good response to lithium, consider yourself very lucky, as this is one medicine that can work for the long term. People who respond to lithium are less likely to need multiple medications because it is so powerful on its own. You may not want to risk losing that good response by coming off. If you're still set on stopping lithium after responding to it, talk with your provider about gradually lowering the dose. This may not give you the prevention you need, but it can prevent the withdrawal effect that makes people lose their response.

Quick facts: Lithium

Brand name	Eskalith, Lithobid
Forms	Instant release: Lithium carbonate Extended release: Lithobid, Eskalith Liquid: Lithium Citrate
Psychiatric benefits	Depression (bipolar and nonbipolar), mania, prevention of suicide, violence, and dementia
FDA-approval	Bipolar disorder
Dose range	The dosage depends on your blood level (see Table 19.1)
Useful tips	Lithium is better tolerated if it's taken all at night, but may need to be divided into morning and night if taking over 1,200 mg per day.
Release date	1949

CARBAMAZEPINE

Carbamazepine works extremely well for some people, particularly for the treatment and prevention of mixed states, but it has a longer list of problems than the medications you've seen so far. Fortunately, most of the serious problems are *really* rare. But there are new warnings about low bone density that have us concerned (Vestergaard, 2015).

Because it's going to sound bad shortly, here is a strong version of carbamazepine's benefits. First, it can *really* help people sleep who've been struggling with insomnia. Second, it's generally regarded as "weight neutral." Third, although it can have temporary side effects in the beginning, most people have no side effects at all once the target dose is reached.

The rare side effects with carbamazepine are:

- *Skin:* Similar to lamotrigine, it has a risk of serious rash, but here it's even less common than on lamotrigine. In people of Asian descent, this reaction can be anticipated with a genetic test (HLA-B*1502).
- *Blood:* Carbamazepine can make your blood counts go down.

White cells in particular can be affected, and you can't feel that, so blood tests are necessary to make sure this is not happening.

- *Liver:* Carbamazepine can bother your liver. Serious problems are *extremely* rare, we've never seen one, but minor liver irritation is possible. A blood test can be done for that too, and one may occasionally have to stop carbamazepine because of it.
- *Bone:* Carbamazepine has been implicated in reducing bone density (osteoporosis), though this is not certain. At this writing, there is still debate as to whether carbamazepine itself (and other antiseizure medications like it) are really the cause of the decreased bone density seen in patients with epilepsy. The risk is greatest in women; weight-bearing exercise, calcium (1,200 mg daily), and vitamin D all lower the risk (Vestergaard, 2015).

Finally, carbamazepine frequently interacts with other medications, lowering their blood levels. This can make it more complicated to use. Most of these interactions are manageable, with the exception of estrogen-based birth control, which can be rendered ineffective by carbamazepine. Another form of birth control (e.g., condoms or an IUD) is needed, because carbamazepine can cause abnormalities in developing fetuses. All pregnancies should be planned, especially for women taking carbamazepine, so that they can get off it before conception.

If you are considering carbamazepine, we hope you're able to work with a psychiatrist or other skilled provider who can help you compare its risks and benefits. This is tricky territory.

Oxcarbazepine (Trileptal) is a related medication that's often used as an alternative to carbamazepine. The main reason to consider oxcarbazepine is that it does not cause the rare blood problems carbamazepine does, nor the liver irritation, so blood tests are not needed. Unfortunately, in our experience it's just not as effective as carbamazepine. Oxcarbazepine also has a greater risk of lowering sodium levels than carbamazepine (this problem can be serious or mild and makes people feel like they have the flu). It also is not free of drug interactions, though the ones it causes are much less pronounced than with carbamazepine.

Quick facts: Carbamazepine

Other names	Carbatrol, Equetro, Tegretol
Forms	Regular release: 200 mg Extended release (Carbatrol, Equetro, Tegretol-XR): 100, 200, 300, 400 mg. These can be opened and sprinkled on food. Equetro is the version that was studied in bipolar. Chewable: 100 mg, Liquid: 100 mg/5 ml
Psychiatric benefits	Bipolar mania, mixed states, and depression; aggression
FDA-approval	Bipolar mania and mixed states, epilepsy, trigeminal neuralgia (nerve pain)
Dose range	400–1,600 mg/day
Tolerability	Dizziness, imbalance, fatigue, nausea, double vision, concentration problems
Health risks	Low blood count, low sodium levels, allergic rash, liver problems, bone thinning
Useful tips	To improve tolerability, use an extended release form and take in the evening. The dose may need to be raised after the first 2–3 months on it because the blood levels drop then (this is called *autoinduction* and only happens after you first start it). Grapefruit juice can raise carbamazepine levels.
Release date	3/11/1968

VALPROATE

Valproate (Depakote) has many of the same benefits as carbamazepine. It's better for the manic than the depressed side, and is very good for mixed states, rapid cycling, and people who have substance abuse along with bipolar (Goodwin & Jamison, 2007).

For some people, it may have more side effects than carbamazepine, especially weight gain, tiredness, nausea, and hair loss. It has about as many medical risks as carbamazepine, but they are different risks:

- *Pancreatitis:* Inflammation of this gland is serious and could lead to diabetes and digestive problems.

- *Liver:* Irritation of the liver is more common with valproate than with carbamazepine.
- *Viral illnesses:* Valproate can make some viruses replicate more, but it won't cause viral illnesses. This is only a problem if you carry a virus (particularly HIV and hepatitis C).
- *Polycystic ovarian disease:* This is a common hormonal disorder in women. It can cause serious problems, such as infertility, weight gain, heart disease, and diabetes. It can also make women grow facial hair and develop a more masculine figure.
- *For people with thyroid disease:* There are rare reports of valproate altering thyroid levels. This is true for most mood stabilizers.

Quick facts: Valproate

Other names	Depakote, Depakene, Valproic Acid, Divalproex Sodium, Valproate sodium
Forms	Tablet: 250 mg Extended release tablet: 125, 250, 500 mg Syrup (Depakene): 250 mg/5 ml Sprinkles (to sprinkle on food): 125 mg
Psychiatric benefits	Bipolar mania, mixed states, and depression; aggression
FDA-approval	Bipolar mania and mixed states, epilepsy, migraines
Dose range	Ideal blood level 50–120, may need to be on higher end for mania. It can be dosed by weight (weight in pounds × 9). The extended-release forms need to be raised by 10% to 20% to achieve the same levels as the regular-release forms.
Tolerability	Stomach distress, tremor, imbalance, fatigue, weight gain, hair loss, irregular menses
Health risks	Liver problems, low blood count, allergic rashes, possible polycystic ovarian disease
Useful tips	The divalproex sodium and ER forms are better tolerated than the others. Evening dosing is also better tolerated.
Release date	1/28/1978

Valproate has a few important drug interactions, but not as many as carbamazepine. It does not interfere with birth control, but it should not be taken while pregnant (serious birth complications, including low IQ, are very likely).

Valproate tends to work better and have fewer side effects if taken with these vitamins: folic acid, selenium, zinc, B6, and B12. This can be achieved by taking certain multivitamins* along with additional folic acid. The ideal dose of folic acid with valproate is 3 mg daily (Behzadi, Omrani, Chalian, Asadi, & Ghadiri, 2009).

ATYPICAL ANTIPSYCHOTICS

These are one of the most popular treatments for bipolar disorder, but we fear that may be because they are the most profitable (and heavily advertised) options. There are many available, and they all differ in their risks and benefits. Only a few are known to treat bipolar depression:

1. Quetiapine (Seroquel)
2. Lurasidone (Latuda)
3. Olanzapine (Zyprexa)
4. Olanzapine-fluoxetine combination (Symbyax)

Nearly all of them can treat mixed states and mania. A few also treat unipolar depression when added to an antidepressant, including quetiapine and olanzapine above, as well as:

1. Aripiprazole (Abilify)
2. Brexpiprazole (Rexulti)
3. Risperidone (Risperdal)
4. Cariprazine (Vraylar)

*Options include Centrum Silver, Puritan's Pride Men's One Daily, or Nature's Way Alive Men's 50+ Ultrapotency; it is fine for women to take men's vitamins.

Information on these drugs is constantly changing, so these lists may be out of date soon. That's one of the good things about popularity: The profits support a lot of research. One of them, lurasidone, was recently shown to work in unipolar mixed states, a diagnosis that identifies people who don't have bipolar disorder but have some manic symptoms during their depression. This diagnosis is brand-new in the *DSM-5*, and lurasidone is the first treatment to prove its benefits in that spectrum condition.

These medications are also used outside of mood disorders. Their main use is actually psychosis and schizophrenia, and they can also help borderline personality disorder, irritability due to autism, and obsessive compulsive disorder.

When used for depression and mania, the atypicals work fast, which means within 2 weeks, and sometimes a few days. So they're a great choice when change is needed quickly. Their side effects are their main drawback, particularly:

- Weight gain (worse with olanzapine and quetiapine)
- Uncomfortable restlessness (called *akathisia*)
- Muscle stiffness or twitching
- Severe fatigue (worse with olanzapine and quetiapine)
- Cognitive slowing and emotional blunting
- Sexual side effects

Some of those side effects (particularly fatigue) can improve with time (e.g., over 2 to 4 weeks). Others don't, however, and over the long term, there are quite a few medical risks to be concerned about:

- Diabetes
- High cholesterol and triglycerides
- Tardive dyskinesia: Potentially permanent involuntary movements.
- Elevated prolactin: A hormonal problem that can cause breast enlargement in men, breast milk-secretion, irregular menses, and bone-thinning.

- Abnormal heart rhythms
- Neuroleptic malignant syndrome: A rare but serious syndrome involving muscle stiffness and fever.
- Early death in people with dementia

There are ways to manage nearly all of these side effects. A remarkable research finding helps put all these medical risks in perspective. People live longer when they take atypicals, *if the medicine improves their mental health.* What that suggests is that a healthy brain is essential to a long life, even if you cross through some medical risks on the way to mental health.

TWENTY

Antidepressants and Other Mood Destabilizers

Key point: *Antidepressants can make things better or worse for people on the bipolar spectrum. It can be difficult to tell what they're doing, especially when they lift depression at first only to make it cycle more frequently down the road.*

Antidepressants are the trickiest medicines for people on the mood spectrum. Depending on how much bipolarity you have, these medications can:

- Help out: 10–20% of the time
- Do nothing: 30–70% of the time
- Make things worse: 20–50% of the time*

So if you're already taking an antidepressant, there's a chance your mood could improve by coming off it. There's also a chance it could get worse. Coming off these medicines is a difficult decision, and we'll give you some guidance on how to do that here. To start with, let's look at how antidepressants can make things worse so you'll know what to look out for.

---

*These percentages are based on review of the research and our own clinical experience (El-Mallakh et al., 2015; Pacchiarotti et al., 2013; Post et al., 2003; Strejilevich et al., 2011; Vázquez, Tondo, & Baldessarini, 2011).

In the short term, antidepressants can bring on a mania or mixed state, usually within 3 months of starting them. Over the long term, such as in the first year, they can cause *rapid cycling,* where the ups and downs of mood happen more frequently.

When antidepressants cause mixed states, most people think the medicine made them more depressed. That's how it feels when anxiety, agitation, and irritability are added onto a depression. It's actually rare for antidepressants to cause a sunny, positive hypomania. The reason is that they don't treat the depression, and instead overlay it with manic symptoms.

Over the long term, rapid cycling can be particularly hard to detect. When it happens, it may even look like the antidepressant helped at first. Consider this scenario for Josh, an imaginary patient.

Josh started to get depressed in January. At first, he figured it was just a post-holiday crash, and he would recover on his own. After 3 weeks, he began to doubt that theory. He was feeling worse. He called his doctor's office and took the next available appointment, which was 2 weeks out. At the visit, he described how he'd been depressed for over a month, and his doctor recommended venlafaxine (Effexor), an antidepressant. "Be patient with this one Josh, antidepressants take about 4 to 6 weeks to work," the doctor advised him as he left the office. Sure enough, Josh started to feel better after a month on the antidepressant. At his follow-up visit he and his doctor were pleased with the results, and he stayed on the venlafaxine. He had been depressed for nearly 3 months and was finally well again.

The problem with this scenario is that most bipolar depressions are brief and go away on their own after 2 to 3 months. That's how long it usually takes to get an appointment and wait for an antidepressant to work. Time would have healed most of these wounds, but the way things play out leaves most patients (and providers) giving credit to the antidepressant. What has actually happened is called the *placebo response.* When people respond to a placebo (or sugar pill), it's not always because their expectations of the pill tricked their mind into recovering—sometimes the illness was simply due to resolve on its own.

To understand rapid cycling, let's follow Josh as he stays on that anti-depressant. He does well through the spring, but gets depressed again in June. This next depression only lasts a month—he calls the doctor in the middle of it, and they raise the antidepressant by phone. He's better again. Then he's depressed again in August. The doctor adds aripiprazole (Abilify) to make the venlafaxine work better, but before Josh fills the prescription, the depression goes away. The episodes are getting shorter—this last one only lasted 3 weeks—but they are also coming on more frequently.

In the past, Josh's depressions came on once a year, but now they're happening every few months, so he's beginning to think something's wrong. His wife is even more concerned. She notices he's a bit hyped up and talkative between those depressions. Neither of them suspect the antidepressant is the problem—after all, it worked at first, and worked again when it was raised.

By autumn, Josh's mood is cycling every week. The hypomania and depression cycle so quickly that they start to overlap. It's like Monday's guest has entered the hotel room before Sunday's guest has checked out. There's confusion, arguing, and luggage scattered everywhere. That's how it feels inside him now—he's in a mixed state. He calls the doctor for an urgent visit. He's anxious, wired, sleeping all day, and up all night. His mind is so restless that he can't work.

What happened? In Josh's case, the antidepressant never worked. Instead, it caused his mood to cycle more frequently. Between his recoveries, he had mild hypomanias, but these were harmless compared with the depressions. The ups and downs eventually became so rapid that they virtually overlapped in a mixed state.

Figure 20.1 shows how Josh's treatment would look on a mood chart.

The best approach at this point would be to slowly withdraw the antidepressant that's aggravating these cycles (Ghaemi, 2010). This won't be easy because depressive episodes will still happen even while you're removing the cause. There will be a lot of days when Josh will want to raise that antidepressant back up. But if he sticks with the plan, the depressions will become milder and less frequent. It will be essential for

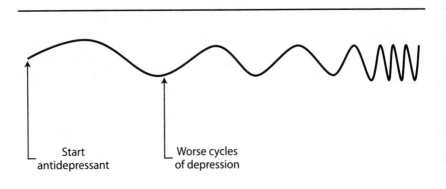

FIGURE 20.1 Mood Gradually Destabilizes after Starting an Antidepressant

him to track them on a mood chart so both he and his provider can check that the frequency is slowing down (see Chapters 16 and 17).

COMING OFF ANTIDEPRESSANTS

Antidepressants can usually be stopped quickly if they bring on a mixed or manic state soon after they're started. If rapid cycling is the problem and you've been on the antidepressant for at least 6 months, you may need to come off more slowly. The exact strategy for rapid cycling is complicated and may require more mood stabilizers; we don't recommend trying this on your own.

Your provider needs to know what you're doing and should be able to help you put together, in advance, a plan for how to handle any worsening of depression you might experience. Going slowly can prevent those kinds of problems. If you lower an antidepressant dose too quickly, things might get worse. Imagine what happens then. You'd want to go back up, wouldn't you? But then the next time someone suggests that you try tapering your antidepressant, you're likely to protest. "We tried that once, but I got worse." Now you're effectively stuck on the stuff.

So the key is to go slowly, and make the *smallest steps* down that you possibly can. This means getting hold of the smallest pill sizes available for your antidepressant and then cutting those into halves, and if you possibly can, into quarters. If it's not precise, no problem. That's a good thing, actually. Cut up several pills and put the big quarters in one bottle, carefully labeled, and the little quarters in another bottle. Start with the big quarters and work your way down to the little quarters. This smoothes the transition even more.

The whole process of tapering your antidepressant should take about 4 months for most patients (Phelps, 2011). This will take a little math to work out with your provider. If you did this in four steps, that would be one step a month. If you can make smaller steps, you might end up going down every 2 weeks, or maybe even every week. The key is to go down gradually, and slowly.

What if your pill only comes in capsules? Venlafaxine is one of those—its smallest capsules are 37.5 mg. You have three choices for capsules:

1. Get a prescription for a local "compounding pharmacy" to make smaller pills for you (e.g., a 5-mg version of venlafaxine), and go down by one such pill.
2. Open your capsules and count out or divide the beads inside. Some medications can then be sprinkled on food. You can even purchase empty gelatin capsules from the pharmacy and rebuild the pills.
3. Ask your provider about switching over to a different antidepressant that's easier to taper.

OTHER MOOD DESTABILIZERS

The key to treating bipolar is to stay clear from things that can destabilize mood. This is particularly true for rapid cycling, mixed states, and mania. Antidepressants are not the only mood destabilizers. In the previous section you learned about a host of lifestyle factors that can destabilize mood, most importantly irregular sleep problems and drugs of abuse.

Besides antidepressants, the two most important medications that can destabilize mood are stimulants and steroids (Yildiz et al., 2015). Stimulants are used to treat ADHD and include versions of amphetamine (Adderall, Dexedrine, Vyvanse) and methylphenidate (Ritalin, Concerta, Focalin). Chapter 22 looks at safer ways to treat ADHD in bipolar disorder.

Steroids are often prescribed for asthma, arthritis, allergic reactions, and inflammation. Examples include prednisone, dexamethasone, hydrocortisone, and prednisolone. They usually don't cause problems in the form of a skin cream or inhaler, but when taken orally, they can cause aggression and manic symptoms, even in people without bipolar.

There are other medicines that may destabilize mood, but the risk is either very low or unproven. These include a few that may be used treat bipolar depression: modafinil (Provigil), armodafinil (Nuvigil), pramipexole (Mirapex), and thyroid hormone. Others in this group include: naltrexone, varenicline (Chantix), testosterone, anticholinergics, ketamine, cyclobenzaprine, and non-steroidal pain medicines (NSAIDs) (Yildiz et al., 2015).

WHEN ANTIDEPRESSANTS WORK

We hope you've gotten an idea of how rapid cycling looks, and how hard it can be to tell when the antidepressant is the problem. But what if the antidepressant really is helping—how do you know when it's best to stay on it? Antidepressants do work for a small minority of people with bipolar depression—about 10% to 20%—but they rarely work all the way. When they work, people feel better on them and don't cycle more frequently in the years ahead (Post et al., 2003).

The trouble is that we don't know how to predict who will respond to antidepressants. A lot more is known about who is more likely to get worse on them. Among the factors that predict a bad response are (Yildiz et al., 2015):

- *Lack of a mood stabilizer.* Taking an antidepressant without a mood stabilizer is so dangerous that it's considered contraindicated in bipolar disorder. Unfortunately, the mood stabilizer that most patients prefer, lamotrigine, offers the weakest protection against mood problems on antidepressants.
- *Bipolar I vs. II.* The further you are toward the manic side of the spectrum, the worse the reactions to antidepressants tend to be. Even if you don't have Bipolar I, simply having more hypomanic than depressive symptoms throughout your life may increase your risk of a bad reaction to antidepressants.
- *Recent manic symptoms.* Starting an antidepressant within 6 months of a hypomania or mixed state is asking for trouble.
- *Rapid cycling.* If you had rapid cycling in the year before starting the antidepressant, it may make it worse.
- *Past worsening.* Any history of worsened mood on an antidepressant increases your risk.
- *Younger age.* The risk is greater for young adults and especially risky for children and teenagers.
- *Substance abuse.* The more recent the abuse, the higher the risk, but the risk is still elevated even if the abuse happened long ago.
- *Suicide.* If you've had a past suicide attempt, there is a greater risk of worsening on antidepressants.
- *Genetics.* Those with the gene for the short-arm of the serotonin receptor (see Chapter 7) are at greater risk for mania as well as suicidal thinking on antidepressants.

We wish we had good information on who is likely to get better on an antidepressant, but we could only find one. Those who responded well to them in the past are likely to respond well again. If you're considering an antidepressant, some are less likely to cause trouble. They are listed here from the most to the least dangerous (Yildiz et al., 2015):

1. Tricyclic antidepressants
2. Serotonin-norepinephrine antidepressants (SNRIs)

3. Monoamine oxidase inhibitors (MAOIs)
4. Serotonin reuptake inhibitors (SSRIs)
5. Bupropion (Wellbutrin)

Let's home in on that last one, bupropion, because if there's one anti-depressant to consider when you have significant bipolarity, bupropion is it. Not only is it the safest antidepressant in bipolar, it also has the least side effects of any antidepressant.

Bupropion has been available since 1986, but it has never been among the most popular antidepressants. If that fact makes you scratch your head, you're not alone. A team of researchers at Brown University once set out to study the reasons behind this surprising fact (Zimmerman et al., 2005). Their results suggested that psychiatrists were not paying enough attention to the side effects of antidepressants and were mislead by pharmaceutical companies who often implied that serotonin medica-tions were superior for anxious depressions (despite scientific evidence that bupropion works just as well when depression and anxiety overlap).

The most popular antidepressants are the serotonin medications, also called SSRIs. Let's take a brief detour to look at the side effects they can cause.

SEROTONIN SIDE EFFECTS

The three main side effects that make people want to stop serotonin antidepressants: low sex drive, weight gain, and apathy. None of these are dangerous, and they should get better off the medication, but for many people, the benefits these drugs bring are not worth those risks. Even in unipolar depression, which they were developed for, these medicines are twice as likely to cause these side effects than they are to treat depression.

Serotonin medications can impair sex life in all sorts of ways. Most commonly, they delay orgasm; sometimes it's delayed indefinitely. They can also decrease pleasurable sensations in the groin area and make people less interested in having sex.

When they cause apathy, people don't feel like themselves. Their emotions are blunted. They don't cry when sad things happen and aren't as concerned about the big issues they once wrestled with. Sometimes this is a serious problem. College students, for example, have told us, "I feel much better, but something is odd . . . I just don't care if I go to class anymore."

Weight gain is difficult to detect on serotonin antidepressants. There usually is none in the first month, but some people have mild weight gain on them over time. It improves when the medication is stopped, and is least likely with fluoxetine (Prozac) (Uguz, Sahingoz, Gungor, Aksoy, & Askin, 2015).

Particularly problematic for people with bipolarity is the way that serotonin medications can disrupt sleep. Sleep is lighter and less restorative on them, which can trigger mood swings or make people more groggy in the daytime (Holshoe, 2009).

These medications also carry physical risks, including:

- *Serotonin syndrome:* A rare and potentially fatal reaction involving muscle breakdown, fever, and confusion.
- *Akathisia:* A sense of restlessness that is so uncomfortable it even elevates the suicide risk (this is a rare side effect and occurs more often on antipsychotics; Hawthorne & Caley, 2015).
- *Other medical problems:* Diabetes (De Long, Stepita, Taylor, & Holloway, 2015), stomach bleeding (Jiang et al., 2015), bone fractures (in postmenopausal women), low sodium (in the elderly), and heart arrhythmias (Diniz & Reynolds, 2014). These are all rare.
- *Withdrawal problems:* Suddenly stopping them can cause imbalance, dizziness, shock-like sensations, tremor, and sweats. This is not dangerous but can be very uncomfortable—withdrawal problems are most common on paroxetine (Paxil), venlafaxine (Effexor), and duloxetine (Cymbalta), and are very rare on fluoxetine (Prozac) and vortioxetine (Brintellix).

We hope that this puts antidepressants in perspective. Even when they do work, they aren't the easiest or safest drugs in the world. Bupropion is an underrecognized gem in that basket. We have never seen cases of blunted emotions, sexual problems, weight gain, or tiredness on it, and it improves concentration more than most antidepressants. But bupropion can certainly worsen mood and cause rapid cycling just as any antidepressant. It also carries a medical risk of its own. It can cause seizures, particularly if the dose is too high.

TWENTY-ONE

Medications for Breakthrough Episodes

Key point: *Preventive medicine makes mood swings less frequent, but they can still break through even with the best efforts. There are several short-term treatments that can help you pull through when that happens.*

When depression starts, something usually needs to be done. That may not involve a new medication. If it's only been a few days, a lifestyle change (see Part 2) may turn things around. Your provider may be able to help by adjusting the dose you're already taking, or you may recover as you get some distance from an active stress.

Adding a new medicine brings new risks, but it may be worth it if the depression is causing problems in your life. We'll call these *active treatments* because they are added onto your preventative treatment. We've just reviewed the most popular active treatment (antidepressants), and you probably guessed they are not our favorite. Let's look at what else is on the menu for bipolar depression.

To start with, you may be able to treat an active episode by raising your mood-lifting stabilizer. Remember that a new depression doesn't mean that your mood-lifting stabilizer isn't working. Its job is to make the episodes less frequent, but it may not make them go away entirely. All of the mood stabilizers in Chapter 19 can be adjusted to treat an active depression, mixed state, or problematic hypomania.

The rest of the options in this chapter can help bipolar depression in the short term, though it's not known if they can prevent mood problems.

They have little to no risk of destabilizing mood, but that's always a possibility to consider (indeed, you may recognize some of them from the list of possible mood destabilizers in Chapter 19).

DOPAMINE AGONISTS

Dopamine agonists are a group of medicines that enhance dopamine in the *nucleus accumbens*, which is the part of the brain that finds life rewarding and meaningful. When things go wrong here, people lose their drive and take little pleasure in what they do. Most treatments for depression eventually restore dopamine through *indirect* mechanisms, including exercise, antidepressants, and even electroconvulsive therapy. The dopamine agonists are the only medications that they restore dopamine *directly*.

Among the dopamine agonists, pramipexole (Mirapex) has the best evidence to treat depression, so we'll focus on that one here. Pramipexole works gradually (over a month) to improve depression, motivation, and drive (Aiken, 2007).

Sometimes this effect can go too far, causing a compulsive drive to get things done. Usually this doesn't cause a problem. We have seen people clean out their entire garage or organize all of their books alphabetically. In more problematic cases, this drive leads to impulsive actions, such as spending too much money, gambling, eating, or hypersexual activity.

That kind of hyperactivity sounds a lot like mania, but those who've had it usually have no other symptoms of mania. This side effect goes by a different name: *hedonistic homeostatic dysregulation*, which is Greek for "I can't get no satisfaction." People with Parkinson's disease, who have very fragile dopamine neurons, are much more vulnerable to this problem. It's extremely rare when pramipexole is used in bipolar.

Pramipexole does not treat mania or mixed states, and it may carry a small risk of mania. Dr. Aiken has only seen two clear cases of mania on it, out of over 800 people he has treated with the drug. Instead, pramipexole is more likely to bring out OCD tendencies, such as repeatedly checking, counting, or sorting things, or worrying about terrible but unlikely

Quick facts: Dopamine agonists

Names	Pramipexole (Mirapex), ropinirole (Requip), rotigotine (Neupro), amantadine (Symmetrel)
Forms	Pramipexole and ropinirole: regular and extended release tablets Rotigotine: skin patch Amantadine: tablet, capsule and liquid
Psychiatric benefits	Depression. Amantadine also treats irritability in traumatic brain injury and autism; fatigue, and may improve OCD.
FDA-approval	Parkinson's disease, restless leg syndrome
Dose range	Most studies were done with pramipexole, which is dosed at 0.5–3 mg/day for depression (average 1.5 mg)
Health risks	Hallucinations, sudden sleep attacks, leg swelling, rare mania. Avoid if you have heart failure.
Useful tips	Fatigue improves by taking it all at night, though people who feel more activated on it should take in the morning. Nausea usually improves with time and can be managed by raising the dose slowly or taking with a proton-pump inhibitor.
Release date	7/1/1997

events. Compulsive physical behaviors, such as nail-biting or hair-pulling, are also possible.

Pramipexole has two siblings—ropinirole (Requip) and rotigotine (Neupro)—and one cousin—amantadine (Symmetrel). These have similar effects in the brain and carry the same risks and side effects as pramipexole, but they don't have as much evidence supporting their use in depression. They might be considered in people who responded to pramipexole but could not tolerate it.

NOVEL STIMULANTS

Stimulants are medicines that treat ADHD and narcolepsy (a rare condition that causes sudden sleep attacks). They have been around for over 50 years, and have an abuse potential, so they are highly controlled. Examples include methylphenidate (Ritalin, Concerta), amphetamine-salts (Adderall), and dextroamphetamine versions (Dexedrine, Vyvanse). Many people with bipolar have symptoms of ADHD, but stimulants are very controversial in depression and bipolar.

Traditional stimulants can make bipolar worse, causing mania and paranoia (Yildiz et al., 2015). At best, they bring needed bursts of energy for a few months and then wear off. They have been tested for depression many times in the past several decades, but the hope never pans out. Most recently, the manufacturer of lisdexamfetamine (Vyvanse) attempted to gain FDA-approval for depression, but the effort was shelved after their large trials showed the drug was no better than a placebo (Grogan, 2014).

A brighter picture emerges with the novel stimulants, modafinil (Provigil), and armodafinil (Nuvigil). These are practically the same drug, so they are referred to here as modafinil*.

Like the traditional stimulants, modafinil treats narcolepsy and fatigue. It also treats ADHD, and was close to FDA-approval for this condition but was denied at the last minute because it carries a risk of severe rash that may be higher in children (Hamilton, 2006).

Modafinil improves depression, fatigue, and concentration. It works in both unipolar and bipolar depression, but does not treat depression completely on its own, so it's usually added to another medication (Goss, 2013).

Modafinil is very well tolerated. It is one of the few medications that patients seem to genuinely like, perhaps because it improves their overall functioning—often helping them return to work and school. Another reason people like it is that they know exactly what it's doing. Modafinil works right away, and only works on the days that you take it.

Modafinil is classified as a "wakefulness promoting agent" or novel stimulant. Hence, it can cause insomnia, which could progress to mania. We recommend stopping or lowering the dose if it keeps you up, and

*Modafinil is a mixture of two drugs that are left- and right-handed versions of each other, called R-modafinil and S-modafinil. Armodafinil was created by isolating the R version of modafinil. Among the two compounds, R-modafinil lasts a little longer in the bloodstream then S-modafinil.

Quick facts: Novel stimulants

Names	Modafinil (Provigil), armodafinil (Nuvigil)
Forms	Modafinil tabs: 100, 200 mg Armodafinil tabs: 50, 150, 250 mg
Psychiatric benefits	Depression, fatigue, concentration, binge eating, cocaine abuse
FDA-approval	Narcolepsy, sleep apnea, shift-work syndrome
Dose range	Modafinil: up to 200 mg in the morning Armodafinil: up to 250 mg in the morning
Tolerability	Insomnia, anxiety, headache. Most side effects improve by lowering the dose.
Health risks	Increased heart rate/blood pressure, rare mania, serious allergic rash
Useful tips	These work immediately and only work on the day they are taken. They can be taken as needed.
Release date	12/24/1998

avoid taking the medicine too late in the day. However, there is also evidence that modafinil can improve sleep by helping people stay awake during the day so their biological clock gets back in order.

THYROID HORMONES

Among all the hormones in the body, thyroid has the strongest effects on mood. It's essential to have a healthy thyroid for any mood treatment to work. Thyroid levels can be supplemented to improve depression when the thyroid levels are in the mild-low or even the normal range (Wartofsky & Dickey, 2005). They are particularly useful when taking lithium, which works better when the TSH (a measure of thyroid hormone) is right in the middle—around 2.4 (Frye et al., 2009).

Thyroid comes in two forms—T3 and T4—and both of these have been used as add-on treatments for depression. The best dose of thyroid for depression is a complex issue. A research team originating at UCLA, now spread around the world, has studied high doses of thyroid hormone as a mood-lifting stabilizer. This strategy carries risks, as elevated thyroid can cause irregular heart rhythms and decrease bone mineral density. On the other hand, it is a well-studied approach for treating both unipolar and bipolar depression and can also improve rapid cycling (Bauer et al., 2003). The safest way to approach this strategy is to back-off on raising the thyroid if you experience symptoms of hyperthyroidism, such as:

- Feeling hot when others are comfortable or even cold
- Sweating
- Thumping heart beats ("palpitations")
- Weight loss
- Anxiety and nervousness
- Frequent bowel movements
- Decreased flow with your menstrual periods, or no period at all

There's a lot more to know about thyroid hormone, and we've included that in our supplementary materials online (moodtreatment-center.com/bipolarnotsomuch).

OTHER OPTIONS

Most psychiatric treatments were originally developed for an entirely different use, and their mental benefits were often discovered by accident. Mood stabilizers were originally anticonvulsants; antidepressants were developed from antipsychotics; and antipsychotics were found while trying to create an anesthetic. That story continues with the medicines in Table 21.1, where researchers have discovered mood-enhancing effects from a surprising array of medical treatments.

Most of these treatments are only supported by small studies and are not fully ready for everyday use. Some were studied in bipolar depression, and others in mania or unipolar depression. They might be worth con-

TABLE 21.1 Medical Treatments that Help Depression

Medicine	Treats	Risks
Calcium channel blockers	High blood pressure. Ultrarapid mood cycles in bipolar.	Low blood pressure.
Statins	High cholesterol. Unipolar depression; prevents dementia.	Muscle pain, memory problems, diabetes.
Allopurinol	Gout. Mania.	Fatigue, rarely renal stones, and liver problems.
Riluzole	Amyotrophic lateral sclerosis (ALS). Treatment-resistant bipolar and unipolar depression, anxiety and OCD (its effects in the brain are similar to those of lamotrigine).	Stomach distress, rare liver problems.
Celecoxib	Pain (anti-inflammatory, nonaddictive). Bipolar and unipolar depression.	Risks of stomach ulcers, heart attack, stroke, and renal impairment.
Pioglitazone	Diabetes. Bipolar and unipolar depression (its effects in the brain are similar to those of lamotrigine).	Bone thinning, risk of bladder cancer, low blood sugar.
Pindolol	High blood pressure. Unipolar depression.	Low blood pressure.

sidering if all else has failed or if you happen to have one of the medical conditions that these also treat.

Among the options in Table 21.1, calcium-channel blockers are supported by the most research. They have been used since the 1980s and are particularly helpful for moods that cycle very rapidly, such as daily or weekly. Examples include verapamil, isradipine, nimodipine, and amlodipine (Post & Leverich, 2008).

TWENTY-TWO

Anxiety, Concentration, and Sleep: The Other Poles of Bipolar

---

Key point: *People on the bipolar spectrum often suffer from other psychiatric conditions. Antidepressants and stimulants are popular in those cases, but they are risky, and there are many safer alternatives for people with bipolarity.*

Bipolarity often comes with other psychiatric conditions. Among them are:

- Anxiety: Panic Disorder, Social Anxiety Disorder, PTSD, and GAD
- OCD
- ADHD
- Bulimia (binging and purging on food)
- Addictions

Sometimes these problems are entirely due to the underlying mood disorder, even when they look like a separate disorder. Bipolar itself can cause symptoms of anxiety, ADHD, and impulsive overeating. When bipolarity is the cause, the problem usually goes away as mood improves, so we recommend treating the mood problem first.

It's tempting to skip mood stabilizers and jump right into treatment for anxiety or concentration, as those other problems can be more distressing than mood symptoms. That's a risky approach, as the main treatments for those problems (antidepressants and stimulants) can wreck havoc when there's untreated bipolarity going on. In this chapter we'll show you some options that can help these associated problems without destabilizing mood.

ANXIETY

Most of the FDA-approved options for anxiety are antidepressants, but don't feel you're missing out if bipolar prevents you from taking them. On average, antidepressants have a very marginal effect on anxiety when compared with a sugar pill.

In contrast, psychotherapy for anxiety usually brings about more lasting changes than antidepressants (Roshanaei-Moghaddam et al., 2011). The therapies that work for anxiety help people encounter their fears with more effective coping skills, such as CBT. This is hard work, and usually involves steady practice outside of the weekly sessions. Therapy is particular helpful when anxiety and bipolar disorder coexit (Deckersbach et al., 2014).

If you are considering a medicine for anxiety, Table 22.1 lists options that are not antidepressants.

TABLE 22.1 Safer Options for Anxiety in Bipolar*

Medication	Notes
Gabapentin (Neurontin)	Particularly good for social anxiety. Few side effects (fatigue, dizziness most common). It may have mild preventative effects for bipolar. It is often given in small doses (300 mg daily), but in the studies for anxiety, the dosage ranged from 900–3,600 mg daily).
Pregabalin (Lyrica)	Similar to gabapentin but greater risk of weight gain. Studied in social anxiety, generalized anxiety, and PTSD (150–600 mg daily).
Mood stabilizers	Some mood stabilizers can help when bipolar and anxiety coexist (e.g., lamotrigine, valproate, quetiapine, lurasidone, olanzapine).

Natural treatments	Silexan (lavender extract), chamomile, probiotics, and aromatherapy (see Chapter 23). These natural treatments improve anxiety and do not worsen bipolar in our experience (we await further research to confirm that).
Propranolol (Inderal)	This blood pressure medicine reduces physical symptoms of anxiety such as tremor and racing heart. If taken within a day after a major trauma, it may prevent PTSD (the steroid hydrocortisone also has this benefit).
Buspirone (Buspar)	Buspirone is the only FDA-approved option for anxiety that is nonaddictive and is not an antidepressant. It may help anxiety in bipolar, but has a slight chance of worsening mood there.
Benzodiazepines	These medicines reduce anxiety quickly but can cause tolerance (where the medication no longer works), addiction or withdrawal problems if taken for more than a few months. They do not worsen bipolar and may help sleep and manic symptoms.

*References on page 321.

OCD

As with anxiety disorders, the main options for OCD are all antidepressants. However, a unique type of behavior therapy (called exposure-response prevention) can be very effective for OCD and even brings about the same changes in the brain as medication (without causing mania). It's hard to find therapists who work with these techniques, but it's worth the effort as behavior therapy teaches skills you'll need to prevent the problem over the long term (Roshanaei-Moghaddam et al., 2011). Table 22.2 details medications for OCD that are not antidepressants.

TABLE 22.2 Safer Options for OCD in Bipolar*

Medication	Notes
Topiramate (Topamax)	This seizure medicine is also used for additions, impulsivity, and weight loss. It can cause concentration problems.
Ondansetron (Zofran), Granisetron (Kytril)	These medications are used to treat nausea, and several studies show remarkable benefits for OCD. They have never been studied in bipolar, but work very differently from antidepressants (they block serotonin) and in our experience do not make bipolar worse.
N-acetylcysteine	This vitamin improves bipolar depression and helps compulsive disorders (mainly compulsive hair pulling but possibly OCD as well). See Chapter 23.
Memantine (Namenda)	Originally for dementia, memantine improved OCD in one study. Not known to worsen bipolar, and small studies suggest it may improve mixed states. Well tolerated.
Atypical antipsychotics	These help OCD when used in combination with an antidepressant, or possibly when used alone. However, they carry many medical risks (see Chapter 19), and there are also reports of them making OCD worse.

*References on page 322.

ADHD AND CONCENTRATION

When people with bipolar disorder have concentration problems, it can be difficult to tell whether they are due to ADHD or result from bipolar itself. Here are a few hints:

- ADHD tends to be worse in childhood and improve with age. In bipolar, the concentration problems begin with the first mood swings (often in teens) and worsen with age.
- In ADHD, the symptoms are always present, though they may worsen with too much stress or too little sleep. In contrast, people with bipolar tend to have extended periods of good concentration and may even have periods of sharpened focus during a sunny hypomania.

TABLE 22.3 Safer Options for ADHD in Bipolar*

Medication	Notes
Modafinil (Provigil), arModafinil (Nuvigil)	These are effective for ADHD and came close to FDA-approval for it. They treat bipolar depression (see Chapter 21).
Clonidine (Kapvay)	This blood-pressure medication is also FDA-approved for ADHD. Its benefits build up over a few weeks. Clonidine is not known to worsen bipolar and has antiaggressive properties that may be beneficial for manic states (it was used for mania in the 1980s). Guanfacine (Intuniv) is a related ADHD medication, but there have been cases of guanfacine causing mania.
VayaRin	VayaRin is a food supplement that's FDA-approved for ADHD. It contains two ingredients that are essential for the brain: omega-3 fatty acids (120 mg daily) and phosphatidylserine (300 mg daily). Although VayaRin's benefits in ADHD are mild, it is worth considering because omega-3s have numerous benefits for bipolar disorder.
EMPowerplus	This compounded vitamin might help bipolar and has at least one scientific study supporting its use in ADHD (see Chapter 23).

*References on page 323.

- ADHD is very heritable, so there are likely traces of it in close family members if it is truly ADHD.

Stimulants are the main treatment for ADHD. They include methylphenidate varieties (Ritalin, Concerta, Focalin, Metadate), dextroamphetamine varieties (Dexedrine, Vyvanse), and amphetamine-salts (Adderall, Evekeo, Adzenys). These are all highly controlled substances as they do have an abuse potential. That brings you to part of the problem. Most people feel better on them whether they have ADHD or not. One difference is that people with ADHD usually feel calmer on them, as they quiet the restless hyperactivity of the disorder. In depression and bipolar they work more like energy boosters.

If used for ADHD, stimulants usually keep working over the long term without tolerance. When used in mood disorders, any initial benefits tend to wear off within a few months, and it's not uncommon to hear requests for higher doses at that point. This can be a problem, as they can have toxic effects on the brain when used for the wrong diagnosis, especially at higher doses. They can cause irritability, mania, and even overt paranoia if this goes on too long (Yildiz et al., 2005). Besides the brain risks, stimulants also stress the heart by raising blood pressure. Given all these concerns, they are not recommended in bipolar unless there is clear-cut ADHD.

There is good news though, for a number of nonstimulants are now available for ADHD. One of these, atomoxetine (Strattera), is actually an antidepressant that was rebranded for ADHD. It should be avoided in bipolar as it has a known potential to worsen mood (Perugi & Vannucchi, 2015), and its benefits in ADHD are so mild that it usually isn't worth that risk (it has a sustained benefit for only 1 in 10 people; Cheng, Cheng, Ko, & Ng, 2007). The other nonstimulants are relatively safe in bipolar and are described in Table 22.3.

The treatments above should be considered in people who have both ADHD and bipolar. We'll turn next to concentration problems that come from bipolar alone. The most common are:

- *Executive functioning:* Prioritizing, planning, managing impulses, making decisions, and learning from mistakes.
- *Processing speed:* The ability to perform routine mental tasks quickly.
- *Verbal memory:* The ability to store and recall information in words.

When the first textbook on this subject came out in 2008, there were no known treatments (Goldberg & Burdick, 2008). Since then, a few options have proven effective (Table 22.4). The most notable advance in this area is a behavior therapy called *functional remediation*, which teaches active exercises to rebuild cognitive skills in bipolar disorder.

TABLE 22.4 Treatments for Concentration and Memory Problems in Bipolar*

Medication	Notes
Sensoril	This formulation of an Indian herb improves growth in the brain's memory center and helps memory, mental speed, and intuitive thinking in bipolar (see Chapter 23).
Modafinil (Provigil), arModafinil (Nuvigil)	These treat bipolar depression, and also help alertness, focus, and mental speed.
Lamotrigine (Lamictal)	Improves concentration in lower doses, but can also cause word finding difficulty if the dose is too high.
Pramipexole (Mirapex)	Treats bipolar depression and has mild benefits in concentration.
Galantamine (Razadyne)	Originally developed for dementia, this medicine has mild benefits for memory and attention in bipolar.
Lithium	Lithium does not improve memory but may help to prevent worsening over time (lithium prevents dementia and causes brain growth).
N-acetylcysteine	This antioxidant treats bipolar depression. Although studies suggest it can improve memory and attention in several conditions (dementia, head injury, and lupus) it did not bring about those improvements when studied in bipolar.

*References on page 323.

Besides ADHD and bipolar, there is a third factor that can cause concentration problems: medication. This can be difficult to tease out, as medications can both improve and worsen concentration. People rarely complain of memory problems when depression is severe, but they do notice them as they start to recover from depression. At that point, they are likely to blame their medications for the problem. Sometimes it's the medicine, and sometimes it's just the slow recovery process (memory is usually the last symptom to recover).

Medications can slow thinking and impair memory. Among the mood stabilizers, all have the potential to do this. This problem usually improves by lowering the dose, so it's often not necessary to come off the medication if it's working well. Mood stabilizers differ in how they impact memory, and we've ranked them below in a rough estimate based on our experience and the research (Gualtieri & Johnson, 2006):

- Least impairment: lamotrigine.
- In the middle: lithium, oxcarbazepine, and the atypical antipsychotics.
- Most impairment: valproate and carbamazepine.

EATING DISORDERS

When eating habits spiral out of control, it usually goes in at least one of three directions: restricting (called *anorexia*), binge eating, and purging (commonly through vomiting, but purging can include anything to make up for a binge, such as overexercise and laxatives). Among these, binging and purging are the ones we see most often in bipolarity.

There's a good reason for this tight connection. Bipolar depression raises appetite, and hypomania causes impulsive actions like overeating and purging. Binging and purging both have addictive qualities, so they can easily spiral out of control.

A binge is excessive eating that feels out of control. It's usually done quickly, in private, and brings on feelings of guilt and shame. When binging and purging occur together, it is called *bulimia*. When binging occurs on its own, it's called *binge eating disorder*. Often these problems resolve with treatment of the underlying mood disorder, but if they develop a life of their own, there are many other ways to address them.

Many treatments that work for bulimia also work for binge eating disorder, and structured psychotherapies like CBT are among the most successful. Simple lifestyle changes can also help, such as eating a protein supplement before each meal, improving sleep, and moderate exercise (as long as it's not done compulsively in response to a binge; Latner & Wilson, 2004, Sundgot-Borgen, Rosenvinge, Bahr, & Schneider, 2002).

When turning to medication options, you face the paradox again

TABLE 22.5 Safer Options for Eating Disorders in Bipolar*

Medication	Notes
Topiramate (Topamax)	Improves binge eating and bulimia. It is usually safe in bipolar but can cause concentration problems.
Zonisamide (Zonegran)	Improves binge-eating; does not worsen bipolar, and speculative studies suggest may help bipolar depression.
Ondansetron (Zofran)	This nausea medicine improves bulimia. It has few side effects and no known risks in bipolar.
Inositol	This natural treatment has mild benefits in bipolar depression and improved bulimia and binge eating in a small study (dose 18 mg daily).
Chromium picolinate	This natural mineral improves binge eating and unipolar depression, as well as blood sugar control. It has no known risks in bipolar (dose 600–1,000 mg daily).

*References on page 324.

that the FDA-approved treatments pose risks for bipolar, such as the antidepressant fluoxetine (Prozac) for bulimia, and the stimulant lisdexamfetamine (Vyvanse) for binge eating disorder. Table 22.5 lists a few medicines that can help eating disorders without undue risks for bipolar.

ADDICTIONS

People with bipolar disorder can do things to excess, and substance abuse is no exception. As many as 70% of people with bipolar have abused recreational drugs at some point. Cocaine and amphetamines are more common in Bipolar I, while marijuana is more prevalent in Bipolar II. Alcohol is common in both.

Therapy is the main treatment for addictions, and this field has become so specialized that there is even a specific licensure for addictions counseling (called *licensed clinical addictions specialist* or LCAS). We wish such specialized attention was paid to therapy for bipolar, as people with bipolar need as much help in rebuilding their lives as those with addiction. Job loss, divorce, legal and financial setbacks, health issues, concentration and mood problems; these are just as prevalent in bipolar as in people with addictions.

In terms of medication, people with bipolar share something else in common with those with significant drug abuse: Neither respond very well to antidepressants (Torrens, Fonseca, Mateu, & Farré, 2005). With the exception of bupropion (Wellbutrin) for nicotine cessation, there is scant evidence supporting the role of antidepressants in addictive disorders. The main treatments for addiction, such as acamprosate (Campral), naltrexone (Revia), topiramate (Topamax), gabapentin (Neurontin), and zonisamide (Zonegram) do not cause major problems in bipolar disorder.

Some controversy exists around the smoking cessation therapy varenicline (Chantix), which carries a warning about suicidal thinking. Since that warning came out, the drug has been studied more extensively in people with depression and bipolar, and the results suggest it is safe and does not tend to worsen mood (Chengappa et al., 2014).

When bipolar and substance abuse occur together, there are ways to adjust the treatment to better address both. For example, the anticonvulsants and the atypical antipsychotics often work better when the two problems overlap (Yildiz et al., 2015). N-acetylcysteine (NAC), a natural treatment for bipolar depression, also helps reduce marijuana use (Gray et al., 2012). Another natural treatment, citicoline, helps both mood and sobriety in people with bipolar and cocaine or amphetamine abuse (Wignall & Brown, 2014). Modafinil, which treats bipolar depression, can help people stay free of cocaine (Kampman, 2015). Memantine can help mixed states, depression, and alcoholism (Muhonen, Lönnqvist, Juva, & Alho, 2008).

SLEEP

Regular sleep is one of the best mood stabilizers. It's so important that we spent half of Part 2 describing natural ways to improve sleep. What if you're doing all of those and still not able to sleep? When insomnia is that

TABLE 22.6 Medications for Sleep

Medication	Notes
Z-Hypnotics (Ambien, Sonata, Lunesta)	Very low risk of dependence, may cause impairment if you are awake after taking them.
Benzodiazepines	Definite risk of dependence and addiction. May increase risk of dementia with long-term use.
Suvorexant (Belsomra)	Appears safe and nonaddictive, but no specific advantages over z-hypnotics.
Ramelteon (Rozerem)	Nonaddictive, little sedating effect, may improve mood in bipolar.
Mood Stabilizers	Those with sedative qualities can improve sleep, as can the anticonvulsant gabapentin.
Antidepressants	Low addiction risk but not well-researched in sleep and may worsen mood in bipolar.
Antihistamines	Nonaddictive, few side effects.
Melatonin	Natural, generally safe.
L-tryptophan	May be unsafe in people with bipolarity or those taking serotonin antidepressants.
Valerian	Plant-based, relatively safe, nonaddictive.

severe, it may be a sign that a mood episode is starting. Sleep medications would be worth consideration then, as would adjusting the mood medications.

Providers vary in how they approach sleep medications. Some are concerned about their addictive potential. Others worry that they may lead to falls or accidents. There is even a risk of death, for example if people take benzodiazepine for sleep along with alcohol or opioid pain medications (Jann, Kennedy, & Lopez, 2014). All of these are legitimate fears, and it's a good idea to show your provider that you understand these risks and can take responsibility for managing them before you ask for a sleep medication.

Besides considering the risks, you'll also want to think about how long you need that sleep medicine to last. Some, like zaleplon (Sonata), leave the body pretty quickly. Others last longer and can be useful if the trouble is staying asleep or waking up early in the morning.

Z-Hypnotics: zolpidem (Ambien), zaleplon (Sonata), and eszopiclone (Lunesta)

Zolpidem is famous for causing sleepwalking behaviors that range from amusing to very concerning. People report getting up at night and eating odd things, not putting things away afterward, and not remembering any of it the following day. So they walk into the kitchen, and it looks like someone's been in there and done some really odd things (one patient put ice cream away in the stove—twice).

More concerning are reports of e-mails and phone calls that aren't remembered the following day. Most extreme are reports of having sex, also not remembered, and even driving around in a trance-like, medicated state (this is not only dangerous but carries the same legal penalties as drunk driving does in many states). Fortunately, these more concerning reports are very rare and can be minimized by keeping the dose low. That message is particularly true for zolpidem, which is a little stronger than its cousins and is often dosed too high in women (Hwang, Ni, Chen, Lin, & Liao, 2010). Zolpidem levels rise twice as high in women compared with men, but the dosing guidelines didn't change to reflect this until 2013.

Sleep medicines are also more likely to trigger problematic behaviors if taken during a manic state. None of these medications were designed for mania, and sometimes they aren't strong enough to bring on sleep during that revved up state. This results in a manic person who is now awake and a little disinhibited from the sedative, so problematic behaviors on sleep meds are seen a little more often in bipolar patients.

Lingering concerns remain about whether these medications are addictive. Imagine what will happen if these medications are stopped, when a person's insomnia has not been addressed in some other way (e.g., working on circadian rhythm with nonmedication approaches; or establishing a new nighttime routine using the sleep hygiene recommendations). The original insomnia is very likely to reappear. If the z-hypnotic was working, and is stopped, is the resulting insomnia the same insomnia as before? If so, this is not withdrawal. But if the insomnia is far worse than it was before, that would suggest the z-hypnotic was addictive in the sense of having changed the person's physiology while on it.

That type of addiction does happen with the benzodiazepine sleep medicines, such as lorazepam (Ativan) and alprazolam (Xanax). The problem is possible, but very rare, with z-hypnotics, unless people keep increasing the dose. In the normal dose, the risk of addiction appears to be very low, almost zero (Roehrs, Randall, Harris, Maan, & Roth, 2012; Voderholzer et al., 2001).

In general, the big problem with this z-hypnotic family is the risk of accidents and falls (Frey, Ortega, Wiseman, Farley, & Wright, 2011). Why would one even consider taking such a risk? Answer: When the risks of not sleeping are at least as great. In Bipolar I, that's the risk of mania. In people in the mood spectrum, it's usually the risk of near-complete functional collapse. For example, there's a risk of losing a job or an important relationship because of symptoms that a good night's rest might easily get rid of.

Benzodiazepines

This is the group that most raises alarms for prescribers. Many people develop tolerance to these medications, which means they no longer bring much benefit, but things are much worse than ever if they are stopped. So why even start them? Answer: In the very short run, two weeks or less, they can be extremely effective for sleep and anxiety. They really work. Almost every time. When people are desperate because of their insomnia or anxiety (or commonly both), and they know these pills exist, they can exert a lot of pressure trying to get some. Feeling that pressure makes prescribers resistant, as they feel like they're the ones taking the risk (which is not the case; the patient is, but that's not how it feels to the prescriber, and they really don't like being in that position).

Many providers would like this family of medicines to just disappear. Some simply announce they won't prescribe them. (At one point the benzodiazepine alprazolam (Xanax) was banned from the entire mental health system of West Virginia).

Turning to these medications for sleep means most everything else has failed or the stakes are really high, and the need for them is predictably short-term. Under those circumstances, they're very useful.

Suvorexant (Belsomra)

This is the first sleep medicine that works by turning down a chemical that keeps us awake (called orexin). It's also the newest to the block, so as of this writing, there is not enough data to compare it with the other options. Overall, it seems to have similar risks to the z-hypnotics. One fact may limit its use: It tends to be given in lower doses, so many on the bipolar spectrum may not think it does the job. So why not just jump to the higher dose? That might be effective, but also carries more risks, so most doctors are not likely to go above the recommended safety level with it.

Ramelteon (Rozerem)

Unlike other sleep medications, this one does not cause much sedation. It works through the melatonin receptor, and gradually helps set the rhythm of sleep over 2 to 4 weeks. That means you have to take it every night for a little while before you'll know if it's working. Sounds like a nice way to fix the broken circadian rhythms of bipolar, right? Possibly so, and we're encouraged that—unlike a lot of sleep medications—ramelteon has actually been studied in bipolar and may improve mood stability and depression in addition to sleep (these results are very preliminary; Norris et al., 2013). In general, ramelteon may be a good option for people who need to completely avoid the risks of falls, sedation, and addiction that come with other approaches.

Mood Stabilizers

Some mood stabilizers have sedative effects and can improve sleep when taken at night, particularly valproate and the atypical antipsychotics. Gabapentin, which is often used for anxiety in bipolar, can improve sleep quality and reduce restless legs.

Antidepressants

To avoid the risks with sleep medications, providers will often turn to sedating antidepressants first, for example trazodone, amitriptyline, mirtazapine, and doxepin (this last antidepressant is also marketed for sleep under the brand Silenor). As mentioned in Chapter 20, antidepressants can worsen mood in bipolar disorder, particularly those in the tricyclic class (which includes amitriptyline and doxepin). Trazodone is less risky in bipolar, but it can leave people sedated the following day, and sometimes it just doesn't work.

Over-the-Counter Sleep Medicines

Melatonin. This hormone occurs naturally in the body where it helps induce sleep. It's also available in a pill form, which is not exactly natural, and usually comes in doses far above the normal levels in the body. Smaller doses, such as 0.3 to 0.5 mg, are more in line with nature (Vural, van Munster, & de Rooij, 2014). The pill form also leaves the body very quickly (a sustained-release version can improve its duration).

A small dose can help set your biological clock, and it can even be used to prevent jet lag (see moodtreatmentcenter.com/bipolarnotsomuch for guidelines on preventing jet lag). It's hard to find small doses in the store, and most people prefer larger amounts (3 to 5 mg at night) because the larger dose makes them groggy. That may not be a natural level, but there doesn't seem to be much risk with taking it. No major problems have emerged since it became popular a few decades ago. Pregnant women and children should steer toward the lowest dose of melatonin or avoid it altogether until more is known (Kennaway, 2015). Remember, it is a hormone.

Histamine Blockers: diphenhydramine (Benadryl) and hydroxyzine (Vistaril). These drugs cause drowsiness by blocking histamine in the brain. They are also used for itch, allergic reactions, and colds. Diphenhydramine is available over the counter, and is often found in "Nighttime" pain medications like Tylenol PM. It's better to use diphenhydramine alone than in these popular combination pills, as the extra pain medicine could damage your liver, stomach, or kidneys. Another antihistamine, hydroxyzine, is available by prescription. Some doctors think hydroxyzine actually has fewer side effects than its over-the-counter cousin, such as less constipation, dry mouth, urine retention, and memory problems (Schiffman, Davis, & Pierre, 2011). That's right—even over-the-counter pills have side effects—and with these antihistamines, we recommend watching out for weight gain and daytime drowsiness. Antihistamines can also have a paradoxical effect—rarely, they hype people up at night.

L-tryptophan. This is an amino acid, a simple molecule that's part of the daily diet. In larger amounts, it causes fatigue, and just as with melatonin, these large doses are not necessarily natural. We have reservations about it, as small studies suggest it may worsen mood in people with bipolar (Applebaum et al., 2007; Sobczak et al., 2002). On the other hand, it has mild antidepressant properties in nonbipolar depression (though it should not be taken if you are on a serotonergic antidepressant, as it can increase the risk of a dangerous reaction called *serotonin syndrome)*.

Valerian. This is derived from a plant and has been used in medicine for over 1,000 years. Today, its main use is for insomnia, and it seems nonaddictive and well-tolerated. Some preparations from Mexico have been associated with contaminants, and rare cases of liver impairment and visual disturbance have been reported. The dose for sleep is 450 to 600 mg at night, and it can take a few weeks to build up. Higher doses do not bring greater benefits (Mischoulon & Rosenbaum, 2008).

TWENTY-THREE

Natural Healers

Key point: *Natural treatments can complement the benefits of lifestyle and medication. It's difficult to filter through the hype and figure out what really works in this area, so we'll focus here on those that are known to work better than a sugar pill.*

"Natural forces within us are the true healers of disease," wrote the ancient Greek physician Hippocrates. We couldn't agree more, but first let's agree on what is meant by *natural*. Just because something occurs in nature doesn't mean it's natural. Many medications are derived from plants and herbs, as are some of the natural options in this chapter (e.g., Sensoril, St. John's Wort, and Rhodiola rosea). Things look a little more natural if they are a regular part of the diet, but then not everything people eat is good for them.

Last, some of the compounds in this section serve an essential function in the human body, such as forming the walls of brain cells. That kind of natural looks even better, but we'll still caution that taking extra doses of a good thing is not necessarily natural.

What Hippocrates meant was that diet and exercise should be tried first to treat disease before jumping to surgery and drugs. Treatment should start with a healthy lifestyle, and you got the full report on that in Part 2 of this book. Now let's take a look at natural supplements that can help depression and bipolar. If you're interested in taking any of the supplements in this chapter, talk with your provider first to make sure they are right for you. Some of them are difficult to find, and others are difficult to find in the right dose. You'll find updated recommendations of specific products at moodtreatmentcenter.com/bipolarnotsomuch.

OMEGA-3 FATTY ACIDS

Omega-3 fatty acids (also called fish oil) make up 30% of the human brain and are naturally obtained from dietary sources like salmon and dark green vegetables. Most people don't get enough from their diet, so the brain substitutes other fats—like cholesterol and omega-6s—which make neurons less flexible (Hirashima et al., 2004; Yildiz et al., 2015). This leads to depression, bipolar, irritability, and just about every psychiatric illness in the book.

When dosed correctly, omega-3s have a real benefit in bipolar and depression, with a potency that comes close to that of some medications. They also reduce irritability in all kinds of people, including people with autism, borderline personality disorder, and substance abuse, as well as irritable people without mental illness (e.g. prisoners, elderly Thai men, and college students during exam time; Sinn, Milte, & Howe, 2010).

Omega-3s are so critical for brain development that baby formula is now supplemented with them. There may be a link between omega-3 depletion and postpartum depression, as much of a woman's omega-3 intake goes to support the developing child during pregnancy. Omega-3s have been used to treat and prevent postpartum depression, but extra caution needs to be taken to ensure the product is free of mercury contamination in these cases (Jans, Giltay, & Van der Does, 2010).

There are two types of omega-3: EPA (ethyl eicosapentaenoic acid) and DHA (docosahexanoic acid). For omega-3 to work, you need a product with both the right amount and the right ratio of EPA to DHA. Specifically, you need at least 1.5 times as much EPA as DHA*. The total daily dose (or EPA + DHA) should be between 1,000 to 3,000 mg daily.

---

*Most fish are higher in DHA than EPA, so if you consume fish regularly you should choose an omega-3 supplement that is close to 100% EPA in order to increase your EPA:DHA ratio.

That 1.5 ratio between DHA and EPA is critical, and unfortunately most products fall just short of it. That's not OK, because you can't round up—omega-3 works no better than a placebo if the ratio is 1.3 or even 1.4 (Sublette, Ellis, Geant, & Mann, 2011). If this is starting to sound confusing, skip to our website where we've highlighted products that have the right specs. We'll walk you through a sample product below so you can see how to do the math on your own. Suppose the back of the bottle reads:

Serving size = 2 capsule
Fish oil per serving: 2,000 mg
DHA per serving: 400 mg
EPA per serving: 800 mg

This product has 1,200 mg of omega-3s (EPA + DHA) in each serving. Note that the "fish oil per serving" is ignored because it's only the EPA and DHA you need. The amount of EPA is two times the amount of DHA, which is greater than 1.5 times so it will work. It takes 2 capsules to equal a serving, so for this product, you could take between 2 to 5 capsules a day to get the recommended dose of 1,000 mg to 3,000 mg daily.

More expensive brands are not necessarily better. Very high doses may not help more (taking more than 4,000 mg a day of EPA may cancel out its benefits). The best brand is one that you can afford and tolerate the taste of. Most products cost between 20 to 40¢ daily.

Importantly, flaxseed oil contains a different kind of omega-3 called n-omega-3 (e.g., alphalinolenic acid). These omega-3s convert to EPA, but at such a low rate (around 10%), that they aren't a good substitute for fish oil. They also appear to increase the risk of prostate cancer in men, while DHA and EPA lower that risk.

Quick Facts: Omega-3 Fatty Acids

How natural?	It is part of a healthy diet and occurs in the body naturally.
Benefits in bipolarity	Depression, mania, irritability.
Other benefits	Unipolar depression, ADHD, memory, schizophrenia, autism, and borderline personality disorder. They help the heart by reducing cholesterol, blood pressure, and inflammation. They lower the risk of cancer, stroke, osteoporosis, psoriasis, inflammatory bowel disease, macular degeneration, and asthma.
Side effects	Fishy taste with some brands, stomach upset. Omega-3s can increase bleeding time, which could be risky if you are undergoing surgery or take blood thinners such as Coumadin, Plavix, Effient, or Brilinta.
How to find it	Omega-3s are available in capsule and liquid forms and as vegetarian options. Odor-neutralized and enteric-coated products reduce the fishy taste, and there are products with flavors as varied as lemon, coffee, and cotton candy. Liquids should be kept in the fridge to prevent oxidation. Gummy forms may be bad for your teeth and usually don't provide the right dose. There are prescription forms (e.g. Lovaza, Epanova, Neurepa), but among these only Neurepa has the correct ingredients for depression; the others are designed for high cholesterol.
Dose	1,000–3,000 mg daily of EPA + DHA, with EPA ≥ 1.5 times the amount of DHA.

N-ACETYLCYSTEINE (NAC)

NAC has been used in medicine for decades, but its mental health benefits are a recent discovery. It helps protect brain cells by increasing the antioxidant glutathione, and improves dopamine transmission in the brain.

Many people with bipolar suffer from a chronic, low-grade depression that is difficult to fully treat. NAC helps this kind of depression, though it takes a long time to work (up to 6 months) (Deepmala et al., 2015). By that time, you may have had so many changes in your life that it's hard to tell what the NAC is doing, but interestingly, those who responded to NAC felt worse within a week of stopping it, so you can stop it after 6 months to figure out if it helps before continuing further on it.

Quick Facts: NAC

How natural?	It's an antioxidant that is found naturally in the body.
Benefits in bipolarity	Chronic, low-grade depression.
Other benefits	Compulsive hair pulling, skin picking, self-cutting, and nail biting; obsessive compulsive disorder, schizophrenia, addictions (e.g., marijuana, alcohol, cocaine, nicotine, gambling), dementia. It is used to treat lung disease, HIV, and Tylenol overdose, and it may reduce the risk of heart disease and cancer.
Side effects	Constipation, unpleasant odor to the pill.
How to find it	Health stores and online shops like Amazon and Drugstore.com. There is a prescription version (Cerefolin-NAC) that contains other vitamins that help depression (methylfolate and B vitamins). You would need 3 pills per day of Cerefolin to reach a therapeutic dose for depression.
Dose	2,000–6,000 mg daily.

INOSITOL

Inositol is a carbohydrate that improves communication between brain cells. It causes some of the same changes in the brain that lithium does, but its effects are much more limited than those of lithium. It has been studied in bipolar depression, and the results are mixed, suggesting that inositol has a small effect at best (Mukai, Kishi, Matsuda, & Iwata, 2014). Inositol and omega-3s each improve brain functioning in different ways, leading some doctors to propose that the two may complement each other when taken together. The initial results of that strategy look promising, and we know of no risks in taking those two compounds together (Wozniak, et al., 2015).

Quick Facts: Inositol

How natural?	It is found in the diet through cantaloupe, grapefruit, oranges, and beans.
Benefits in bipolarity	Depression.
Other benefits	Panic disorder, obsessive compulsive disorder, binge eating.
Side effects	Rare.
How to find it	Available in powder form at health stores and online shops like Amazon and Drugstore.com.
Dose	5–25 grams/day. Start at 2.5–6 grams/day and raise every 2 to 7 days as tolerated. Can be taken all at once or divided into three daily doses.

SENSORIL (ASHWAGANDHAIS)

Sensoril is an extract of an Indian form of ginseng (also called Ashwagandhais or *Withania somnifera*). It has been used for centuries in Indian medicine where it is thought to protect the body from disease and stress. Two compounds in the plant (glycowithanolides and sitoidosides) help protect cells in the brain's memory center (called the *hippocampus*). The hippocampus is fragile and can be injured by stress or depression. In one study, Sensoril helped depressed mice rebuild their hippocampus, reducing 80% of the damage that stress had caused.

Sensoril is one of only a few treatments that can improve concentration in mood disorders. Those who took it had better short term-recall, faster mental responses, and were more tuned in to the nonverbal cues in their relationships (what you might call social intuition; Chengappa et al., 2013).

Quick Facts: Sensoril

How natural?	Not very. It's a plant and isn't naturally found in the body or in the diet (though it is used to age cheeses).
Benefits in bipolarity	Concentration.
Other benefits	Anxiety, energy, cholesterol, diabetes, and arthritis.
Side effects	Rare stomach upset or tiredness. Possible risks of irregular heart rhythms, hyperthyroidism, and kidney problems.

How to find it	Sensoril is a formulated extract of Ashwagandhais which contains:
	    8% withanolides, 32% oligosaccharides, and no more than 2% withaferin-A.
	    This proprietary formulation is used by many brands. Other forms of Ashwagandhais are not recommended as they have not been tested and may be unsafe.

Dose	250 mg/day for 7 days then 250 mg twice/day (can be taken all at once).

PROBIOTICS

Probiotics are "healthy bacteria" that aid digestion. They are mainly used in irritable bowel syndrome but appear to have psychological benefits as well. They help colic (excess crying) in babies and anxiety in adults. It's likely they help by reducing inflammation in the body, which has been linked to anxiety and depression.

There are many types of probiotics available. The study of anxiety used a combination of *Lactobacillus helveticus* and *Bifidobacterium longum* (Messaoudi et al., 2011).

Quick Facts: Probiotics

How natural?	They are the healthy bacteria that occur naturally in the gut and are part of the diet (e.g., yogurt, kefir, kombucha, raw apple cider vinegar, nonpasteurized sauerkraut, kimchi, and pickles).
Benefits in bipolarity	Unknown.
Other benefits	Anxiety, diarrhea, and irritable bowel syndrome. They improve immune function and may prevent urinary tract and vaginal infections, gastrointestinal cancers, and the common cold.
Side effects	Headache, insomnia, rare risk of mania.
How to find it	The specific probiotic used in the anxiety study was Lallemand's Probio'stick, which is difficult to find. We list alternative brands with the same strains at moodtreatmentcenter.com/bipolarnotsomuch.
Dose	3 billion (or $3×10^9$) CFU per day.

CITICOLINE, CYTIDINE, AND LECITHIN

These three supplements are used by the brain to create cell membranes. Among them, citicoline has the most research behind it and helps a unique aspect of bipolar where medications are not very helpful. It improves mood, memory, and sobriety in people with bipolar who have abused cocaine or methamphetamine (Wignall & Brown, 2014). It seems to do this by helping rebuild the dopamine neurons that are damaged by that kind of drug abuse. Citicoline's role in brain repair has also proven useful in neurologic disease like stroke and dementia.

The research on cytidine and lecithin is more scant. Cytidine (available as cytidine choline) seems to improve bipolar depression, while lecithin may have antimanic effects. Neither have significant side effects. Lecithin is actually a group of molecules, called phospholipids, that help form brain cell membranes. The bipolar studies, which were done in the early 1980s, used a type of lecithin that is hard to find today (called phosphatidylcholine, or phospholipon-100; Cohen, Lipinski, & Altesman, 1982). However, a similar type of lecithin has recently gained popularity as an FDA-approved food supplement for memory and ADHD (phosphatidylserine, available by prescription as VayaCog and VayaRin).

Quick Facts: Citicoline

How natural?	It occurs naturally in the body.
Benefits in bipolarity	Problems associated with methamphetamine or cocaine abuse.
Other benefits	Depression related to a stroke; dementia, Parkinson's disease, traumatic head injury, glaucoma.
Side effects	None known, but it is expensive ($2–3/day).
How to find it	Health stores and online shops like Amazon and Drugstore.com.
Dose	Start at 500 mg daily and raise by 500 mg every week toward a dose of 2,000 mg daily. It can be taken all at once or spread throughout the day.

Quick Facts: Cytidine

How natural?	Part of the diet, found in yeast and organ meats.
Benefits in bipolarity	Depression.
Other benefits	Possible in Parkinson's disease.
Side effects	None, but expensive ($2–4/day).
How to find it	Search for "cytidine choline" or "cytidine CDP choline."
Dose	1 gram (1,000 mg) twice a day.

Quick Facts: Lecithin

How natural?	Part of the diet, found in eggs, soybeans, nuts, and whole grains.
Benefits in bipolarity	Manic symptoms.
Other benefits	Possible memory benefits.
Side effects	Possible depression with long-term use. In high doses, it can cause stomach upset, sweating, salivation, and low appetite. Avoid if allergic to soy.
How to find it	It is difficult to find the form used in the research, called Phospholipon-100 (>90% pure lecithin). It is made by www.lipoid.com but not sold commercially. Other versions of lecithin are available through natural health stores and Amazon.
Dose	Start at 15 mg/day, raise to 30 mg/day after 1 week.

MAGNESIUM

Like lithium, magnesium is a natural mineral. Dietary deficiencies of magnesium have been linked to depression, and magnesium has effects in the brain that are beneficial in bipolar (e.g. blocking calcium and N-methyl-D-aspartate transmission).

Magnesium can help in rapid cycling bipolar, particularly when used with the medication verapamil (Giannini, Nakoneczie, Melemis, Ventresco, & Condon, 2000).

Quick Facts: Magnesium

How natural?	It occurs naturally in the body and is a part of the diet.
Benefits in bipolarity	Rapid cycling bipolar.
Other benefits	Migraines, restless legs, muscle cramps, premenstrual syndrome (PMS).
Side effects	Rare. Possible low heart rate, nausea, diarrhea.
How to find it	Online stores (Amazon, Drugstore.com) or specialty supplement shops.
Dose	375 mg magnesium oxide daily.

EMPOWERPLUS

EMPowerplus is trademarked preparation of 36 ingredients (16 minerals, 14 vitamins, 3 amino acids, and 3 antioxidants). Seven of those ingredients are known to help either bipolar disorder (inositol and magnesium) or unipolar depression (vitamin B6, B12, folate, chromium, and L-methionine), but the doses it provides are generally below those known to be effective. Most of the remaining ingredients in EMPowerplus would be found in an average multivitamin.

EMPowerplus is advertised for bipolar, depression, anxiety, autism, and ADHD. Among these, it's only in ADHD that EMPowerplus has past the test of a placebo-controlled study. There are, however, numerous reports of children and adults whose depressive and manic symptoms improved on it. We hope that someone will compare this promising therapy to a sugar pill so we can be more assured of those results (Yildiz et al., 2015).

Quick Facts: EMPowerplus

How natural?	Most ingredients are part of the diet or occur naturally in the human body.
Benefits in bipolarity	Depression, mania (but not proven).
Other benefits	ADHD (proven in one study)
Side effects	None known.
How to find it	www.truehope.com
Dose	2 tablets or capsules daily.

LIGHT THERAPY

Seasonal mood changes are common in bipolarity. Most often there is depression in the winter and manic or mixed symptoms in the spring. Seasonal shifts also occur in nonbipolar depressions.

The intensity of seasonal depression depends on where you live. The rates start to go down in South Carolina and the lower states, and nearly go away in places like Florida. In Northern Europe, where winters are particularly dark, light therapy is so common that people go to light bars to soak up light instead of cocktails.

Light therapy has been known to treat seasonal depression for over 30 years, and it's one of the few natural treatments that works as well as medication. Amazingly, light therapy even treats depression in the summertime, maybe because people spend too much time indoors (Wirz-Justice, Benedetti, & Terman, 2013).

The treatment involves sitting under a lightbox for about 30 minutes in the morning. This resets the biological clock, which is a little broken in mood disorders. The timing of light therapy is critical. If used in the late afternoon or evening, it can actually cause depression by setting the clock the wrong way. There are two approaches to the timing, and the research isn't clear yet on which path you should take. For bipolar depression, the lightbox seems to work well and have less risk of destabilizing mood when used around noon (Geoffroy et al., 2015). For unipolar depression, most research points toward early morning use (e.g., 6–8 a.m.; Wirz-Justice et al., 2013). There is even a self-test that can tell you the optimal time to turn it on in the morning if you're using the early-morning strategy. You can take that test on this book's website (moodtreatmentcenter.com/bipolarnotsomuch).

However, these rules are not hard and fast, especially for people near the middle of the mood spectrum, so you may need to use some trial and error and talk with your provider about when to turn it on.

Regardless of whether you turn it on in morning or noon, you should sit under the box for 30 minutes each day. If there's no improvement after 1 to 2 weeks, increase the time (up to 2 hours). You can read or eat while under the box, but should remain close under it during the treatment. Don't look directly into the box, but let it hang over you at a 30- to 45-degree angle just like the sun hangs over your head.

Light therapy can trigger manic symptoms, though the risk of this is much less than once thought. The risk is greater if you have Bipolar I. If manic or mixed symptoms develop while using it, you should decrease the time you spend under it or stop it altogether.

It's best to start light therapy about 2 weeks before you anticipate winter depression coming on. As spring comes on, you can slowly reduce the time you spend under it and stop it altogether 2 weeks after you would expect your winter depression to go away on its own.

If sitting under a light box doesn't fit your schedule, consider a dawn simulator. This requires no effort (it turns on gradually while you are asleep) and has a mild benefit in depression. Turn back to Chapter 10 to learn more.

There's a lot to know about light therapy, and those details would fill another book. Indeed they have, and we recommend *Reset Your Inner Clock* (Terman, 2013). The most difficult step is purchasing the right box. Be careful: The most popular models are small and sit on a table instead of hanging over your head. They are more attractive, but do not work. The bulbs need to be replaced every 2 to 3 years, which may be before

Quick Facts: Light Therapy

How natural?	Almost as natural as sunlight.
Benefits in bipolarity	Depression, energy, sleep.
Other benefits	Unipolar depression, ADHD, bulimia.
Side effects	Headache, insomnia, rare risk of mania.
How to find it	Look for these specifications in a lightbox: Intensity: at least 2,000 lux; 10,000 lux is optimal Screen size: at least 12 × 17 inches Wavelength: around 509 nM (white light)
Dose	Usually 30 minutes in morning, but may need to be personalized.

they burn out, as their wavelengths may fade enough in that time to lose the antidepressant effect. Our website lists models that have proven their merit in clinical tests.

NATURAL TREATMENTS FOR ANXIETY

There are two natural treatments for anxiety that might also be found in your kitchen and garden. Chamomile comes in a tablet form, and those with 1.2% apigenin can help sleep and anxiety at a dose of 220 mg daily (Amsterdam et al., 2009). Lavender has also been extracted into a form called Silexan, and a study of this extract found it improved generalized anxiety disorder even better than paroxetine (Paxil), one of the most popular antidepressants for anxiety (Kasper, 2014). Silexan is a prescription product in Germany where it is approved for anxiety, and it's available over-the-counter in the United States as Calm Aid (made by Nature's Way).

It's not known if chamomile and lavender can trigger manic symptoms, but the risk appears very low. One of us (Aiken) has used them in over 100 patients with bipolar disorder without inducing mania.

AROMATHERAPY

It's not surprising that scents have an effect on the brain, as the olfactory nerves which detect smell go straight from the nose to the brain. The studies of aromatherapy are numerous, and though none are very scientifically designed, the gist of them suggest that lavender scents improve anxiety and sleep, while citrus and mint help depression and concentration. There are no known risks with aromatherapy.

NATURAL THERAPIES FOR UNIPOLAR DEPRESSION

There are many other natural treatments for depression that haven't yet been studied in people with bipolarity. Among those that have at least one controlled trial supporting their use in unipolar depression are*:

- Rhodiola rosea (200–400 mg daily)
- Chromium picolinate (600 mcg daily)
- L-methylfolate (Deplin, 7–15 mg daily, taken with an antidepressant)
- Saffron (30 mg daily)
- Creatine (5 grams daily; effective when used with an SSRI antidepressant in women)
- Acetyl-L-carnitine 1,000–3,00 daily
- St. John's Wort (Hypericum perforatum) 900–1,800 mg daily
- SAMe 400–1,600 mg daily
- Vitamin supplementation with folate 2 mg daily and vitamin B12 400–600 mg daily

Among these, SAMe has the best evidence to treat unipolar depression, where it works as well as an antidepressant. Unfortunately, it does not work in bipolar depression and has about the same risk of causing mania as an antidepressant (Yildiz et al., 2015). Like SAMe, St. John's Wort works a lot like an antidepressant and can trigger mania. We've seen many people with bipolarity try it on their own but we know of no successes.

*Lopresti & Drummond, 2014; Lyoo et al., 2012; Mischoulon & Rosebaum, 2008; Wang et al., 2014.

TWENTY-FOUR

Knowing When to Stop Medications

Key point: *Depression has a high chance (up to 90%) of coming back, but that doesn't mean you have to stay on every medication you've ever taken. The best way to minimize medication is to stay out of depression. Tapering medications slowly and carefully helps minimize that risk.*

"Will I have to take this for life?" It's an important question, and one we hear often. The answer depends on whether you are taking the medicine for active treatment or prevention. Active treatment is what gets you out of a mood episode, and prevention is what keeps them from returning.

The textbook answer is that active treatments should be taken for at least 6 months after recovery. That's about how long it takes the brain to heal. If the active treatment is stopped too soon, it's likely that the old symptoms will return because the brain is still in a vulnerable place. As for preventative treatments, the textbook advice is that people with bipolarity need to stay on them because the risk of new episodes is just too high (over 90%; Yildiz et al., 2015).

Now for a more practical answer. No one wants to think about taking a medication "for the rest of their life." Even if that was true, which is uncertain (what new treatments, including nonmedication approaches, might emerge in the next few decades?), it's not a very useful way to look at the future.

Instead, think of it this way. You'll be taking the medication until you're doing really well. Then, after you've enjoyed a good long period of recovery, you'll start wondering whether you need to stay on it.

When you reach that point, have a conversation with your provider. Hear out their concerns. Then, if you're still determined to try it, ask them to help you plan out how to gradually taper off, and only come off one medication at a time. That conversation should include how to know when it's time to say "oops, bad idea" and what you'll do then. Will you go back up, or switch to something else? What are the pros and cons of the alternatives?

HOW TO AVOID MEDICATION OVERLOAD

Sometimes it can look like a medication helped when the recovery would have happened naturally with time. We showed you a case like that ("Josh") in Chapter 20. That kind of problem happens a lot for people on the mood spectrum, and it can lead to a laundry list of medications. Here are some ways to avoid medication overload.

Focus on Prevention

Take at least one medication that can prevent mood episodes from returning. Good options include lithium, lamotrigine, carbamazepine, valproate, and, for some people, the atypical antipsychotics. Talk with your provider about which medicines are necessary for prevention, and don't try to come off those unless you're having side effects you can't tolerate. In that case, talk with your provider about your options. Sometimes you just have to turn down the one you're on until the side effect goes away and add a tiny bit of another mood stabilizer (even fish oil counts here) to make up the difference.

Come Off Other Medicines Slowly, One at a Time

It's easy to stop medications; it's hard to do it successfully. Too often people stop all their medications in a moment of desperation, only to crash into a depression and have to restart them all again out of a different kind of desperation. Here are some tips to avoid that cycle:

- Lower them slowly (e.g., over 2 to 4 months). New episodes are less likely to come on if you go slow.
- Lower them one at a time. That way you won't have to restart them all if there's a misstep.
- Lower them after your mood has been stable for at least 6 months. That gives your brain time to build up strength.
- Avoid lowering them when you're under major stress. Again, the goal is to stack the odds in your favor.

Do All You Can to Prevent Bipolarity Outside of Medication

Lifestyle and natural approaches are an essential part of this package. As for pills, though: The best way to avoid being on too many medications is to take the ones that work. The more mood episodes you have, the more frequent and difficult to treat they may become. This vicious cycle is called *kindling,* which means that episodes change the brain in ways that make them more likely to occur. What this means for you is that the earlier you intervene and treat them, the easier it will be to recover and the fewer medications you will need.

When bipolarity goes on too long, it can become complicated, twisting into rapid cycles and mixed states, and overlapping with anxiety. It can also cause you to lose the healthy supports and habits that keep depression away. There are four reasons why bipolarity might go on too long:

- The medications you are taking haven't worked.
- You've stopped treatments that you needed.

- Other factors are overpowering the medications (e.g., substance abuse, medical illness, or severe stress).
- And there are a few people who just inherited a combination of genes that makes their bipolarity hard to keep under control even when they're doing everything right.

HOW MANY MEDICINES ARE TOO MANY?

If mood stabilizers, vitamins, sleep medicines, and antidotes for side effects are starting to crowd your pill box, you might be wondering where all this is heading. We've got some surprising answers below, but first a note on the pill box. Anyone taking more than two medications a day should consider a daily pill box. It's far too easy to forget whether you took that pill and end up missing a day or double dosing.

For many people, the number of pills they are taking has a strong personal meaning, and it's usually a negative one. "This must mean I'm really sick," "I feel like an old man every morning," "All these pills must be doing some damage," are common reactions. Less often is the thought, "I'm finally taking care of myself like I'm worth something," or "I'm lucky to be alive in an age where we have so many treatments."

While many people donate time and money to support medical research, it doesn't feel so good when the fruits of that research end up in our medicine cabinet. The number of available medications has more than doubled since the 1980s, and this explosion takes some getting used to (Figure 24.1). Five medications a day may have meant you were seriously ill in the 1980s, but might mean something very different in the 2010s.

We do live in a very different world then the one our grandparents were born into. Before 1937, pharmaceutical companies were not required to prove that their drugs were safe. It was not until 1963 that they were required to also show their drugs worked. On the other hand, a quick glance at any processed food label will likely reveal more chemicals than would fit in a pill box, and those chemicals don't have to prove that they're beneficial to health.

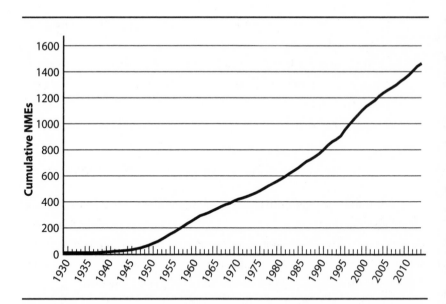

FIGURE 24.1 Available FDA-Approved Medications by Year (Psychiatric and Nonpsychiatric). Source: Kinch, M. S., Haynesworth, A., & Kinch, S. L. (2014). An overview of FDA-approved new molecular entities: 1827–2013. *Drug Discovery Today, 19,* 1033–1039.

This is not to minimize the risks of medications. The bottom line is that it makes more sense to focus on how many health risks you have, and how they are being reduced, than on the number of medications you take. The next section has some frightening and reassuring data on that note.

TWENTY-FIVE

Live Long and Minimize Side Effects

Key point: *Despite their risks, taking mood stabilizers can actually increase the life span. There are many ways to make medications affordable, safer, and more tolerable.*

As you weigh the risks of medications, it's critical to remember that untreated mood disorders have side effects of their own. You'll recall from Chapter 2 that mood disorders are not emotional illnesses. Well, some doctors think they should even be reclassified as physical illnesses because they can harm the body as much as the mind.

Consider this statistic: A study of 10.5 million people found that those with bipolar died 10 years earlier than the rest of the population, and the main cause of premature death was not suicide but medical problems.

Top Causes of Premature Death in Bipolar

Heart disease
Stroke
Cancer
Diabetes mellitus
Chronic obstructive pulmonary disease (COPD)
Pneumonia and influenza
Accidental injuries
Suicide

About 82% of these deaths were from medical problems, while suicide and accidents accounted for the remaining 18% (Crump, Sundquist, Winkleby, & Sundquist, 2013).

No one is sure how bipolar causes all these health problems, but it is not simply due to lifestyle, and even substance abuse only modestly raised the risks. Bipolar affects the body in many ways that might explain these illnesses. It raises levels of inflammation and oxidative stress, disrupts steroids and other hormones that circulate between the mind and body, and raises adrenaline during agitated or manic states.

Now for the hopeful part. Despite all the risks that mood stabilizers carry, the risk of medical problems was highest among those with bipolar who did not take medication. Those who started treatment early had the lowest risk of premature death, suggesting that long-term use of mood stabilizers can prevent these problems (Crump et al., 2013).

This relationship between the mind and body goes both ways. Treating depression will improve your physical health, and taking care of your body will improve your mental health. Let's look at that more closely.

PHYSICAL HEALTH

Without a doubt: Psychiatric medications work better when people are in good physical health. This is true for mood stabilizers as well as antidepressants. But all health problems are not equal. We'll focus here on the top conditions that impact mental health.

Thyroid

Thyroid hormones influence so many mood symptoms (energy, appetite, concentration, anxiety) that it may as well be called the mood hormone. Indeed, thyroid problems are more common among people with bipolarity. Low thyroid levels contribute to depression, while elevated ones tend to cause anxiety and agitation, but the reverse can also be true, and any thyroid problem can cause rapid cycling.

Thyroid hormone is produced by the thyroid gland, which sits just above your collarbone in the front of your neck. This hormone regulates your body's metabolic rate. When it's too low, people generally feel cold, as though their furnaces weren't burning hot enough. When it's too high, people can feel hot when others are comfortable, and sometimes kind of wired, like too much strong coffee. Their furnaces are turned up too high. But thyroid hormone does far more than this. It is an essential brain signal as well, with many roles, some of which affect mood.

When a provider orders a blood test for thyroid, she will usually test something called thyroid stimulating hormone (TSH). TSH is the signal from your brain to your thyroid gland that says "make more thyroid hormone." When your thyroid level is too high, TSH goes down. When your thyroid level is too low, TSH goes up. It's all backward.

Thyroid levels that are normal for general health may not be good enough for people with mood disorders. The higher the TSH, the more likely patients are to have rapid cycling, and the less likely that treatment for depression will work. This is true even when TSH is in the normal range, so careful attention to the TSH level is an important part of a good mood management (Bauer et al., 2003).

Sex Hormones

Although it's clear that changes in reproductive hormones in women contribute to mood disorders, it's not clear exactly how or what to do about it. Mood swings before menses are so widely recognized that they have their own diagnosis (Premenstrual Dysphoric Disorder, or PMDD). Other critical periods where women experience more mood problems are around menopause, after childbirth, and after changes in hormone replacement therapy (HRT).

The highest risk period for mood disorders in a woman's life is after childbirth, and these postpartum episodes tend to peak about 1 month after delivery. Postpartum depression is not the same as the baby blues, which refers to a brief period of tearfulness that is common in the first week after childbirth. The baby blues are normal and do not require treatment, but postpartum depression can be severe and treating it will make a positive difference for your child as well as yourself.

PMDD and PMS. Some women have troublesome shifts in mood that start about 1 week prior to menses. PMDD is only diagnosed if the mood changes are severe; milder forms are considered normal and are called premenstrual syndrome or PMS. For readers of this book, however, the most important thing to know is that PMDD is not diagnosed when an underlying mood disorder gets worse in the premenstrual phase. Most women with mood disorders will experience worse symptoms in that phase, but that doesn't mean they have PMDD.

PMDD is a unique disorder where the mood symptoms are limited to the week or two before menstruation. It also involves physical symptoms like bloating, breast tenderness and muscle aches. PMDD is usually treated with antidepressants, which can cause problems if it's really bipolarity instead of PMDD that's driving the mood swings. There are nonantidepressant options for PMDD, including calcium, black cohosh, and chasteberry, but these were not studied in bipolar individuals.

Women with mood disorders usually feel worse before their menstrual cycle for the same reason that people feel worse under stress. Both stress and menstruation involve surges of steroid hormones, and when these go into the brain irritability and depression tend to come out. The same is true for people taking steroids. In those situations the best thing to do is treat the underlying mood disorder. This may involve raising a mood stabilizer in the premenstrual phase if there is bipolarity going on, or raising an antidepressant if there is not. Lifestyle changes would be helpful for either.

Menopause. Depression has been associated with the menopausal phase as well, and it's controversial whether HRT can help that. Around a dozen controlled studies looked at this question, and only one found a benefit. HRT may improve quality of life in other ways without treating depression, but evaluating its risks is a complex issue most psychiatrists don't get into (e.g., risk of developing breast or uterine cancer).

Fortunately, after menopause, mood problems usually slowly diminish. It can take a long while, and improvement is slow. It's as though the erratic estrogen levels that preceded menopause sensitized the brain, increasing the mood problems that were there a decade before but much more subtle. And then it takes several years for that sensitization to gradually decrease. Unfortunately, this aspect of mood disorders has been remarkably understudied.

Birth Control Pills. Although HRT has a potential benefit for mood, birth control pills (BCP) can make mood better or worse. There are two key hormones in BCP: progestin and estrogen. When mood gets worse, it's usually the fault of the progestin, but you can't simply take progestin away. Without it, there's a risk that the estrogen may cause cancer. One type of progestin is less harmful for mood: desogestrel. This is used in "third generation" BCPs like Yasmin and Yaz. Other formulations, which contain the progestin levonorgestrel, tend to cause a little more trouble for women with mood problems (Goldberg, 2012).

Testosterone. Men's testosterone levels tend to decline after age 40, and low testosterone may play a role in depression, but the risks of testosterone supplementation usually outweigh the benefits unless the levels are extremely low. Testosterone has both psychiatric and medical risks. Too much testosterone can cause—yes, you guessed it—irritability and mania. Medical risks with testosterone supplementation include blood clots, stroke, sleep apnea, acne, prostate growth, and breast enlargement.

Sleep Apnea

Sleep apnea means that breathing stops while you're asleep. As you age, the tissues near your windpipe get softer. When you sleep, they sag and can obstruct your airway. Snoring is one marker of this problem, though you can have complete obstruction without snoring. When you can't get air into your lungs because of this obstruction, you wake up, briefly, take a few gasping breaths, then go back to sleep. This all happens so fast that you never really wake up enough to know it's happening. But the next day, it's as though you didn't sleep much—because you didn't. You were waking up all night.

Anything that impairs sleep can cause mood disorders, but sleep apnea does a little more than this. It deprives the brain of oxygen at night. It's hard for any medication to work when that is going on. Depression, fatigue, irritability, headaches, and concentration problems are common daytime complaints for people with sleep apnea.

Rates of sleep apnea are increasing as obesity rises. Since 1991, there has been a 75% increase in obesity in the United States. Can you believe that? One in every five Americans is obese. Unfortunately, the standard test for sleep apnea, an overnight sleep study in which breathing is monitored during sleep, is very expensive. Frankly, we're not sure we can afford, as a country, to test everyone who might need to be tested.

So, how are you supposed to figure out whether sleep apnea might be contributing to your mood problem? Most sleep specialists consider a screening tool called STOP-BANG to be a good way to look for apnea (Table 25.1). How many of these questions would get a "yes" from you?

If you answered yes to five or more of these questions, you should

TABLE 25.1 Looking for Sleep Apnea: The STOP-BANG Questionnaire

S	Do you Snore loudly (loud enough to be heard through closed doors or your bed partner elbows you for snoring at night)?
T	Do you often feel Tired, fatigued, or sleepy during the daytime (such as falling asleep during driving or talking to someone)?
O	Has anyone Observed you stop breathing, or choking/gasping during your sleep?
P	Do you have or are you being treated for high blood Pressure?
B	Body mass index more than 35 kg/m^2? (Use an online calculator: You need only your height and weight).
A	Age older than 50?
N	Neck Size large? (Measured around Adam's apple) For male, is your shirt collar 17 inches / 43 cm or larger? For female, is your shirt collar 16 inches / 41 cm or larger?
G	Gender = male?

ask your provider about sleep apnea. Even if you just answer yes to two of the STOP questions, or 3 to 4 of all the questions together, sleep apnea should remain a concern (Chung, Abdullah, & Liao, 2015).

Weight

Obesity can reduce the benefits of antidepressants. This isn't simply due to body image. Obesity causes inflammation in the body that interferes chemically with treatment. This problem is more pronounced when the body mass index (or BMI) rises above 30 (Woo et al., 2016).

Other Health Problems

Just about any medical condition can cause or contribute to depression. It's a good idea to screen for these when you first start treatment or if treatments are not working well. Examples include anemia (low blood count) and low vitamin levels (folate, B12, and vitamin D).

Diseases that raise inflammation in the body can cause depression, including allergies, infections, and immunologic disorders. Viral inflammation can impact the brain. People with bipolar disorder who carry the herpes virus report better concentration when they take the antiviral medicine valacyclovir (Valtrex) (Jancin, 2013).

Chronic pain is another common cause, and some medicines for pain have possible benefits in bipolar (gabapentin (Neurontin), pregabalin (Lyrica)) while others can make bipolar worse (antidepressants).

Nonpsychiatric medications can also affect mood. Among these, prednisone is the most important, as it can easily cause mania or depression even in people without bipolar disorder. Prednisone is often given for brief periods to quickly reduce inflammation. Long-term use of opioid pain medicines or benzodiazepine anxiety medicines can cause depressive symptoms, such as cognitive slowing and emotional numbing.

The full list of medications that have been linked to depression is quite long, and in most cases, the linkage is speculative, so it's best to follow your own experience before concluding that a medicine is causing your symptoms. This can be done through careful on/off experiments as guided by your physician. Many medications on the "may cause depression" list also have studies suggesting they can improve mood, such as statins, beta-blockers, anticonvulsants, nonsteroidal anti-inflammatory pain medicines, melatonin, and estrogens.

MANAGING SIDE EFFECTS

Side effects come in two varieties: short-term and long-term. Those that come on soon after starting a medicine, particularly fatigue and stomach problems, usually improve with time.

For those that don't go away, it's a good idea to ask your provider whether the side effect is dangerous and whether it's treatable. There are medicines that can reduce unpleasant side effects, and though this sounds like a risky venture, it often allows people to live comfortably with a treatment that has made a big difference in their life. Many of these antidotes have simple effects on the body, often through a mechanism that directly reverses the unwanted side effect (Table 25.2).

PREGNANCY AND BREASTFEEDING

Pregnancy, and the postpartum period that occurs in the 6 months after delivery, is one of the highest risk periods for mood episodes in a woman's life. Actually, in a man's life as well (there's a high risk of mania in men after child birth, perhaps because of the shifting routines and sleep disruption).

Men need not worry about the effects of their medication on a developing baby, nor should women before they are pregnant. The testes and ovaries are protected by a tight barrier that keeps medications out, so medicines cannot impact the sperm and egg that may one day turn into a pregnancy.

During pregnancy, the highest risk period for negative effects from

TABLE 25.2 Strategies to Reduce Side Effects

Side effect	Antidotes	Notes
Weight gain	Topiramate, orlistat, zonisamide, naltrexone. For weight gain on atypical antipsychotics: Metformin, nizatidine, melatonin 3 to 5 mg at night.	Start with diet and exercise, as most of these antidotes carry risks.
Sexual dysfunction	Viagra, Cialis, Levitra, ginkgo, maca root, Zestra, Arginmax. For men taking lithium, aspirin 240 mg daily.	Viagra-type compounds can help women and men.
Fatigue	Modafinil, armodafinil.	Take sedating medications at night.
Tremor	Propranolol, vitamin B6 (900–1,200 mg daily), primidone.	Often improves with lowering doses.
Restlessness (akathisia)	Propranolol, benzodiazepines, betaxolol, vitamin B6 (900-1,200 mg daily), pramipexole, ropinirole, gabapentin.	
Muscle stiffness (dystonia)	Benztropine.	
Tardive dyskinesia	Ginkgo extract (egb-761), Keppra, vitamin B6 (1,200 mg daily).	Vitamin E (1,200 IU daily) has preventative effects.
Teeth grinding (bruxism)	Propranolol, benzodiazepines, gabapentin.	Talk to your dentist as a mouth guard may be needed.
Nausea	Ginger tabs, ondansetron, promethazine.	Try taking medications with food.
Constipation	Colace, methylcellulose, psyllium seed, senna, metoclopramide, bethanechol.	Increase fiber, stay hydrated, and exercise.
Diarrhea	Probiotics, loperamide, metamucil, milk of magnesia, amphojel, bismuth subsalicylate.	Stay hydrated.
Dry mouth	Sugar-free gum (e.g., Spry, SmartMouth), Biotene, Evoxac, pilocarpine.	Avoid caffeine and sugary drinks. Watch for dental problems.
Acne	Doxycycline, tetracycline.	

continued

Sweating	Terazosin, clonidine, oxybutynin, benztropine, glycopyrrolate, aripiprazole.	
Hair loss	Biotin, Rogaine. If taking valproate: multivitamin with selenium and zinc (see page 168).	
Itch	Hydroxyzine, doxepin, Aveeno oatmeal bath, Sarna lotion.	
Leg cramps	Gabapentin, vitamin E, vitamin B-complex, calcium.	
Vivid dreams	Take offending medications in the morning.	Taking a hot bath at night, sleep in a colder room, exercise in the afternoon, and keep the lights down at night.

Source: Goldberg, 2012

medicine is in the first trimester. That is when the major organs are developing and would be most sensitive to harm.

Any risks that medications pose to the pregnancy need to be weighed against the known risks of depression. Study after study has found that children born to mothers with depression do not develop as well emotionally and intellectually. Part of this may be due to the interactions between the mother and child, and part could be due to hormonal changes that depression brings on during pregnancy.

The only mood stabilizer that should be completely avoided in pregnancy is valproate. Children who were exposed to valproate during pregnancy have lower IQ scores and can have serious spinal cord problems. Other mood stabilizers have known risks, but the risks are much smaller. The safest mood stabilizers during pregnancy are lamotrigine and the atypical antipsychotics. These have the most data supporting their safety, with little evidence of causing problems (Khan, 2015).

During breastfeeding, most medications pass through the breast milk, but it's not known whether this harms a young baby. On the other hand, the benefits of breastfeeding are so well known that one should think twice before forgoing it. Although it makes intuitive sense to bottle-feed if you are taking a psychiatric medication (especially valproate), consider this surprising fact: Children who were bottle-fed to avoid exposure to anticonvulsant medications ended up with lower IQs than those whose mothers breastfed them while taking anticonvulsants. Valproate was one of those anticonvulsants, as were other mood stabilizers we've discussed like lamotrigine and carbamazepine (Meador et al., 2014).

It's best to plan pregnancy when your mood is in a good place and you've found medications that work for you. Sticking with what works will help you avoid new medication trials during pregnancy, which keeps the number of medication exposures to a minimum. More importantly, it will help you stay well, as there is some truth in this bottom line: A healthy mother makes a healthy child.

BRANDS, GENERICS, AND COSTS

We are often unpleasantly surprised to see brand-name drugs in the top ten list of commonly prescribed medications, especially when good generic options are available. It takes around 7 to 10 years for a branded medication to go generic. In the first year that it's generic, the price remains high because only one generic manufacturer is allowed to produce it. After that, the market opens, and prices drop dramatically.

Sometimes newer medicines have real advantages over the older generics, such as lurasidone (Latuda), which causes less weight gain and fatigue than its generic alternative quetiapine (Seroquel). On the other hand, there is a very good reason to trust generics more than the newer brands: They've stood the test of time. It's not uncommon to see new warnings added to medications within the first few years of their release.

A separate question is whether you should continue taking the branded version after a medication becomes generic. Usually there is no meaningful difference between the two. The FDA requires generics to achieve the same levels in the blood as the brand, plus or minus 20%. If you feel the generic is not as effective or has more side effects, a reasonable first step would be to ask your provider to raise or lower the dose by 20%. You could also try different generic manufacturers, which may require shopping at different pharmacies.

When there have been problems with generics, it usually happens with those that have complex release mechanisms, such as extended release (XR or XL) and controlled release (CR). Problems with these would cause the medicine to release too quickly or too slowly, as seen in 2012 when a generic version of bupropion (Wellbutrin) XL was pulled from the market (it was later replaced with an improved version).

If you do take a brand-name medication, ask your doctor or check the manufacturer's website for coupons. If you don't have health insurance, check our website for programs that can help you find low cost or free medications (moodtreatmentcenter.com/bipolarnotsomuch).

Hard Pills to Swallow

All medications should be taken with liquid, unless advised otherwise (e.g., asenapine (Saphris) should be taken alone). There's a small chance that pills could get lodged in your esophagus without fluid to wash them down.

If you have difficulty swallowing pills, try these techniques:

- Put the pill in applesauce, yogurt, or another thick liquid.
- Crush, cut, or grind the pill and add it to a thick liquid (you can purchase a pill-splitter from the pharmacy).
- Ask your pharmacist if it's ok to cut or crush the pill. This is usually fine with tablets but can cause problems with capsules and time-released or enteric-coated pills. The pharmacist can also tell you if the medicine comes in liquid or other forms (such as lamotrigine-ODT—which dissolves under the tongue).

If that doesn't work, try these more advanced techniques:

Pop-bottle method for tablets:

1. Fill a flexible water bottle with water (the kind you could crush by sucking on the opening).
2. Place the tablet on your tongue and close your lips tightly around the bottle. Then drink the water by sucking it down. Your lips should form a tight seal to keep air from getting in the bottle, so that the bottle squeezes in on itself as you suck the water down.

Lean-forward method for capsules:

1. Place the capsule on your tongue.
2. Take a medium sip of water, but don't swallow yet.
3. Bend your head down by tilting your chin toward your chest and swallow the water and capsule.

(Schiele, Schneider, Quinzler, Reich, & Haefeli, 2014)

TWENTY-SIX

Beyond Medication: Electricity,

Magnets, and Depression

Key point: *Electroconvulsive therapy and transcranial magnetic stimulation are two procedures that treat depression when medications haven't worked. There's a lot of myths around these, so they're worth a fresh look.*

What do you do when medications and lifestyle changes haven't worked? There are a number of medical procedures which can treat depression, and we'll focus here on the top two that are worth your consideration: electroconvulsive therapy (ECT) and transcranial magnetic stimulation (TMS) have a lot in common. Both work by causing electrical changes in the brain, and both can work when medications haven't.

ELECTROCONVULSIVE THERAPY

Electroconvulsive therapy (ECT) has been used for over 80 years, longer than any psychiatric medication, and the reason for this is that it remains the most effective treatment for depression. Over those years, the treatment has been refined to make it safer and better tolerated.

ECT works by inducing a seizure in the brain. This resets brain chemistry in a way that breaks through intractable depression. It does not harm the brain, in fact it causes brain cells to grow and strengthen (neuroprotection). ECT uses an electrical wave to induce the seizure, because brain cells communicate in part through electrical signals, but the electricity is not necessary for the procedure. In the 1920s and 1930s, doctors used medicines to induce the seizure, but electricity turned out to be much safer.

Today, ECT can be done with anesthesia to keep the seizure from affecting the body. There have also been advances in the electrical wavelengths used and the placement of the electrodes. For example, people have fewer concentration and memory problems when the electrodes are placed on the right, rather than on both, sides of the brain (however, placing them on both sides can be more effective).

The main safety risk in ECT comes from the anesthesia, which is a mild one that carries similar risks to the anesthetics dentists use to remove wisdom teeth. Beyond that, ECT is surprisingly safe; for pregnant women, it is even safer than medication.

Memory loss is usually the most troublesome side effect. People usually don't remember things that happened during the month they had ECT. Day to day, they may forget what they did or ate, and years later, that time period is likely to be a blur. It's controversial whether ECT can cause long-term memory problems. A lot of research has gone into that question, and the results suggest that many people have better memory after ECT (perhaps because they are less depressed); others have memory problems due to the effects of chronic depression; and a rare minority have memory problems due to ECT (Mankad & Beyer, 2010).

For many years, ECT was used mainly for unipolar depression, as it can be twice as effective as antidepressant medication. The most exciting update to ECT's benefits came in 2015, when it was proven to work for bipolar depression as well. The results were impressive. More than twice as many people with bipolar depression responded to ECT than they did to medication (Schoeyen et al., 2015).

Not as much is known about how ECT works in mania and mixed states, and there are cases of it causing as well as helping mania.

There is one down side to ECT's benefits. It doesn't keep people from going back into the depression. Fortunately, many people are able to use preventative medication and lifestyle changes to keep depression at bay. When that doesn't work, monthly ECT treatments can be used to help people stay well.

Transcranial Magnetic Stimulation

Like ECT, transcranial magnetic stimulation (TMS) also relies on electricity to stimulate brain cells, but uses magnets to create that electrical effect. The brain stimulation that TMS brings is lighter than that of ECT, which means it's better tolerated but less effective (it's about 60% as effective as ECT; Micallef-Trigona, 2014). There are studies underway for high intensity versions of TMS that may work better. This therapy can definitely help people on the unipolar side who haven't responded to antidepressants (Kedzior, 2015). Less is known about its effects in bipolar depression, but so far the results look promising (Berlim, van den Eynde, Tovar-Perdomo, & Daskalakis, 2013). Table 26.1 reviews the key differences between these two therapies.

TABLE 26.1 ECT vs. TMS

	ECT	TMS
Treats unipolar depression when medication hasn't worked	Yes	Yes
Treats bipolar depression when medication hasn't worked	Yes	Probably
Is the most effective option	Yes	No
Prevents depression	No	No
Uses anesthesia	Yes	No
Requires a hospital stay	Sometimes	No
Requires someone to drive you home	Yes	No

Number of sessions	8–12 (3 per week)	20–30 (5 per week)
Total cost of treatment	$25,000	$15,000
Covered by insurance	Usually	Sometimes
Side effects	Headaches, muscle aches, temporary memory loss	Headaches, risk of seizures
Mechanism of stimulating brain cells	Electricity	Magnets (which create electricity)
Endorsed by Dr. Oz?	Yes	Yes

S

TWENTY-SEVEN

Good Therapy

Key point: *Therapy works for bipolar and depression. When it comes to anxiety and insomnia, therapy often works better than medication. Finding a therapist who's a good fit for you and understands how to work with these conditions can be a challenge, but a worthwhile one.*

There are some good reasons to consider therapy:

1. It works for bipolar. On average, an effective therapy can cut the rate of depression and mood swings in half, and that benefit continues years after ending therapy (Scott, Colom, & Vieta, 2007).
2. It may help you reduce medications (but unfortunately therapy doesn't work well enough to completely replace mood stabilizers).
3. It helps many of the problems that go along with bipolar better than medication does. These include anxiety, addictions, eating disorders, PTSD, and borderline personality.
4. Therapy not only improves symptoms; it helps the problems that bipolar causes in your life and relationships.

There are also reasons to avoid therapy:

1. *Time.* Therapy works best when you attend for at least an hour a week. Your therapist will also call on you to make changes and practice new skills outside of session. It doesn't have to go on forever—many people get significant benefits after about 12

sessions. After that, people may cut back to monthly sessions or stop therapy and return as needed.

2. *Expense.* Therapy sessions run from $60 to $300 per hour. These days many insurance plans have high deductibles, but using your insurance can still bring savings. If your therapist is in-network with your insurer, they will usually offer you a reduced rate (often a 20–50% discount), which can ease the burden these deductibles bring. Group therapy costs even less.

3. *You're not ready.* Therapy should not become another check on your list of failures, but keep in mind that a good therapist will meet you where you're at and help you take on things where you can find success. Even if your depression is so severe that you can barely hold a conversation, therapy can still bring benefits by offering support and basic behavioral guidance. If your motivation for therapy is truly 0%, and the only pressure to attend is from your relatives, consider family therapy for bipolar (which is just as effective as individual).

THERAPIES FOR BIPOLAR

A handful of therapies have proven effective for bipolar disorder (both Bipolar I and II):

- Interpersonal social rhythm therapy (IPSRT)
- Cognitive behavioral therapy for bipolar (CBT-B)
- Family-focused therapy for bipolar
- Group psychoeducation
- Group functional remediation

The challenge is finding a therapist who knows how to use these techniques. Don't fret if that's not possible in your area. It's more important to find a good therapist who understands mood disorders, and whom you are comfortable opening up with. Here are some tips:

- Ask your psychiatrist whom they recommend. If the therapist works closely with your doctor, that can help them both stay up to date, and on the same page, with you.
- Check the therapist's website or online database (we have a few selections at www.moodtreatmentcenter.com/bipolarnotsomuch).
- Look for therapists who have done additional training in mood disorders or who belong to societies that advocate for mood-focused therapies (see Appendix D).
- Call your local depression or bipolar support group leader and ask for their recommendations (see Appendix E).
- Call your insurer to find out who is in-network.

Once you've found some names, you should feel free to ask the therapist a few questions by phone before scheduling. If you're still unsure whom to pick, it's fair to consider your first appointment a trial session. Therapists understand that they are not a good match for everyone, and you won't hurt anyone's feelings by meeting with a few before choosing. This is an area of individual preferences, so below are some areas that patients have cited as important to them.

Past vs. Future

"My therapist only wanted to talk about my father, and that just made me more depressed so I quit."

"I have a lot of baggage and really want a therapist who can help me work through that so I don't repeat the past."

Mood and memory are tightly linked, and mood can worsen when people spend too much time thinking about negative past events. In fact, rumination about the past is a symptom of depression, and a good therapist should help you break free of that habit rather than encourage it.

Problems happen when this tendency to ruminate on negative past events gets confused with PTSD. Trauma creates symptoms that are very similar to bipolarity, but the similarity is only surface deep. In PTSD, the cause of the problem is a phobic avoidance of the traumatic memory. Trauma is different from stress; it means there was a serious threat to your life or your body (or when you saw that in someone else). PTSD actually improves when people confront and reprocess those traumatic memories.

In depression, the problem is not traumatic memory but selective memory. The mood center accentuates negative memories and blurs positive ones. This causes more depression and makes people think the future is just going to be more like the past no matter what they do. Good therapy for depression helps you balance those negative memories with positive ones, and move forward to create more positive experiences.

On the other hand, sometimes people with depression want to revisit the past to understand themselves better. There is an effective therapy that's built around this idea, called cognitive behavioral analysis system of psychotherapy (CBASP). This therapy takes a serious look at how past relationships affect depression, particularly those that were hurtful, neglectful, or rejecting. Those relationships can leave a stamp on a person. For example, someone with depression may relate to others in a timid, avoidant way as though they were still dealing with their harsh, critical father. This therapy is particularly helpful for chronic, lifelong depression. It is difficult work that requires a skilled therapist (McCullough, 2003). You can learn more about it at www.cbasp.org.

Active Advice vs. Empathic Listening

"I don't need someone to nod and say 'I understand'—I need some guidance here!"

"There's no one I can talk to about these problems, and have a lot to get off my chest. I'm not looking for simple advice—I need someone who can take the time to understand me."

This is an area where therapists can differ widely. Structured therapies, such as CBT, usually focus the session on active problems and solutions. In some versions of CBT, the therapist may even limit the amount of venting that goes on to ensure you have time to work toward goals.

On the other end of the spectrum are therapies that allow the session to unfold spontaneously with little structure. This can help the therapist get to know you better and work directly with what is going on in the room.

Not sure which to choose? That's OK; a good therapist will usually be able to shift flexibly as needed, but you may need to speak up about your preferences.

Seeing the Real Me vs. Understanding My Mood Disorder

"I don't think my therapist gets it that I have bipolar. She expects me to do things that I just can't, and she acts like it's my fault for not trying hard enough."

"No offense but I really don't want to hear anymore about bipolar. I want to move beyond that and need a therapist who can help me find myself again."

On this one, most people want a mix of both, and rightly so. Most therapists are pretty good at seeing the real you. Problems start when they misinterpret your mood symptoms as the real you—no one wants to feel like they're being blamed for the problems that brought them to treatment. So, the more difficult part in this balance is finding a therapist who understands bipolarity. Hopefully, they'll use that knowledge to shine a light on the parts of you that aren't bipolar. You have a lot to work from on that side, and therapy tends to work best when it draws on a person's strengths.

People tend to think more about bipolarity when they first realize they have it. Later on, they put that on the back burner and start to live again. Ideally, bipolarity will be in your mind enough that you stick with your medicines, maintain good sleep and exercise, and have a plan to deal with new symptoms that don't go away on their own.

Involving Family vs. Creating Your Own Space

Mood disorders impact the whole family, and there may be times when you want your family to come to sessions. Family can help your therapist understand symptoms that you may not see (like the hypomanic ones). Your therapist can guide your family to tone down any excess pressure or blame they might be sending your way.

A wise therapist will understand when to bring them in and when to limit their involvement. Therapy sessions shouldn't be a place where everyone gets to vent about you—if that happens too often, your family may need to see a counselor of their own.

Family-focused treatment is a type of family therapy that was developed just for bipolar (Miklowitz, 2010). Although family are involved in most sessions, the aim of the work is to help you. The therapist helps people improve communication and reduce the types of stresses in the home that can worsen bipolar. Your family would learn to:

- Understand the nature and symptoms of bipolar.
- Communicate more effectively with you (these methods are outlined in Chapter 30).
- Adjust roles and expectations so you can get some space.
- Turn down the pressure for you to change faster than you can.
- Problem-solve family conflicts in a structured way so that every random moment of the day doesn't turn into a heated debate.
- Develop a plan that everyone can agree on for managing future episodes.

Ideally, this kind of work builds understanding and respect. Boundaries are a big part of respect, and therapy can help restore those boundaries. For example, if your relatives are starting to act like your therapist, getting one of your own may help them retire from that job.

ADAPTING THERAPY FOR BIPOLAR

Most of the effective therapies for bipolar have a few key ingredients that can be woven into any therapeutic program, whether individual, group or family therapy. These are:

- Regulation of sleep and daily routines (see Chapters 9-11).
- Staying active during depression (see Chapter 12).
- Managing the effects of mood on relationships (see Chapter 28).
- Identifying early signs of a new episode, and developing a plan to address those.
- Education on the nature of bipolar and addressing the impact of the diagnosis on your life and identity.
- Education about medications and actively addressing factors that make it hard to stay on medications.

GROUP THERAPY AND SELF-HELP GROUPS

Group therapy may be a no-go for those who like to keep things private or don't want to hear horror stories about other people's mood problems. If that sounds like you, here is a little reassurance. The types of groups that work for bipolarity are much more structured and don't require you to reveal much personal information. They operate more like a college seminar or study group. Sharing is usually optional, but remarkable benefits do result when people learn from each other in group. Many have never met another person with similar problems, or at least not at a place where people speak openly.

Free support groups can also serve that role, such as those run by the depression and bipolar support alliance (DBSA). These groups vary in quality. They usually include seasoned members who have kept up their recovery as well as new ones in their first episode. Often the members are educated, determined people who want to learn how to manage their lives and give back to others in the process.

There are also groups for family members. The National Alliance for the Mentally Ill (NAMI) is a good resource for those.

FUNCTIONAL REMEDIATION FOR COGNITION

This is the latest advance in therapy for bipolar and takes things in an entirely new, and much needed, direction. This one departs from the core ingredients listed above and focuses instead on memory, social skills, and everyday functioning.

It is taught in a group format and involves active practice outside of session. People learn exercises that can improve their cognitive symptoms and ways to compensate for those that don't get better. Some of these exercises are similar to the popular "brain training" programs and apps (see Appendix D). Others involve social skills, such as making small talk or handling job interviews. If there is not a functional remediation group in your town, you could read the book—*Functional Remediation for Bipolar Disorder* (Vieta, 2014)—and look for a therapist who can work on those skills with you. Therapists who work in specialized centers for vocational rehabilitation (often through the public mental health sector) or cognitive rehabilitation (often in centers that focus on neurologic or memory disorders and head injuries) may have the skills to help.

PART FOUR

RECLAIMING YOUR LIFE

TWENTY-EIGHT

Relationships

Key point: *Relationships are difficult when you're having mood problems, in part because they affect the areas of the brain that read and respond to people intuitively. In particular, there's a tendency to read negative, hostile intentions in other people's body language.*

The brain spends a lot of its time figuring out how to manage relationships. Most of this happens beneath the surface as you intuitively read and respond to other people. Intuitions come from the brain's *amygdala*. Another area of the brain, the *frontal lobes*, sorts through those intuitions and decides which should be acted on and which are best ignored. These two parts of the brain—the frontal lobes and amygdala—are exactly the parts that bipolarity disrupts, so it's no surprise that mood disorders take a toll on relationships.

A lot of the wiring in the amygdala is devoted to reading other people's faces. To fully grasp that point, look at your palm. Would your friends recognize you by your palms? Probably not, yet your palms are just as unique as your face. The brain doesn't have a center for reading palms, but it has a whole area—the amygdala—that reads faces.

Relationships also have a powerful effect on mood. We'd rank them right up there with sleep, light/dark, and physical activity. Human touch and conversation impact brain chemistry, as do human scents (called *pheromones*). The types of stress that cause depression are usually relationship stresses, even if they don't seem that way on the surface. Consider Jennifer, a marketing specialist who went into depression shortly after being promoted to account manager. At first she wondered if the new responsibilities were too much of a burden, but she had always thrived on that type of challenge. Through therapy, she realized what was wrong. The coworkers she'd grown close to now worked under her, and they no longer related to her as a friend. She felt lonely. What looked like a job stress was really a relationship problem.

HOW DEPRESSION AFFECTS RELATIONSHIPS

Besides robbing life of pleasure, depression can bring a sense of dread that makes people avoid whole areas of life. Most often, it's other people that are avoided. Let's look now at how depression affects relationships, symptom by symptom.

- *Reading faces:* During depression, the brain tends to read hostility, criticism, or rejection in other people's faces, even when that's not what's going on. Neutral or expressionless faces are particularly ripe for this misreading, as are fearful looks (which the depressed brain often mistakes for anger; Fitzgerald, 2013). This type of error makes every day interactions painful.
- *Rejection sensitivity:* This symptom makes people feel easily disliked or excluded. For example, Matt's mind would fill with dejected thoughts whenever he wrote a personal e-mail. "Why haven't they written back? Do they not like me?" The thoughts would become more and more intense and painful until he got a reply (then, a new cycle would begin).
- *Agoraphobia:* This is a fear of being in public places, like shopping malls or crowded theaters. It probably relates to basic fears that we share with the animal kingdom, such as the fear of being attacked or hunted. It impairs social life during depression because it keeps people from leaving the house.
- *Shame:* Guilt and shame are cardinal symptoms of depression, as is the feeling that you're a burden on others. These symptoms have

many effects on relationships. For example, you may delay in returning a phone call, and then delay even more because you're embarrassed by your own procrastination.

Low confidence: Depression saps confidence and keeps people from asserting themselves even in the simplest ways. Low confidence causes people to hide away, averting eye contact and speaking in mumbles. This can make others uneasy, as they genuinely want to know where you stand but are met with only vague answers like, "I don't know, whatever you want," when they seek your input. Relationships work better with some give and take, but depression can make it easier to be a giver than a taker.

HOW HYPOMANIA EFFECTS RELATIONSHIPS

Even when hypomania is positive and happy, it can strain relationships. You may become impatient with people who can't keep up with you. When hypomania darkens, it makes you mistrust the intentions of others. The facial-reading part of the brain is altered in hypomania so that everyday faces appear more threatening, angry, or menacing (Samamé, Martino, & Strejilevich, 2012).

Hypomanic arguments often proceed like this:

- You mistrust the intentions of others.
- Something happens that makes you feel betrayed, and you lash out without thinking it through.
- The other person is shocked and looks afraid.
- Your brain misreads their fear as anger, which turns the fight up a notch.
- As the argument unfolds, your focus narrows. You can no longer see the other person's point of view and lose sight of all the things you once valued about them. Hypomania is single-minded, but also easily distracted, which makes you jump into new arguments, bringing up unrelated conflicts from the past in a way that con-

fuses your opponent. At every step along the way, your heightened confidence is there to remind you that you are right, and they are wrong.

- Now the cognitive symptoms of hypomania start to cause trouble. Part of the brain (the frontal lobes) keeps track of events so you know what happened first and can evaluate cause and effect. This sequencing breaks down in hypomania, so at some point in the fight you are likely to believe that the other person started it all and you have just been defending yourself all along.

- By this point, the other person has probably become genuinely angry and accusatory toward you. That's understandable, but it only serves to further confirm your suspicions about them.

- As exhaustion sets in, your frenemy tries to compromise so the fight can come to an end. However, hypomania is not easily satisfied, so it's unlikely their offering will feel big enough to compensate for the painful injustice you've endured.

- Thus, you persist in pursuing a greater apology, which further offends your partner.

The reward center in the brain lights up when you take revenge on those who've wronged you, so there's an addictive quality to "getting even" (de Quervain et al., 2004). That's true for anyone, but particularly so in hypomania, which makes that reward center even more sensitive. Combine that with the mistrustful, irritable, single-minded, uncompromising, forgetful state of hypomania, and terrible fights ensue.

It's hard to do much about these fights when they're happening, so it's better to come up with a plan that you and your significant other can agree on in advance. Sketch that out when you're both cool-headed. A common strategy is to step away when either person seems hot-headed. This usually means going to another room (and may require a special signal, like a scarf tied to the door). Time often heals this kind of anger more than words, and after a day, you may both have forgotten what the fight was about. In contrast, attempts to resolve these fights verbally often pull people back into the vicious cycle above.

HOW TO APOLOGIZE

Hypomania needs grace and forgiveness. To find that, you either have to choose your friends wisely or get very good at apologizing. Otherwise, people end up managing hypomanic problems by hiding them or just avoiding relationships altogether (that's not a solution we recommend).

There's an art to apologizing, and it's not an entirely rational one. Simply saying the plain truth—that you spent your family's savings on a new motorcycle because you were hypomanic—is usually not enough. It's likely your spouse will think, "Oh great, now they have a medical excuse for anything they do."

A good apology focuses on the *effect* your actions had on the other person rather than the reasons behind your mistake. Here is a step-by-step guide:

1. *Acknowledge what you did.* Describe it factually without getting into why you did it.
2. *Acknowledge the effect it had on them.* Try to be as accurate and specific as possible. If you're not sure how it affected them, ask them or couch your guesses with phrases like "I imagine" instead of "I know."
3. *Acknowledge that what you did was wrong.* If it was clearly an accident—and not a moral lapse—acknowledge that you could have been more careful. Emphasize that you are sorry for how it affected them.
4. *Offer something to repair the relationship.* If you can't think of anything, try "I'd like to make up for this but am not sure how. Let me know what I can do that would make this better for you," or "I really value your friendship and hope we can rebuild that."

Depending on your relationship, it may be appropriate to bring up hypomania at some point in the conversation. If you're concerned they'll think you're using your diagnosis as an excuse, say something like, "I think I was in a hypomanic state when I did that, but that's no excuse for how I hurt you."

Sometimes, the chaos and fighting that hypomania brings can leave your loved one feeling traumatized. This is a dicey problem, because trauma causes people to remember everything in stark detail, while hypomania makes people forget. You'll have to keep reminding yourself that they have a good reason to be tense, anxious or upset. Trauma makes people react to life as though the terror is still going on, long after it has passed. If your loved one has been traumatized by your hypomania, they may keep reacting to you as though you're moody and unreliable even after you've recovered. What kind of warm welcome is that?!? This is a tough one, and it requires a great deal of sensitivity on your part. Tread lightly, speak softly, and be kind.

TO TELL OR NOT TO TELL

You do not need to tell people close to you that you have bipolar. This is a difficult and very personal choice. Those in your support network (doctors, therapists, and others like clergy) should know. Those close to you (spouse or partner, children older than 13, close friends) may need to know as well.

The hard part in all this is usually the *bipolar* word, because to most people that means "Bipolar I" and conjures up images of hospitalization, violence, and losing one's mind. Another approach is to say that you have a mood disorder and describe the symptoms, starting with depression. After all, depressions are far more common than hypomania in most people with bipolarity, so this isn't far from the truth. See how they react to that. If comfortable, you can add "my depression also causes mood swings where I . . ." and describe the other symptoms that are important to relate. If you do go on to say you have bipolarity, cyclothymia, or Bipolar II, you could add "this isn't the same as bipolar disorder—which means mania. Instead, it's a form of depression with milder mood swings."

In the end, it's more important that they know how it affects you than the diagnostic term. Emphasize you are getting help; this will increase their trust. Talk to them about how this may impact your relationship and let them know specific things they can do to help (see below). This last step is critical—giving them a role can keep them from getting overwhelmed with fear and hopelessness. It may also keep them from making up their own role (which isn't always the best one).

Outside of that close circle, you may or may not want to tell others. Before you tell, consider how it may help or hurt you, and whether you can trust them to keep the matter private. Think about how you'll feel in the relationship if they know, and how that person may view mental illness.

WAYS FOR OTHERS TO SUPPORT YOU

- Help me preserve sleep by keeping the lights out and sounds down at night.
- Reach out when I'm down to let me know you're thinking of me.
- Invite me out for low-stress activities, and let me know you understand when I can't say "yes."
- Try not to hold grudges (I'll do the same). Sometimes I'll say things I really don't mean in a fight—try to move on with grace instead of dissecting every fight in long discussions.
- Learn about bipolarity without turning into a local expert on it (that can lead to power struggles, even with the best intentions). Read the "For Friends and Family" section in this book.
- Treat me like I'm more normal than not. When I'm not doing well, notice the ways that I'm still holding it together.
- Know that I'll probably be flooded with guilt when I'm depressed. Don't lose hope that I'll recover; we'll need to keep that hope from turning into more guilt because I *should* recover and I haven't. Let me know you love me as I am.
- My mind can't process very well when I'm in an episode, so let's

come up with a signal (like a scarf tied to a door knob) for when I need to be alone to cool down.

- Sometimes we'll need to save intense discussions for later. I promise not to avoid them though—let's schedule time for them so I can be prepared.
- Help me with chores or child care when I'm not doing well.
- Please don't resent me for having this problem.

TWENTY-NINE

Work and School

Key point: *Most employers in the United States are legally required to allow reasonable accommodations and sick leave for people with mood disorders. Fear of discrimination keeps many from using those benefits, and there are definite pros and cons to revealing your diagnosis in the workplace.*

The only good thing about mood disorders is that they can go away completely. People with bipolarity have held jobs at every level (psychiatrists have suggested that Presidents Lyndon Johnson and Theodore Roosevelt had Bipolar I, but we won't get into that debate; Davidson, Connor, & Swartz, 2006). In a survey of professionals with a history of mental illness, 73% were able to maintain full-time work in their chosen career. Those people held high-level jobs, and their psychiatric histories were not mild (all had been hospitalized or were on psychiatric disability in the past; Ellison, Russinova, Lyass, & Rogers, 2008).

The bad thing is that mood episodes can come back, and when they do, it can derail work and school. Nine out of ten people with bipolar say it caused problems at work (Depression and Bipolar Support Alliance, 1998). Two-thirds of people with significant mental illness say it caused them to drop out of college (Gruttadaro & Crudo, 2012), and the problems that lead to the highest rates of college drop-out are mania and substance abuse (Hunt, Eisenberg, & Kilbourne, 2010).

People with bipolarity can succeed in work and school, but they need skills to minimize the problems their symptoms bring and get back in the game when those symptoms go away. As reviewed in Chapter 8, there are strengths that come with bipolarity, and for many, the main issue with work is inconsistency, with times of industriousness and times of sluggish procrastination.

TO TELL OR NOT TO TELL AT WORK

Bipolar is just one of the illnesses in the World Health Organization's list of the top ten medical causes of disability, but it can be the loneliest one (Chisholm, van Ommeren, Ayuso-Mateos, & Saxena, 2006). Many suffer through it in silence, preferring to take the blame at work than risk the stigma of revealing their diagnosis. Although the Americans with Disabilities Act (ADA) protects those with mood disorders from overt discrimination, patients fear more subtle forms of discrimination that would be difficult to prove in a court of law. On one blogger's list of the top ways to survive in the workplace with bipolar, the first and last rules encouraged secrecy (Tracy, 2013):

- Don't tell
- Work hard
- Don't stress
- Take time off when you need to
- Be discrete

The responses that followed online were even more telling. All but a small minority agreed and added their own stories of being excluded from projects or passed up for promotions after making the revelation. Those who recommended revealing the diagnosis reported a sense of relief after doing so and felt that being transparent helped squelch the rumor mill. They cautioned that you should not tell unless your workplace has a supportive culture and you are valued by the company.

That last caution is alarming. It sounds like the ones who should use the ADA's protection are the ones who need it the least, because people who are valued by their company probably aren't at risk of being fired. They may still benefit from accommodations for minor problems and brief time off. It's those who are having trouble at work who need the ADA the most, and they may be the ones at most risk of discrimination when they seek it out.

Several lawsuits have ruled in favor of persons who were fired because of their bipolar. In each of these, it was pretty clear that the firing was directly related to the employee taking medical leave, and that the company had systemic problems with neglecting disability rights. The amounts awarded were in the ballpark of $100,000, depending on the person's original salary.

There are some areas where the laws offer more clear-cut guidance in this dilemma. For example:

- You should not reveal a bipolar diagnosis before being hired. According to the ADA, it is illegal for employers to require psychiatric screening before hiring, "unless such examination or inquiry is shown to be job-related and consistent with business necessity." Telling a prospective employer that you have bipolar puts them at risk, for they could be sued if they decide not to hire you after that revelation. Even in situations where your mental health may be relevant to the job (such as driving trucks), only the minimum amount of information should be revealed (e.g., a letter from your doctor could say you have no psychiatric or medical impairments that would affect your driving, without listing your diagnosis).
- You should know your company's policies on medical leave and disability accommodations (available through human resources). The Family Medical Leave Act (FMLA) requires most companies to allow employees a reasonable amount of medical leave for illness (up to 12 weeks), though sick-pay for this is optional. The FMLA form also has a place for your doctor to indicate that you

may require brief intermittent leave for future episodes or time off to attend medical appointments.

- You do not need to reveal the nature of your diagnosis to qualify for medical leave, but may need to reveal it to request accommodations.

ACCOMMODATIONS

The ADA requires employers to make reasonable accommodations for illness. *Reasonable* is in the eye of the beholder; usually it means that the accommodations cannot cause such a burden that they make it difficult for the company to operate.

Typical accommodations for bipolar include:

- Flexible scheduling or part time work when in an episode
- Regular schedule to prevent episodes
- Working from home
- Allowing more breaks
- More frequent feedback
- A quiet working environment
- Access to a window or sunlight
- Avoiding work that interferes with sleep (e.g., travel, on-call, late hours, or overtime work)
- Avoiding early morning work if your nighttime medications cause drowsiness
- Time off for mental health appointments

The exact accommodation may require some creative thinking. For example, suppose you are part of a team that shares on-call duties to ensure that the computer systems stay operational 24/7. It may be unreasonable to request that you never take part in this call. On the other hand, it might work to take on other responsibilities (such as holiday work) in exchange for a lighter call schedule.

DISABILITY

Disability takes many forms, from private policies to state or federal disability benefits. Private policies are purchased in advance or as part of an employment package, and they vary in whether they define disability as "unable to work at your usual job level" or "unable to work at any job." These plans also have different terms for short-term and long-term disability.

Disability status is never permanent, which is a good thing, as it means there's always a chance of recovery. One of the most frustrating parts of psychiatric disability, for doctors and patients, is proving that a person cannot work. It is often surprising what people are capable of, even in the midst of depression, so we try not to underestimate patients. On the other hand, we don't want insurers to use that optimism to deny benefits that are truly deserved.

Part of the difficulty is that people with mood disorders often fluctuate between periods of high and low functioning. Disability forms ask about how you are doing at the current moment, but you and your provider need to consider the whole pattern of episodes to accurately assess your ability to work. You may need to discuss this with your provider, and ask them to emphasize how the frequency of episodes makes you unable to hold a steady job.

WORK AND MOOD

"To love and work," answered Sigmund Freud when he was asked to define the essence of mental health. Many aspects of work are beneficial to mood. Regular structure helps prevent mania, while social connection and productivity ward off depression.

Interestingly, research consistently finds that people are happier when they volunteer than when they do the same type of work for pay (Borgonovi, 2008). This sounds a little hard to believe, but time and again, we see two patients doing exactly the same job, where one cites it as the source of their stability and the other says it's causing their depression. The only difference is that the first one is a volunteer. Doing things for others helps you get out of your own head, and that role is all the more meaningful when given freely.

The impact of volunteering is greatest when it involves helping strangers through direct, personal contact. Why strangers? When giving to people you don't know, you are giving *freely*. Helping out family is also rewarding, but it doesn't feel as free. There's a sense of obligation with family.

One more word about money. It can buy happiness, but only to a point. Happiness tends to increase with income, but it levels off at around $75,000 per year in 2010 dollars (Kahneman & Deaton, 2010). The wealthiest among us (those in the Forbes 500 list) report only slightly higher levels of happiness than the average American (Deiner, Horwitz, & Emmons, 1985). It seems our ability to create wealth and luxury has surpassed the brain's capacity to enjoy it all the way.

So think twice before working long hours to double your income, as depression starts to set in with too much time at the office. People who work over 10 hours a day (5 days a week) have more than twice the risk of depression (Virtanen, Stansfeld, Fuhrer, Ferrie, & Kivimäki, 2012). That 10-hour threshold applies to people who had no history of depression; we wonder if it would be even lower for those on the mood spectrum.

Not surprisingly, your commute to work can have a big impact on your mood and health. Long commute times (especially greater than 45 minutes one-way) are associated with depression, obesity, insomnia, chronic pain, and marital stress (Lowrey, 2011).

Shift work is a more complicated subject. People with bipolar tend to be night owls, and they often find the night shift suits their natural rhythm. That may be fine for some, but on average, night shift work increases the risk of depression. It has also been linked to stomach problems, heart disease, obesity, and sexual dysfunction (Vogel, Braungardt, Meyer, & Schneider, 2012). If you do work a late shift, it may be easier on your biological clock (and mood) to stick with the same sleep routines on your days off.

SCHOOL

Bipolar often comes on around age 18, just as a young person is building the confidence they need to launch into the world. It can be intimidating to start again after that kind of setback.

Fortunately, most schools follow the ADA laws and allow students to take medical leave and return when they are ready. The school's disability office can help students manage these transitions and secure the accommodations they need. Examples might include:

- A single dorm room
- Taking tests in a quiet environment
- Allowing extra time on tests
- Front row seating in the classroom
- Flexibility with due dates if symptoms prevented the completion of assignments
- More frequent feedback
- Access to tutoring

If a mood episode takes you out for a semester, it's best to go back to school as soon as you can. We have seen young people stay out of school for prolonged periods out of a fear that they will fail again, even when they are in recovery. "Seize the day," is a useful guide for living with a recurrent mood disorder. You don't know if or when it will come back, but you need to take full advantage of the periods of recovery you have. Fortunately, most medical leave policies allow students to minimize their losses if their best laid plans go wrong again.

THIRTY

For Friends and Family

Key point: *Emotional warmth, empathy, and positive comments can help your relative recover. Mood disorders worsen when families scrutinize mood or get too involved in their relative's life, well-intentioned though those efforts may be. Conflict is hard to avoid, but families can minimize the harm by scheduling time for intense discussions, so they don't spring up randomly in the house.*

Mood disorders affect the whole family. Moods are contagious: the irritability or excitement of mania, the gloom of depression. A severe episode will often send your family into crisis mode. It's hard to see the big picture in the emotional reactivity of a crisis, and that tunnel-vision usually makes the situation worse.

Researchers have studied how families live with mood disorders, and their conclusions are clear. There are a few things you can do that improve mood problems, and a few things you can do that make them worse. This chapter is written for your family and will lay out those dos and don'ts, but first a few guiding principles:

1. Much of the advice will focus on nonverbal behaviors, like body language and vocal tone, because those have the most significant effect on the mood center in the brain.
2. Don't strive for perfection. What matters is getting it right most of the time, not all the time. There's a reason for that. It's the

frequency and duration of your actions that matter to the brain, just as the skin is affected by *how long* it's exposed to the sun.

3. This advice is not easy to follow, and often goes against your natural reactions. Don't be hard on yourself if you slip up now and then.

4. Follow this advice, and don't try to do much more. There isn't a lot you can do to help or hurt the illness, and grander attempts to help your loved one will only frustrate the both of you. It takes a lot of strength to face a catastrophe without diving in to rescue, but in the case of bipolarity, trying to do too much is a lot like banging on a computer to get it to work. Focus on the basic principles below, and respond to the rest with grace and acceptance.

WHAT TO INCREASE: FOUR THINGS THAT HELP

Each of the interactions below has a positive effect on the brain, and sprinkling them throughout the day can speed recovery from a mood disorder.

Emotional Warmth

This first part is all about body language. *Emotional warmth* is conveyed by a gentle smile, compassionate eyes, and an accepting posture. It sends people the message that you are genuinely interested and pleased to see them. The voice is soothing, with an almost musical quality that mixes soft and slow with a slightly upbeat tone that's both cheerful and calming. Movements are relaxed and gentle, without pressure, sending the message that you accept things as they are. In its most profound form, warmth is the gleam in a mother's eye that conveys unconditional love.

Emotional warmth is welcoming, so your arms are likely at your side with your palms open. Crossing your arms around your chest conveys defensiveness, as if you're trying to protect yourself. Also to be avoided are postures of dominance that will come across as an attack, such as wagging your hands in the air or arching your hands on your hips like a scolding school teacher.

Warmth is a scarce resource when there are intense mood swings in the home. Your body is more likely to shift towards fight-or-flight than emotional warmth. In fight-or-flight mode, your heart races, hands shake, and breath becomes rapid and shallow. Muscles tighten up in fight-or-flight, which shifts your posture into an urgent stance. Your facial muscles tense, creating a look that will likely be mistaken as anger. Your vocal chords constrict, making your voice sharp, fast, and harsh.

What's going on inside you is fear, but the problem is that mood disorders alter the amygdala (the part of the brain that reads faces) so that fearful faces are read as angry ones (Samamé et al., 2012). To your loved one, your concern will look like an attack, and they might fight back. This makes you even more defensive, and you can see how the problem escalates from there.

A neutral face is probably better than a fearful one, but even these tend to be misinterpreted as angry when people are in a mood episode. The same problem applies to the thoughtful, serious look you might adopt while reading a book: It looks angry to someone in a mood episode. It's hard to show emotional warmth when there's stress in the family, but it's the expression that works best.

Last, a word about eye contact. In most social interactions, it's best to make enough eye contact to communicate interest, but not so much as to make the other person feel stared at. During a mood disorder, you may need to shift that balance away from the long stare. Like a lion in a cage, mood disorders can cause a slightly paranoid state where too much eye contact makes them feel attacked or hunted.

Empathy

Empathy accepts people as they are without judgment. It seeks to understand and appreciate them rather than change them. Empathy is also compassionate and communicates genuine caring for the other person.

It can be hard to empathize with a person who's having mood problems. It's likely that you don't agree with their point of view, whether depressive hopelessness or hypomanic invincibility. It's particularly hard to empathize when their behavior is the source of your stress. Empathy doesn't mean you feel the same way they do, just that you understand them or at least seek understanding. In that way, empathy respects the boundaries between you and them, and we'll see how important those boundaries are in the section on *overinvolvement*.

Empathic comments usually reduce tension; they rarely invite a fight. Empathy goes hand in hand with emotional warmth, and both have a healing effect on mood, in part by reducing the isolation that mood episodes bring. The frequency of empathic comments in a family influences recovery rates in bipolar (Miklowitz, 2012). These can include simple empathic statements such as, "I see your point," "I get it," and "I know what you mean," as well as more specific ones like:

"It must be hard to go through the motions each day when you're depressed."

"Though I've never been through the kind of depression you're having, I can tell it's a terrible place to be and you certainly don't deserve it."

Positive Comments

Positive comments also help recovery from depression. The best positive comments are accurate and specific, such as "I appreciate how you put the kids to bed last night."

In general, what you shine a light on is what will grow. There's a paradox to deal with here, for mood disorders draw the family's attention toward a problem that can't be readily fixed, and shining a light there just leads to more frustration. It takes some mental training to do the opposite.

First, you need to retire from the role of problem-solver, fixer, and psychiatric detective. Instead of cataloguing all the depressive or bipolar things your loved one does, make it your job to search for anything about them that is *not consistent* with a mood disorder. It helps to first know what the signs of the illness are, and the first section of this book can help with that. Then look for the opposite of those symptoms. How is your depressed friend being active in life? What are some ways that your hypomanic husband is exercising patience and responsibility? Shift your attention away from the illness. If they oversleep, ignore that. Focus instead on the fact that they got out of bed—many depressed people never take that step.

This advice applies to treatment, as well. We often see families talk at great length about the doses of medication their loved one missed, instead of focusing on the ones they took. Nearly half of people with serious mood problems don't stick with treatment (but they may come back), and the illness itself contributes to this problem by impairing self-awareness. When someone stops their medication, but still comes to treatment, remind yourself that she is at least showing up, which puts her ahead of most people with a mood disorder.

Optimism about the Illness

Depression robs people of hope, and causes them to blame themselves for the disorder. If you live with someone who has depression, don't let yourself fall into that trap. Dr. Mark Frye, Chair of Psychiatry at the Mayo Clinic, tells his patients with bipolar that they should expect a full recovery (Frye, 2013). He is right: Most people with bipolar and depression can fully recover.

Always remember that the manic and depressive behaviors are what they have, not who they are. As striking as those episodes can be, they don't reveal much about the person behind them. People have acted the same way during depression and mania for thousands of years. There are descriptions of the illness dating back to ancient Greece that sound identical to what is seen today (Goodwin & Jamison, 2007).

On that note, one word of warning: Be careful when reading about personality disorders. Every sign of a personality disorder, from the narcissist to the paranoid, can come out during a mood episode. These are usually signs of the episode rather than character traits of the person. Instead of sleuthing for pathology, your efforts will be better spent recalling how your loved one was before the episode, and relaying the optimism that they'll be that way again.

WHAT TO DECREASE: FIVE THINGS THAT HARM

The brain is wired to react to negative events more than positive ones, so the interactions below are particularly important to reduce. This won't be easy, as mood disorders tend to bring exactly the kinds of negative interactions that you'll want to steer clear of to help your relative heal.

Critical Comments

These are comments that find fault, pass judgment, suggest bad motivations, or simply point out problems. Often they come from a good place (after all, pointing out problems might help people fix them). Whether or not a comment is critical is in the eye of the beholder, but you can bet that mood problems will make people more sensitive to criticism.

Usually, critical comments are made out of frustration, or when forgetting that your friend has a real impairment. Here are a few strategies to reduce them:

- Watch for the word "should" in your mind and in your words. Try not to communicate that things "should" be different: They aren't.
- Think about your expectations. If your loved one is having an episode and you haven't already lowered your expectations, you may need to. Most critical comments stem from a mismatch between ideals and reality.
- If you cannot lower your expectations on an issue (you are not alone in that), lower the frequency with which you remind them about it. Schedule weekly times to talk about your concerns rather than bringing them up randomly throughout the day. This last point is crucial. The brain follows a psychological law called *inter-*

mittent reinforcement, which means it reacts to random comments as though they are happening *all the time.*

- Check in with your loved one. Ask about ways you may come across as overly critical. Bringing this up at the weekly meeting can keep them from feeling like it's a weekly complaint session with them as the target.

Scrutinizing Mood

It's important to monitor for relapses when someone is in recovery, but too much focus on this may come across as a critical attitude. In general, you should respond to your relative's emotions just as you would to someone who never had a mood disorder. Don't be too quick to evaluate whether each emotion represents a new episode or a medication reaction.

On the other hand, relatives are often the first to pick up on the early signs of an episode. Still, it's impossible for anyone to determine if a few hours of emotional swings represent a mood disorder or not. *Mood* refers to changes over days or weeks, while *emotion* refers to changes over minutes or hours. Emotions, in themselves, are not disorders. It's important to step back and focus on the big picture when evaluating mood. Ask your loved one how they'd like you to share your observations.

Trying to Win or Resolve Arguments

President Jimmy Carter said that one secret of his successful marriage is that he and Rosalynn always "try to resolve our . . . differences before we go to bed at night" (Carter, 2015). This may work for the Carters, but it is terrible advice for a couple with a mood disorder. Hypomania is known to argue for the sake of arguing, and that kind of quarrel is more likely to implode than resolve. Couples reading this book need to put a premium on sleep, which is the main healer for mood swings. Often the arguments of hypomania are forgotten and no longer need resolution after a good night's sleep.

If we could pick one rule for marriages with mood problems, it would be to avoid any serious interaction when either person is hot-headed. That could mean hypomanic, angry, stubborn, anxious, or reactive. Unfortunately, the hot-headed mindset usually comes with a pressure to keep up the argument, so this rule is hard to follow.

If a conversation seems to be escalating toward a fight, and the back-and-forth is causing each person to get more entrenched in their position, it's best to drop it and—if needed—retreat to separate rooms until cooled down. Make an agreement to do this in advance of those fights, and you can even add that stepping away from the fight is an invitation to return to the issue later (when you're both calm).

There will be times when you step away as agreed, only to find the other person banging on your door. There will be times when one of you uses this rule as a stonewalling technique to avoid discussion. There will even be times when you both fight intensely about who is breaking this rule. Let that be—it's a small price to pay for the benefits the rule brings.

Overinvolvement

Just as with medications, overinvolvement is a side effect of a potentially good thing. It can happen when you take a strong, active role in your relative's recovery. While this is a natural and caring reaction, it can stress your relative. Mood disorders can cause people to feel guilty, controlled, or like they've lost their self. Overinvolvement from relatives can intensify those feelings.

There's a fine line between overinvolvement and positive support, and where this line falls will be different for each family. It may even move over time. Driving your son to his psychiatric appointment may be supportive when he's too depressed to start the car, but overinvolved when he's entering recovery. In the end, your family member will be more likely to stick with treatment if they take it on themselves. An open discussion with them and their treatment provider can help you navigate this area.

Another form of overinvolvement warrants special caution because it's slightly addictive. Relatives can literally get hooked on the ups and downs of their loved one's mood. At the sign of any improvement, they light up, searching for clues as to what brought on a better day. That's good, right? Didn't we just preach to look on the bright side? But we meant to look for the real person, not the illness. The illness cycles randomly, and that's where the trouble comes from: Anything that's random tends to become addictive. Psychologists call this *intermittent reinforcement*, and casinos use this property (programming slot machines to randomly give out big prizes) to their advantage.

In this cycle, the family gets hooked on trying to figure out what they did to make the illness better or worse. They take on too much of the responsibility, and burden, for the illness. Yes, there are a few positive things you can do, and they are listed here, but these are really meant to help over the long haul (not in the moment). Remember: outside the advice in this chapter, you can't control, and aren't responsible for, the mood disorder. We've heard relatives fret about every possible decision, "Should we make him eat dinner with us?," "Should we go away for the weekend—she seems better when she has space, but we're worried she is not ready to stay by herself?" Those are important questions—but they aren't going to change the disorder—so you'll usually need to make those decisions based on factors other than your loved one's diagnosis.

Hostility

Hostility is an attitude that can set in after years of living with a mood disorder. It happens when people blame their relative for all the problems the illness brought (and then some). In a hostile view, the person and their illness are one and the same, and there's contempt for both.

Critical comments flow from hostility. A person with a warm, positive attitude may slip into critical comments, but that doesn't make them hostile. In hostility, the comments are almost always critical, as is the entire way of seeing things.

Attitudes are hard to change, and we recommend you seek the counsel of a therapist, clergy, or friend if hostility has set in. To avoid hostility, watch out for beliefs that blame your relative or question their motivation, such as:

- "He wouldn't be like this if he tried harder."
- "She doesn't want to get better."
- "She just wants an excuse for her behavior."
- "He may have a disorder, but he has more self-control than he lets on. I've seen him change around his friends—he's like a totally different person with them!"

That last one is particularly important. Mood disorders change in different contexts, and they aren't the only brain problem to do this. Parkinson's patients who are unable to move have been known to stand up and walk when bold, bright lines are placed on the floor in front of them (Morris, 2010). The visual novelty of the lines probably alters dopamine levels in the brain, but the effect is short-lived—it doesn't cure Parkinson's. Likewise, your relative may briefly become friendly when out in public, but sink into sullen depression or harsh irritability when alone with family.

Different neurotransmitters circulate in the brain depending on whom you're with. Consider your own behavior. Are you more likely to put your feet on the coffee table, scratch your armpits, or pick your nose when you are home alone or when you are at a business meeting?

When someone has a mood disorder, the worst face usually comes out with close family. Psychiatrists even measure mania by the setting it comes out in. If the fighting is just with family, it is probably hypomania or normal. When fights extend into the workplace, it is at least hypomania and possibly mania. When a patient fights with the police, it's a good guess that the line between hypomania and mania has been crossed.

This tendency for symptoms to change in different environments causes two problems for the family. First, it makes them think their loved one has more self-control than they really do, which can lead to blame and hostility.

Second, it prevents families from seeing the progress their loved one is making. Because family conflict represents the mildest level of irritability, it's often the last symptom to resolve. Sometimes the first sign of recovery is when a person no longer fights in public, even if they are still just as argumentative at home. Unfortunately, relatives may not notice that change, and if they do, they may see it as proof that the meanness they see at home is intentional. That dampens two things the family needs: optimism and positive comments.

KNOW YOUR LIMITS

Does it sound like we've been telling you to accept everything your relative does during a mood episode? Not at all. The message so far is that words are not going to solve the problem, and can even make it worse. In fact, if verbal reminders and rational conversations could solve the problem, then you're probably not dealing with a mood disorder.

It's also crucial to know your limits and have a plan of action if a situation becomes dangerous or destructive. This involves *action*, not words. Anticipate the worst and develop an emergency plan in advance. Examples include:

- Violence
- Suicidal behavior
- Drug or alcohol intoxication
- Conflict that impacts children in the home
- Financial crises from overspending

Potential solutions could include allowing family to come to a crisis appointment, temporarily living apart, hospitalization, locking away extra meds to prevent overdose, and placing a hold on credit cards. The person with the mood disorder should take an equal role in creating a crisis plan, which ideally would be made when they are not in an episode.

TALKING WITH CHILDREN ABOUT BIPOLAR

Children are naturally sensitive to their parents' behavior and will usually pick up on mood problems in the family. Talking with kids can help. Speak to them about the changes that are likely affecting them and explain that it is due to a treatable illness. How much detail you go into about the illness will depend on their age, but either way you should tell them it's treatable. Children, especially under 12, often blame themselves for problems in the family, so emphasize that it is not their fault.

Tell them that the whole family is working together on it and help them feel empowered by giving them specific things to do. This could include helping out with chores or giving their parent a hug and saying "I love you." What they do is not as important as having something to do. People respond better to stress when they can take action.

Remind them that they are loved, and their parents will be there for them. Encourage them to ask questions and talk about how they feel. Strengthen the support they can get from places that aren't affected by the problem, such as friendships, extended kin, exercise and extracurricular activities.

Mothers and Bipolar

"It is often the mother who carries the brunt of the illness' burden [in bipolar]," wrote Dr. Hagop Akiskal (Akiskal & Tohen, 2011). Mothers carry a strong sense of responsibility for their children and may blame themselves for the problem. They don't need extra help with that guilt, but that doesn't stop other people from lending an unhelpful hand. If she's supportive and nurturing, she's accused of enabling the illness; if she steps back, she's cold and neglectful. It's rare for all family members to see the problem for what it is: a mood disorder. Family members go through their own cycles of denial about the illness, or hope and despair about recovery.

Watching the Kids Grow Up

Bipolar disorder is one of the most heritable psychiatric conditions. Many parents with bipolarity or depression worry that their children may get it too. What to do about that? This is a large topic, but here's a short answer: Focus on things you can control (genetics is not one of them).

Good parenting can lower your child's risk. Everyone can benefit from reminders here, especially if they didn't have good models from their own childhood. Children don't come with a manual, but some good manuals have been written (you'll find some on our website: moodtreatmentcenter.com/bipolarnotsomuch).

To improve your parenting, focus on the strategies that don't already come naturally for you. Make a list of them, and at the end of each day, jot down specific things you did to put them into action.

Second, know what to look for. Part 1 talked about how mood symptoms look in adults, but how do they look in children? What are the earliest signs? Here are two important ones:

1. Changing social interactions: Used to be engaged with other kids and family, now not very interested, perhaps seems preoccupied.
2. Changing sleep patterns: Although staying up late and sleeping late into the morning is a normal pattern for adolescents, a *shift*, particularly an extreme one (e.g., staying up most of the night or waking up at 5 A.M. ready to go), warrants attention.

Third, have a rough idea of what kinds of specialists and services are available in case you need them. If you're already seeing signs of mood trouble, get on wait-lists early because in many areas these are long.

Finally, develop a mantra such as "If I do my job well, the chances are lower" or "I'll take action if there's a problem; for now, focus on today." You may use it a lot because your mind will find reasons to invite more worry. Be gentle with your mind as you decline the invitation, softly repeating your mantra.

CONCLUSION

Thank you for picking up this book. We have tried to give you a good introduction to depressions that are not fully bipolar, but more than unipolar—the middle of the mood spectrum.

We hope what you've learned here will help you or your loved one experience fewer and less severe depressions, and a smoother course overall.

—Chris Aiken and Jim Phelps

APPENDIX

Medication Glossary

Mood Stabilizers

Carbamazepine (Tegretol, Equetro), lamotrigine (Lamictal), lithium (Lithobid, Eskalith), oxcarbamazepine (Trileptal), valproate (Depakote)

Atypical Antipsychotics

Aripiprazole (Abilify), asenapine (Saphris), brexpiprazole (Rexulti), cariprazine (Vraylar), clozapine (Clozaril), iloperidone (Fanapt), lurasidone (Latuda), olanzapine (Zyprexa), olanzapine/fluoxetine combination (Symbyax), paloperidone (Invega), quetiapine (Seroquel), risperidone (Risperdal), ziprasidone (Geodon)

Novel Medications for Mania, Rapid Cycling, and Mixed States

Allopurinol, amlodipine, galantamine, isradipine, levetiracetam (Keppra), memantine (Namenda), nimodipine, verapamil

Novel Medications for Bipolar and Unipolar Depression

Amantadine, armodafinil (Nuvigil), atorvastatin, botulinum (Botox), buspirone (Buspar, treats depression when used with melatonin), celecoxib, cyproheptadine, ketamine, lovastatin, minocycline, modafinil (Provigil), pindolol, pioglitazone (Actose), pramipexole (Mirapex), riluzole (Rilutek), ropinirole (Requip), scopalamine, thyroid T3 (Cytomel), thyroid T4 (Synthroid), topiramate (Topamax)

SSRI Antidepressants

Citalopram (Celexa), escitalopram (Lexapro), fluoxetine (Prozac), fluvoxamine (Luvox), paroxetine (Paxil), sertraline (Zoloft)

Other Serotonergic Antidepressants

Vilazodone (Viibryd), vortioxetine (Trintellix)

SNRI Antidepressants

Desvenlafaxine (Pristiq), duloxetine (Cymbalta), levomilnacipran (Fetzima), milnacipran (Savella), venlafaxine (Effexor)

MAOI Antidepressants

Isocarboxazid (Marplan), phenelzine (Nardil), selegiline (Emsam), tranylcypromine (Parnate)

Tricyclic Antidepressants

Amitriptyline (Elavil), clomipramine (Anafranil), desipramine (Norpramin), doxepin (Sinequan), imipramine (Tofranil), nortriptyline (Pamelor), protriptyline (Vivactil), trimipramine (Sumontil); Tetracyclic versions: maprotiline, amoxapine

Other Antidepressants

Bupropion (Wellbutrin, Budeprion, Aplenzin, Forfivo), mirtazapine (Remeron), nefazodone (Serzone), trazodone (Desyrel)

Sleep Medications: Z-Hypnotics

Eszopiclone (Lunesta), zaleplon (Sonata), zolpidem (Ambien, Ambien-CR, Edluar), short-acting zolpidem (Intermezzo)

Other Sleep Medicines

Diphenhydramine (Benadryl), doxepin (Silenor), gabapentin (Horizant, Neurontin, Gralise), hydroxyzine (Vistaril), ramelteon (Rozerem), suvorexant (Belsomra), trazodone (Desyrel)

Medications for Nightmares

Cyproheptadine, prasozin, tiagabine (Gabitril)

Anti-Anxiety Medications

Buspirone (Buspar), gabapentin (Neurontin), pregabalin (Lyrica), riluzole (Rilutek), propranolol (Inderal)

Benzodiazepines

Alprazolam (Xanax), chlordiazepoxide (Librium), clonazepam (Klono-pin), clorazepate (Tranxene), diazepam (Valium), estazolarn (Prosom), flurazepam (Dalmane), lorazepam (Ativan), oxazepam (Serax), quazepam (Dural), temazepam (Restoril), triazolam (Halcion)

ADHD Treatments: Stimulants

Methylphenidate (Ritalin, Concerta, Metadate, Methylin, Daytrana, Quillivant, Aptensio), dexmethylphenidate (Focalin), amphetamine salts (Adderall, Evekeo, Adzenys), dextroamphetamine (Dexedrine, ProCen-tra, Zenzedi), lisdexamfetamine (Vyvanse)

ADHD Treatments: Nonstimulants

Armodafinil (Nuvigil), atomoxetine (Strattera), clonidine (Kapvay), guanfacine (Intuniv), modafinil (Provigil)

Hypomania in 900 Words

Hypomania has many faces. Most of the words below came from patients who experienced it.

Thoughts move like a ping-pong ball
Cleaning the house all night
Strong desire to reconnect with old friends or lovers
Interest shifts from one thing to another, can't finish anything
More puns or plays on words
Easily overstimulated
Seductive or flirtatious as if playing a role
Tired and wired at the same time
Buying things with pleasure
Engaging in lots of new pursuits
No verbal filter—blurt things out
Heightened sensations, colors are brighter, sounds are louder
Acute sense of humor or irony
Spending too much money
Intense romantic life
Full of plans and projects
Never met a stranger
Disregard for authority
Dramatic or high-fashion clothing
Frequently changing lovers
Feeling people stare or laugh at you

Not bound by everyday social etiquette

Like to be the center of attention

High curiosity, interested in everything and everybody

Driving recklessly or speeding

Over-commit: Could not say "no" to opportunities, even with no time to
do them

Felt particularly strong and invulnerable, resistant to illnesses and accidents

Doing things to excess

Very assertive

Enjoy your work more

Sudden travel plans

When your daily routines are disrupted, you get irritable or have trouble
functioning

A slightly paranoid feeling, feeling that comments are directed at you

So many thoughts and ideas all at once that it's hard to express them

Others were attracted to your confidence, energy, and enthusiasm

So noisy, for example, with music or TV, that others complained

Very impatient

Others thought you were irresponsible

Overreactive

Puns or word play

Warm, extroverted, and social

People can't keep up with you

Hearing things, even just your name being called

Emotionally expressive

Emotions shift rapidly from happy to sad

Making foolish business or major life decisions

Tended to ignore rules or broke the law a little

Self-assured, charismatic, a natural leader

Restless

Suddenly changing hair styles, color, or other fashions

Greater mental clarity

Taking risks easily

Seeing things, such as shadows or bugs

Collecting, buying multiples of the same thing

Enjoy dangerous, risky, challenging, or emotionally intense activities

Easily distracted

Frequently changed jobs, homes, friends, hobbies

Charismatic

Feeling overly certain about your own ideas

More interested in sex

Do things more quickly and easily

Stubborn, one-track mind

See connections in things that others miss

Exhausting or irritating to others

Mistrusting the intentions of others

More optimistic

Hostile

Vigorous, much livelier than usual, and full of energy

Felt really good about how you looked

Can't think before you act

Unusually high self-esteem, feelings of superiority, or unrealistic ideas that you had amazing abilities, talents, knowledge, or powers

Multiple trains of thought, like you can carry on a conversation while another track is writing a short story

Intense enjoyment or appreciation of artistic works

Overly carefree

Felt you could make decisions for others because you knew their thoughts, intentions, or wishes

More fluent with words

You went for days without sleeping or with much less sleep than usual but didn't feel tired

Overly talkative, spoke rapidly, and loudly

Sped up inside

Easily caught up in addictive things, like gambling, sweets, porn, drugs

If, for some reason, you get much less sleep than is normal for you, you found that you actually had more energy rather than less the next day

Interrupting others

Mystical experiences or visions

Driven to do something but don't know what to do

Giving lots of presents

A lot of activity makes it hard for you to wind down and sleep at night

The smallest thing makes you very enthusiastic

Self-assured, feeling you are incapable of making mistakes, and indifferent to criticism

Perfectionist

Felt like you had extrasensory perception (ESP)

Time moves quickly

Made very important decisions (such as selling or buying a house or car, or changing jobs) quickly

Vivid tastes and smells

An irresistible urge to communicate by phone, letters, e-mails, or texts

Drawn to bright colors or red hues

The life of the party

You often see humor where others miss it

A sense of oneness with others

Gravitate toward colorful clothing

Ideas came and went with unusual ease

Urges to self-medicate, to calm your nerves

Ending relationships suddenly

Particularly sensitive to shapes, forms, and harmony in nature

Spent a lot of time on social, political, or religious causes

Vindictive, a need to even the score

Leaving big tips

More physically active

Did the opposite of what people wanted you to do or played the devil's advocate

Artistic and creative

Crying and laughing at the same time

Unusually spiritual or mystical

Binging on food

Critical or sarcastic

Unusually argumentative

Felt you were mentally very sharp, brilliant, and clever

Mood and energy heightened in the spring

Musical, rhyming, or dancing a lot

Irritable at small things

A lot of daydreaming, fantasy

Decorating or reorganizing the house a lot

Great difficulty seeing others' points of view

Felt unappreciated because others did not understand or share your optimistic or imaginative ideas

Your mood, energy, interest, and efficiency improved if you were in a regular routine

Thoughts jump from topic to topic

Wanting to decorate your body with tattoos, piercings, or make-up

Inappropriate jokes

150 Things to Try When You're Depressed

This list is meant to be used with the therapy techniques in Chapter 12 ("Getting Active").

Constructive Ideas

Exercise
Work in a garden
Clean your room
Write a poem
Wash your car
Reorganize your room
Plant a tree
Decorate your room
Work on your car
Clean out one closet
Learn to draw
Clean something
Get to work early
Try a new, easy recipe
Organize your apps, bookmarks, or bookshelves
Practice a sport, karate, or yoga
Work on a photo album
Plan how to lose weight
Throw out old papers you no longer need
Gently stretch your muscles

Take a class in something that interests you
Read the Bible or a spiritual text
Plan your career
Plan how to save money or get out of debt
Recycle old items
Make plans for finishing school
Give things you don't need to a charity
Complete a task (any task)

Relaxation

Take a warm bubble bath
Practice breathing slowly
Practice mindfulness
Go buy an ice cream cone
Walk in the rain
Think about things that you've accomplished
Sit by a warm fire
Eat a strawberry
Walk barefoot on soft cool grass
Eat a slice of fresh-baked bread
Find a quiet place to sit outside and enjoy nature
Make a list of things you are thankful for
Sit in a coffeehouse and read
Have breakfast in bed
Buy yourself a rose
Walk on a scenic path in a park
Drink some hot cocoa, tea, or cider
Write in your journal
Pet a friendly dog or cat
Have a manicure or pedicure
Stop and smell some flowers
Think about finishing school
Try a food you've never tasted
Wake up early and watch the sunrise

Watch the sunset

Relax with a good book or soothing music

Play your favorite music and dance to it by yourself

Go to bed early

Sleep outside under the stars

Fix a special dinner just for yourself

Go for a walk

Light candles

Sing or whistle around the house

Pray

Take a sauna

Daydream

Laugh

Give yourself more time than you need to accomplish whatever you're doing

Get a massage

Take a cozy nap

Listen to your favorite music

Get a facial

Have a day with nothing to do

Paint your nails

Fun, Travel, and Entertainment

Go see a film or show

Go to a pet store and play with the animals

Visit a zoo

Visit a town you've never been to

Explore a new hobby

Watch a funny movie

Go out to your favorite restaurant

Go to the beach

Take a scenic drive

Buy new clothes

Browse in a book store for as long as you want

Buy yourself something special that you can afford

Go to the park—feed the ducks, swing on the swings, and go down the slide
Visit a museum or another interesting place
Work on a puzzle book or adult coloring book
Go dancing
Research your family tree
Read a book
Go bowling or skating
Go shopping
Start an aquarium
Go to a sporting event
Learn a magic trick
Go fishing
Play cards
Bake cookies
Take some pictures
Plan a day trip
Throw snowballs
Learn to needlepoint
Go swimming
Watch a ballet
Read or memorize a poem
Listen to a symphony
Read a story curled up in bed
Look at a work of art
Do something you've never done before
Feed the birds
Memorize a joke
Go on a picnic
Take a different route to work
Play solitaire
Window shop on your favorite street
Play a board game
Learn to sail, canoe, or ride horses
Do a crossword puzzle

Shoot pool
Plan an easy, restful vacation
Listen to an audiobook
Go out to your favorite restaurant
Look through travel brochures and dream
Visit your local library and browse the shelves
Take pictures of your family
Write your life story
Plan a hike or camping trip
Read magazines or newspapers

Social

Call a good friend or several good friends
Play an intramural sport
Go to church or a prayer group
E-mail a friend
Smile
Practice listening to others
Plan a surprise birthday party
Meet new people
Join or start a book club
Plan lunch with a friend
Go on a date or spend time alone with your partner
Make a gift for family or a friend
Watch children play
Do volunteer work
Get involved in a club
Teach a child to fly a kite
Take acting lessons
Say something nice to someone
Play with a toddler or baby
Write a note to a far away friend
Freely praise other people
Tell a friend how much you appreciate them

Online Resources

Educational Sites

www.moodtreatmentcenter.com/bipolarnotsomuch (supplementary
materials for this book)

www.psycheducation.org (Dr. Phelps)

www.beyondbipolar.com (Dr. Mountain)

www.pubmed.org (index of all research articles)

www.bipolarnews.org (research updates)

www.bbrfoundation.org/bipolar-disorder (research updates)

www.cet.org (light and other environmental therapies)

www.tara4bpd.org (borderline personality disorder)

www.thebalancedmind.org (for children with bipolar)

www.activeminds.org (for students)

www.bipolarcaregivers.org (for family)

Find a Therapist or Provider

Many websites can guide you toward providers who have expertise in
certain areas. Below are some examples: (for a more complete list, see
www.moodtreatmentcenter.com/referrals.htm).

www.psychiatry.org

www.isbd.org

therapists.psychologytoday.com

www.goodtherapy.org

www.academyofct.org

www.contextualscience.org
www.cbasp.org
www.ipsrt.org
www.iptinstitute.com
www.motivationalinterviewing.org
www.emdria.org

Online Therapy Programs

Bipolar: www.mycompass.org.au
Depression: moodgym.anu.edu.au
Anxiety: ecouch.anu.edu.au
Mindfulness: marc.ucla.edu/body.cfm?id=22
Positive psychology: www.authentichappiness.sas.upenn.edu
Suicide: www.metanoia.org/suicide

Parenting

www.parentingstrategies.net
www.triplep-parenting.net
www.loveandlogic.com

Cognitive Brain Training

www.lumosity.com
www.elevateapp.com
www.fitbrains.com
www.brainhq.com
www.brainworkshop.sourceforge.net

Medications

Drug interaction checker: reference.medscape.com/drug-interaction checker

Find the lowest local price for medications: www.goodrx.com

People with low incomes may be eligible for free medication programs. Note: This often won't work if you have insurance or there are generic versions of the medication, but there are exceptions. Resources include: www.pparx.org, www.togetherrxaccess.com, and www.rxassist.org.

Rating Scales

Mood and other spectrum disorders: www.spectrum-project.org

Mood Disorder Questionnaire (for mania): www.dbsalliance.org/pdfs/mdq.pdf

MoodCheck (to screen for bipolar): psycheducation.org/primary-care-provider-resource-center/moodcheck

Depression and anxiety: www.phqscreeners.com

Personality testing: www.npsp25.com

Other rating scales: www.outcometracker.org/scales_library.php

Further Reading

A textbook version of this book is available for providers, professionals, and anyone who wants more technical detail:
A Spectrum Approach to Mood Disorders: Not Fully Bipolar but Not Unipolar—Practical Management. James Phelps. W. W. Norton, 2016.

Workbooks for Bipolar, Depression, Anxiety, and Insomnia

The Bipolar II Workbook. Stephanie Roberts, Louisa Sylvia, and Noreen Reilly-Harrington. New Harbinger, 2013.
Overcoming Depression One Step at a Time. Michael Addis and Christopher Martell. New Harbinger, 2004.
The Feeling Good Handbook. David D. Burns. Plume, 1999.
The Anxiety and Phobia Workbook. Edmund J. Bourne. New Harbinger, 2011.
The Insomnia Workbook. Stephanie Silberman. New Harbinger, 2009.

Memoirs and Biographies of Bipolar and Depression

An Unquiet Mind: A Memoir of Moods and Madness. Kay Redfield Jamison. Vintage, 1996.
Touched With Fire: Manic Depressive Illness and the Artistic Temperament. Kay Redfield Jamison. Free Press, 1996.
A First-Rate Madness. Nassir Ghaemi. Penguin, 2012.
Lincoln's Melancholy. Joshua Wolf Shenk. Mariner, 2006.

Support Groups

Depression and Bipolar Support Alliance, www.dbsalliance.org
  1–800–826–3632
Child and Adolescent Bipolar Foundation, www.bpkids.org
  1–847–492–8519
Mental Health America, www.mentalhealthamerica.net
  1–800–969–6642
National Alliance for the Mentally Ill, www.nami.org
  1–800–950–NAMI
Anxiety and Depression Association of America, www.adaa.org
  1–240–485–1001
Active Minds (for students and young adults), www.activeminds.org
Suicide prevention hotlines: www.crisistextline.org
  1–800–273–TALK (8255)

References

Addis, M., & Martell, C. (2004). *Overcoming depression one step at a time: The new behavioral activation approach to getting your life back*. Oakland, CA: New Harbinger Publications.

Aiken, C. B. (2007). Pramipexole in psychiatry: A systematic review of the literature. *Journal of Clinical Psychiatry, 68*(8), 1230–1236.

Aiken, C. B., & Orr, C. (2010). Rechallenge with lamotrigine after a rash: a prospective case series and review of the literature. *Psychiatry (Edgmont), 7*(5), 27-32.

Aiken, C. B., Weisler, R. H., & Sachs, G. S. (2015). The Bipolarity Index: A clinician-rated measure of diagnostic confidence. *Journal of Affective Disorders, 177,* 59–64.

Akiskal, H. S., Hantouche, E. G., & Allilaire, J. F. (2003). Bipolar II with and without cyclothymic temperament: "Dark" and "sunny" expressions of soft bipolarity. *Journal of Affective Disorders, 73*(1–2), 49–57.

Akiskal, H. S., & Tohen, M. (2011). *Bipolar psychopharmacotherapy: Caring for the patient*. West Sussex, UK: Wiley.

Al-Karawi, D., Al Mamoori, D. A., & Tayyar, Y. (2016). The role of curcumin administration in patients with major depressive disorder: Mini meta-analysis of clinical trials. *Phytotherapy Research, 30*(2), 175–183.

Amminger, G. P., Schäfer, M. R., Papageorgiou, K., Klier, C. M., Cotton, S. M., Harrigan, S. M., . . . Berger, G. E. (2010). Long-chain omega-3 fatty acids for indicated prevention of psychotic disorders: A randomized, placebo-controlled trial. *Archives of General Psychiatry, 67*(2), 146–154.

Amsterdam, J. D., Li, Y., Soeller, I., Rockwell, K., Mao, J. J., & Shults, J. (2009). A randomized, double-blind, placebo-controlled trial of oral

Matricaria recutita (chamomile) extract therapy for generalized anxiety disorder. *Journal of Clinical Psychopharmacology, 29*(4), 378–382.

Angst, J., & Dobler-Mikola, A. (1984). The Zurich study. II. The continuum from normal to pathological depressive mood swings. *European Archives of Psychiatry and Neurological Sciences, 234,* 21–29.

Applebaum, J., Bersudsky, Y., & Klein, E. (2007). Rapid tryptophan depletion as a treatment for acute mania: A double-blind, pilot-controlled study. *Bipolar Disorder, 9*(8), 884–887.

Babyak, M., Blumenthal, J. A., Herman, S., Khatri, P., Doraiswamy, M., Moore, K., . . . Krishnan, K. R. (2000). Exercise treatment for major depression: Maintenance of therapeutic benefit at 10 months. *Psychosomatic Medicine, 62*(5), 633–638.

Bagby, R. M., Quilty, L. C., Segal, Z. V., McBride, C. C., Kennedy, S. H., & Costa, P. T. (2008). Personality and differential treatment response in major depression: A randomized controlled trial comparing cognitive-behavioural therapy and pharmacotherapy. *Canadian Journal of Psychiatry, 53*(6), 361–370.

Bao, Y., Han, J., Hu, F. B., Giovannucci, E. L., Stampfer, M. J., Willett, W. C., & Fuchs, C. S. (2013). Association of nut consumption with total and cause-specific mortality. *New England Journal of Medicine, 21*(369), 2001–2011.

Bauer, M., Adli, M., Bschor, T., Heinz, A., Rasgon, N., Frye, M., . . . Whybrow, P. C. (2003). Clinical applications of levothyroxine in refractory mood disorders. *Clinical Approaches in Bipolar Disorder, 2,* 49–56.

Bauer, M., Glenn, T., Alda, M., Andreassen, O. A., Ardau, R., Bellivier, F., . . . Whybrow, P. C. (2012). Impact of sunlight on the age of onset of bipolar disorder. *Bipolar Disorder, 14*(6), 654–663.

Bauer, M., & Grof, P. (2006). *Lithium in neuropsychiatry: The comprehensive guide.* Abingdon, UK: Informa UK.

Bearden, C. E., Glahn, D. C., Caetano, S., Olvera, R. L., Fonseca, M., Najt, P., . . . Soares, J. C. (2007). Evidence for disruption in prefrontal cortical functions in juvenile bipolar disorder. *Bipolar Disorder, 9,* 145–159.

Bedrosian, T. A., & Nelson, R. J. (2013). Influence of the modern light environment on mood. *Molecular Psychiatry*, 18(7), 751–757.

Behzadi, A. H., Omrani, Z., Chalian, M., Asadi, S., & Ghadiri, M. (2009). Folic acid efficacy as an alternative drug added to sodium valproate in the treatment of acute phase of mania in bipolar disorder: A double-blind randomized controlled trial. *Acta Psychiatrica Scandinavica*, 120(6), 441–445.

Belsky, J., Jonassaint, C., Pluess, M., Stanton, M., Brummett, B., & Williams, R. (2009). Vulnerability genes or plasticity genes? *Molecular Psychiatry*, 14(8), 746–754.

Benazzi, F., & Akiskal, H. S. (2006). The duration of hypomania in bipolar-II disorder in private practice: Methodology and validation. *Journal of Affective Disorders*, 96(3), 189–196.

Benedetti, F., Riccaboni, R., Poletti, S., Radaelli, D., Locatelli, C., Lorenzi, C., . . . Colombo, C. (2014). The serotonin transporter genotype modulates the relationship between early stress and adult suicidality in bipolar disorder. *Bipolar Disorder*, 16(8), 857–866.

Berchtold, N. C., Kesslak, J. P., Pike, C. J., Adlard, P. A., & Cotman, C. W. (2001). Estrogen and exercise interact to regulate brain-derived neurotrophic factor mRNA and protein expression in the hippocampus. *European Journal of Neuroscience*, 14(12), 1992–2002.

Berlim, M. T., van den Eynde, F., Tovar-Perdomo, S., & Daskalakis, Z. J. (2013). Response, remission and drop-out rates following high-frequency repetitive transcranial magnetic stimulation (rTMS) for treating major depression: A systematic review and meta-analysis of randomized, double-blind and sham-controlled trials. *Psychological Medicine*, 44(2), 225–239.

Beyer, J. L., & Weisler, R. H. (2016). Suicide behaviors in bipolar disorder. *Psychiatric Clinics of North America*, 39(1), 111–123.

Birmaher, B., Axelson, D., Monk, K., Kalas, C., Goldstein, B., Hickey, M. B., . . . Brent, D. (2008). Lifetime psychiatric disorders in school-aged offspring of parents with bipolar disorder: The Pittsburgh Bipolar Offspring study. *Archives of General Psychiatry*, 66(3), 287–296.

Borgonovi, F. (2008). Doing well by doing good. The relationship between formal volunteering and self-reported health and happiness. *Social Science and Medicine, 66*(11), 2321–2334.

Carey, B. (2013, November 18). Sleep therapy seen as an aid for depression. *New York Times.*

Carter, J. (2015, September 27). The secret to Jimmy and Rosalynn Carter's nearly 70-year marriage [television interview]. Retrieved from http://www.supersoul.tv

Caspi, A., Sugden, K., Moffitt, T. E., Taylor, A., Craig, I. W., Harrington, H., . . . Poulton, R. (2003). Influence of life stress on depression: Moderation by a polymorphism in the 5-HTT gene. *Science, 18*(301), 386–389.

Cheng, J. Y., Chen, R. Y., Ko, J. S., & Ng, E. M. (2007). Efficacy and safety of atomoxetine for attention-deficit/hyperactivity disorder in children and adolescents-meta-analysis and meta-regression analysis. *Psychopharmacology (Berlin), 194*(2), 197–209.

Chengappa, K. N., Bowie, C. R., Schlicht, P. J., Fleet, D., Brar, J. S., & Jindal, R. (2013). Randomized placebo-controlled adjunctive study of an extract of withania somnifera for cognitive dysfunction in bipolar disorder. *Journal of Clinical Psychiatry, 74*(11), 1076–1083.

Chengappa, K. N., Perkins, K. A., Brar, J. S., Schlicht, P. J., Turkin, S. R., Hetrick, M. L., . . . George, T. P. (2014). Varenicline for smoking cessation in bipolar disorder: A randomized, double-blind, placebo-controlled study. *Journal of Clinical Psychiatry, 75*(7), 765–772.

Chisholm, D., van Ommeren, M., Ayuso-Mateos, J. L., & Saxena, S. (2005). Cost-effectiveness of clinical interventions for reducing the global burden of bipolar disorder. *British Journal of Psychiatry, 187,* 559-67.

Chung F., Abdullah H.R., Liao, P. (2015). STOP-Bang Questionnaire: A practical approach to screen for obstructive sleep apnea. *Chest* (2015).

Clos S., Rauchhaus P., Severn A., Cochrane L., Donnan P. T. (2015). Long-term effect of lithium maintenance therapy on estimated glomerular filtration rate in patients with affective disorders: a population-based cohort study. *Lancet Psychiatry, 2*(12), 1075-1083.

Cohen, B. M., Lipinski, J. F., & Altesman, R. I. (1982). Lecithin in the treatment of mania: Double-blind, placebo-controlled trials. *American Journal of Psychiatry, 139*(9), 1162–1164.

Colcombe, S. J., Erickson, K. I., Raz, N., Webb, A. G., Cohen, N. J., McAuley, E., & Kramer, A. F. (2003). Aerobic fitness reduces brain tissue loss in aging humans. *The Journals of Gerontology Series A: Biological Sciences and Medical Sciences, 58*(2), 176–180.

Cooney, G. M., Dwan, K., Greig, C. A., Lawlor, D. A., Rimer, J., Waugh, F. R., . . . Mead, G. E. (2013). Exercise for depression. *Cochrane Database Systematic Reviews, 9*, CD004366.

Crump, C., Sundquist, K., Winkleby, M. A., & Sundquist, J. (2013). Comorbidities and mortality in bipolar disorder: A Swedish national cohort study. *JAMA Psychiatry, 70*(9), 931–939.

Dankoski, E. C., Agster, K. L., Fox, M. E., Moy, S. S., & Wightman, R. M. (2014). Facilitation of serotonin signaling by SSRIs is attenuated by social isolation. *Neuropsychopharmacology, 39*(13), 2928–2937.

Davidson, R. T., Connor, K. M., & Swartz, M. (2006). Mental illness in U.S. presidents between 1776 and 1974: A review of biographical sources. *The Journal of Nervous and Mental Disease, 194*, 47–51.

De Long, N. E., Stepita, R. A., Taylor, V. H., & Holloway, A. C. (2015). Major depressive disorder and diabetes: Does serotonin bridge the gap? *Current Diabetes Review, 11*(2), 71–78.

de Quervain, D. J., Fischbacher, U., Treyer, V., Schellhammer, M., Schnyder, U., Buck, A., & Fehr, E. (2004). The neural basis of altruistic punishment. *Science, 27*(305), 1254–1258.

de Souto Barreto, P., Demougeot, L., Pillard, F., Lapeyre-Mestre, M., & Rolland, Y. (2015). Exercise training for managing behavioral and psychological symptoms in people with dementia: A systematic review and meta-analysis. *Ageing Research Reviews, 24*(Pt B), 274–285.

Deckersbach, T., Peters, A. T., Sylvia, L., Urdahl, A., Magalhães, P. V., Otto, M. W., . . . Nierenberg, A. (2014). Do comorbid anxiety disorders moderate the effects of psychotherapy for bipolar disorder? Results from STEP-BD. *American Journal of Psychiatry, 171*(2), 178–186.

Deepmala, Slattery, J., Kumar, N., Delhey, L., Berk, M., Dean, O., . . . Frye,

R. (2015). Clinical trials of N-acetylcysteine in psychiatry and neurology: A systematic review. *Neuroscience and Biobehavioral Reviews*, 55, 294–321.

Deiner, E., Horwitz, J., & Emmons, R. (1985). Happiness of the very wealthy. *Social Indicators Research*, 16, 263–274.

Depression and Bipolar Support Alliance. (1998). *Bipolar disorder statistics*. Retrieved from http://www.dbsalliance.org

Devinsky, O., Marsh, E., Friedman, D., Thiele, E., Laux, L., Sullivan, J., . . . Cilio, M. R. (2015). Cannabidiol in patients with treatment-resistant epilepsy: An open-label interventional trial. *Lancet Neurology*, 2015(December 23).

Devore, E. E., Kang, J. H., Breteler, M. M., & Grodstein, F. (2012). Dietary intakes of berries and flavonoids in relation to cognitive decline. *Annals of Neurology*, 72(1), 135–143.

Diniz, B. S., & Reynolds, C. F., III. (2014). Major depressive disorder in older adults: Benefits and hazards of prolonged treatment. *Drugs and Aging*, 31(9), 661–669.

Dong, X., Yang, C., Cao, S., Gan, Y., Sun, H., Gong, Y., . . . Lu, Z. (2015). Tea consumption and the risk of depression: A meta-analysis of observational studies. *Australian and New Zealand Journal of Psychiatry*, 49(4), 334–345.

Edinger, J. D., & Carney, C. E. (2014). *Overcoming insomnia: A cognitive-behavioral therapy approach*. New York, NY: Oxford University Press.

Egeland, J. A., Hostetter, A. M., & Eshleman, S. K., III. (1983). Amish study, III: The impact of cultural factors on diagnosis of bipolar illness. *American Journal of Psychiatry*, 140(1), 67–71.

Ellison, M. L., Russinova, Z., Lyass, A., & Rogers, E. S. (2008). Professionals and managers with severe mental illnesses: Findings from a national survey. *The Journal of Nervous and Mental Disease*, 196(3), 179–189.

El-Mallakh, R. S., Vöhringer, P. A., Ostacher, M. M., Baldassano, C. F., Holtzman, N. S., Whitham, E. A., . . . Ghaemi, S. N. (2015). Antidepressants worsen rapid-cycling course in bipolar depression: A

STEP-BD randomized clinical trial. *Journal of Affective Disorders*, *184*, 318–321.

Fiala, S. J. (2004). Normal is a place I visit. *Journal of the American Medical Association*, *23*(291), 2924–2926.

Fitzgerald, P. J. (2013). Gray colored glasses: Is major depression partially a sensory perceptual disorder? *Journal of Affective Disorders*, *151*(2), 418–422.

Foster, R. G. (2005). Neurobiology: Bright blue times. *Nature*, *433*(7027), 698–699.

Frances, A. (2013). *Saving normal: An insider's revolt against out-of-control psychiatric diagnosis, DSM-5, Big Pharma, and the medicalization of ordinary life*. New York, NY: HarperCollins.

Frank, E. (2007). *Treating bipolar disorder: A clinician's guide to interpersonal and social rhythm therapy*. New York, NY: Guilford Press.

Frey, D. J., Ortega, J. D., Wiseman, C., Farley, C. T., & Wright, K. P., Jr. (2011). Influence of zolpidem and sleep inertia on balance and cognition during nighttime awakening: A randomized placebo-controlled trial. *Journal of the American Geriatric Society*, *59*(1), 73–81.

Frye, M. (2013, June 15). *Joint presentation with Depression & Bipolar Support Alliance*. 10th International Conference on Bipolar Disorders, Miami Beach, FL.

Frye, M. A., Yatham, L., Ketter, T. A., Goldberg, J., Suppes, T., Calabrese, J. R., . . . Adams, B. (2009). Depressive relapse during lithium treatment associated with increased serum thyroid-stimulating hormone: Results from two placebo-controlled bipolar I maintenance studies. *Acta Psychiatrica Scandinavica*, *120*(1), 10–13.

Galvez, J. F., Thommi, S., & Ghaemi, S. N. (2011). Positive aspects of mental illness: A review in bipolar disorder. *Journal of Affective Disorders*, *128*(3), 185–190.

Geddes, J. R., Gardiner, A., Rendell, J., Voysey, M., Tunbridge, E., Hinds, C., . . . Harrison, P. J. (2016). Comparative evaluation of quetiapine plus lamotrigine combination versus quetiapine monotherapy (and folic acid versus placebo) in bipolar depression (CEQUEL): A 2 × 2 factorial randomised trial. *Lancet Psychiatry*, *3*(1), 31–39.

Geoffroy, P. A., Fovet, T., Micoulaud-Franchi, J. A., Boudebesse, C., Thomas, P., Etain, B., & Amad, A. (2015). Bright light therapy in seasonal bipolar depressions. *Encephale, 41*(6), 527–533.

Ghaemi, S. N. (2006). Hippocratic psychopharmacology for bipolar disorder—An expert's opinion. *Psychiatry (Edgmont), 3*(6), 30–39.

Ghaemi, S. N. (2007). Feeling and time: The phenomenology of mood disorders, depressive realism, and existential psychotherapy. *Schizophrenia Bulletin, 33*(1), 122–130.

Ghaemi, S. N. (2010). *A first-rate madness: Uncovering the links between leadership and mental illness.* London, UK: Penguin Press.

Ghaemi, S. N., Ostacher, M. M., El-Mallakh, R. S., Borrelli, D., Baldassano, C. F., Kelley, M. E., . . . Baldessarini, R. J. (2010). Antidepressant discontinuation in bipolar depression: A Systematic Treatment Enhancement Program for Bipolar Disorder (STEP-BD) randomized clinical trial of long-term effectiveness and safety. *Journal of Clinical Psychiatry, 71*(4), 372–380.

Giannini, A. J., Nakoneczie, A. M., Melemis, S. M., Ventresco, J., & Condon, M. (2000). Magnesium oxide augmentation of verapamil maintenance therapy in mania. *Psychiatry Research, 93*(1), 83–87.

Goldberg, J. F., & Burdick, K. E. (2008). *Cognitive dysfunction in bipolar disorder: A guide for clinicians.* Washington, DC: American Psychiatric Publishing.

Goldberg, J. F., & Ernst, C. L. (2012). *Managing the side effects of psychotropic medications.* Washington, DC: American Psychiatric Publishing.

Goodwin, F. K., & Jamison, K. R. (2007). *Manic-depressive illness: Bipolar disorders and recurrent depression,* 2nd ed. New York, NY: Oxford University Press.

Goss, A. J., Kaser, M., Costafreda, S. G., Sahakian, B. J., & Fu, C. H. (2013). Modafinil augmentation therapy in unipolar and bipolar depression: A systematic review and meta-analysis of randomized controlled trials. *Journal of Clinical Psychiatry, 74*(11), 1101–1107.

Gotlib, I. H., & Hammen, C. L. (2010). *Handbook of depression,* 2nd ed. New York, NY: Guilford Press.

Gray, K. M., Carpenter, M. J., Baker, N. L., DeSantis, S. M., Kryway, E.,

Hartwell, K. J., . . .Brady, K. T. (2012). A double-blind randomized controlled trial of N-acetylcysteine in cannabis-dependent adolescents. *American Journal of Psychiatry, 169*(8), 805–812.

Grogan, K. (2014, February 7). Shire ADHD drug Vyvanse fails in depression studies. *PharmaTimes Digital.*

Grosso, G., Micek, A., Castellano, S., Pajak, A., & Galvano, F. (2016). Coffee, tea, caffeine and risk of depression: A systematic review and dose-response meta-analysis of observational studies. *Molecular Nutrition and Food Research, 60*(1), 223–234.

Gruttadaro, D., & Crudo, D. (2012). *College students speak: A survey report on mental health.* Retrieved from http://www.nami.org/collegesurvey

Gualtieri, C. T., & Johnson, L. G. (2006). Comparative neurocognitive effects of 5 psychotropic anticonvulsants and lithium. *Medscape General Medicine, 8*(3), 46.

Hallowell, E. M., & Ratey, J. J. (1995). *Driven to distraction: Recognizing and coping with attention deficit disorder from childhood through adulthood.* New York, NY: Touchstone.

Hamilton, J. (2006, March 24). FDA committee rejects ADHD use for Modafinil. *National Public Radio News.*

Hamilton, S. P. (2015). The promise of psychiatric pharmacogenomics. *Biological Psychiatry, 77*(1), 29–35.

Hashimoto, K. (2010). Brain-derived neurotrophic factor as a biomarker for mood disorders: An historical overview and future directions. *Psychiatry and Clinical Neurosciences, 64*(4), 341–357.

Haspel, T. (2013, September 24). Farmed vs. wild salmon: Can you taste the difference? *The Washington Post.*

Hawthorne, J. M., & Caley, C. F. (2015). Extrapyramidal reactions associated with serotonergic antidepressants. *Annals of Pharmacotherapy, 49*(10), 1136–1152.

Hayes, S. C., Strosahl, K. D., Wilson, & K. G. (2003). *Acceptance and Commitment therapy: An experiential approach to behavior change.* New York, NY: Guilford Press.

Henriksen, T. E., Skrede, S., Fasmer, O. B., Hamre, B., Grønli, J., & Lund,

A. (2014). Blocking blue light during mania—Markedly increased regularity of sleep and rapid improvement of symptoms: A case report. *Bipolar Disorder, 16*(8), 894–898.

Hirashima, F., Parow, A. M., Stoll, A. L., Demopulos, C. M., Damico, K. E., Rohan, M. L., . . . Renshaw, P. F. (2004). Omega-3 fatty acid treatment and T(2) whole brain relaxation times in bipolar disorder. *American Journal of Psychiatry, 161*(10), 1922–1924.

Hirschfeld, R. M. (2001). Bipolar spectrum disorder: Improving its recognition and diagnosis. *Journal of Clinical Psychiatry, 62*(14), 5–9.

Holshoe, J. M. (2009). Antidepressants and sleep: A review. *Perspectives in Psychiatric Care, 45*(3), 191–197.

Hou, L., Heilbronner, U., Degenhardt, F., Adli, M., Akiyama, K., Akula, N., . . . Schulze, T. G. (2016). Assessment of response to lithium maintenance treatment in bipolar disorder: A Consortium on Lithium Genetics (ConLiGen) report. *Lancet*, S0140-6736(16)00143-4.

Hunt, J., Eisenberg, D., & Kilbourne, A. M. (2010). Consequences of receipt of a psychiatric diagnosis for completion of college. *Psychiatric Services, 61*(4), 399–404.

Hutchinson, M. (2010). At first it was fun. *On the Living Side* [CD]. Saint Paul, MN: Red House Records.

Hwang, T. J., Ni, H. C., Chen, H. C., Lin, Y. T., & Liao, S. C. (2010). Risk predictors for hypnosedative-related complex sleep behaviors: A retrospective, cross-sectional pilot study. *Journal of Clinical Psychiatry, 71*(10), 1331–1335.

International Society for Psychiatric Genetics. (2014, April 22). *Genetic testing statement.* Retrieved from http://ispg.net/genetic-testing-statement

Jacobs, G. D., Pace-Schott, E. F., Stickgold, R., Otto, M. W. (2004). Cognitive behavior therapy and pharmacotherapy for insomnia: a randomized controlled trial and direct comparison. *Archives of Internal Medicine, 164*(17), 1888-1896.

Jacka, F. N., Pasco, J. A., Mykletun, A., Williams, L. J., Hodge, A. M., O'Reilly, S. L., . . . Berk, M. (2010). Association of Western and traditional diets with depression and anxiety in women. *American Journal of Psychiatry, 167*(3), 305–311.

Jaffee, W. B., Griffin, M. L., Gallop, R., Meade, C. S., Graff, F., Bender, R. E., & Weiss, R. D. (2009). Depression precipitated by alcohol use in patients with co-occurring bipolar and substance use disorders. *Journal of Clinical Psychiatry, 70*(2), 171–176.

Jamison, K. R. (1995). *An unquiet mind: A memoir of moods and madness.* New York, NY: Knopf.

Jancin, B. (2013, June 5). Valacyclovir improves cognition in bipolar patients. *Clinical Psychiatry News Digital Network.*

Jann, M., Kennedy, W. K., & Lopez, G. (2014). Benzodiazepines: A major component in unintentional prescription drug overdoses with opioid analgesics. *Journal of Pharmacy Practice, 27*(1), 5–16.

Jans, L. A., Giltay, E. J., & Van der Does, A. J. (2010). The efficacy of n-3 fatty acids DHA and EPA (fish oil) for perinatal depression. *British Journal of Nutrition, 104*(11), 1577–1585.

Jiang, H. Y., Chen, H. Z., Hu, X. J., Yu, Z. H., Yang, W., Deng, M., . . . Ruan, B. (2015). Use of selective serotonin reuptake inhibitors and risk of upper gastrointestinal bleeding: A systematic review and meta-analysis. *Clinical Gastroenterology and Hepatology, 13*(1), 42–50.

Kahneman, D., & Deaton, A. (2010). High income improves evaluation of life but not emotional well being. *Proceedings of the National Academy of Sciences, 107*(38), 16489–16493.

Kampman, K. M., Lynch, K. G., Pettinati, H. M., Spratt, K., Wierzbicki, M. R., Dackis, C., & O'Brien, C. P. (2015). A double blind, placebo controlled trial of modafinil for the treatment of cocaine dependence without co-morbid alcohol dependence. *Drug and Alcohol Dependence, 155,* 105–110.

Kasper, S., Gastpar, M., Müller, W. E., Volz, H. P., Möller, H. J., Schläfke, S., & Dienel, A. (2014). Lavender oil preparation Silexan is effective in generalized anxiety disorder—A randomized, double-blind comparison to placebo and paroxetine. *International Journal of Neuropsychopharmacology, 17*(6), 859–869.

Kedzior, K.K., Gellersen, H.M., Brachetti, A.K., Berlim, M.T. (2015). Deep transcranial magnetic stimulation (DTMS) in the treatment of major depression: An exploratory systematic review and meta-analysis. *Journal of Affective Disorders*, 15(187), 73-83.

Kelly, M. E., Loughrey, D., Lawlor, B. A., Robertson, I. H., Walsh, C., & Brennan, S. (2014). The impact of exercise on the cognitive functioning of healthy older adults: A systematic review and meta-analysis. *Ageing Research Reviews*, 16, 12–31.

Kennaway, D. J. (2015). Potential safety issues in the use of the hormone melatonin in paediatrics. *Journal of Paediatrics and Child Health*, 51(6), 584–589.

Kessing L. V., Gerds T. A., Feldt-Rasmussen B., Andersen P. K., Licht R. W. (2015). Use of lithium and anticonvulsants and the rate of chronic kidney disease: A nationwide population-based study. *JAMA Psychiatry*, 72(12), 1182-1191.

Ketter, T. (2009). *Handbook of diagnosis and treatment of bipolar disorders.* Washington, DC: American Psychiatric Publishing.

Khan, S. J., Fersh, M. E., Ernst, C., Klipstein, K., Albertini, E. S., & Lusskin, S. I. (2016). Bipolar disorder in pregnancy and postpartum: Principles of management. *Current Psychiatry Reports*, 18(2), 13.

Kinch, M. S., Haynesworth, A., & Kinch, S. L. (2014). An overview of FDA-approved new molecular entities: 1827–2013. *Drug Discovery Today*, 19(8), 1033–1039.

Kiyosaki, R. T. (1997). *Rich dad poor dad: What the rich teach their kids about money that the poor and middle class do not!* New York, NY: Warner Books.

Kotin, J., & Goodwin, F. K. (1972). Depression during mania: Clinical observations and theoretical implications. *American Journal of Psychiatry*, 129, 679–686.

Kyaga, S., Lichtenstein, P., Boman, M., Hultman, C., Långström, N., & Landén, M. (2011). Creativity and mental disorder: Family study of 300,000 people with severe mental disorder. *British Journal of Psychiatry*, 199(5), 373–379.

Kyaga, S., Lichtenstein, P., Boman, M., & Landén, M. (2015). Bipolar disorder and leadership—A total population study. *Acta Psychiatrica Scandinavica, 131*(2), 111–119.

Lanni, C., Racchi, M., & Govoni, S. (2013). Do we need pharmacogenetics to personalize antidepressant therapy? *Cellular and Molecular Life Sciences, 70*(18), 3327–3340.

Latner, J. D., & Wilson, G. T. (2004). Binge eating and satiety in bulimia nervosa and binge eating disorder: Effects of macronutrient intake. *International Journal of Eating Disorders, 36*(4), 402–415.

Leasure, J. L., & Decker, L. (2009). Social isolation prevents exercise-induced proliferation of hippocampal progenitor cells in female rats. *Hippocampus, 19*(10), 907–912.

Leibenluft, E. (2014). Categories and dimensions, brain and behavior: The yins and yangs of psychopathology. *JAMA Psychiatry, 71*(1), 15–17.

Leidy, H. J., Bossingham, M. J., Mattes, R. D., & Campbell, W. W. (2009). Increased dietary protein consumed at breakfast leads to an initial and sustained feeling of fullness during energy restriction compared to other meal times. *British Journal of Nutrition, 101*(6), 798–803.

Lera-Miguel, S., Andrés-Perpiñá, S., Calvo, R., Fatjó-Vilas, M., Fañanás, L., & Lázaro, L. (2010). Early-onset bipolar disorder: How about visual-spatial skills and executive functions? *European Archives of Psychiatry and Clinical Neuroscience, 261*(3), 195–203.

Letenneur, L., Proust-Lima, C., Le Gouge, A., Dartigues, J. F., & Barberger-Gateau, P. (2007). Flavonoid intake and cognitive decline over a 10-year period. *American Journal of Epidemiology, 165*(12), 1364–1371.

Lidz, G. (2007, October 27). My adventures in psychopharmacology. *New York Magazine.*

Lopresti, A. L., & Drummond, P. D. (2014). Saffron (Crocus sativus) for depression: A systematic review of clinical studies and examination of underlying antidepressant mechanisms of action. *Human Psychopharmacology, 29*(6), 517–527.

Lowrey, A. (2011, May 26). Your commute is killing you. *Slate.*

Lyoo, I. K., Yoon, S., Kim, T. S., Hwang, J., Kim, J. E., Won, W., . . . Renshaw, P. F. (2012). A randomized, double-blind placebo-controlled trial of oral creatine monohydrate augmentation for enhanced response to a selective serotonin reuptake inhibitor in women with major depressive disorder. *American Journal of Psychiatry, 169*(9), 937–945.

MacCabe, J. H., Lambe, M. P., Cnattingius, S., Sham, P. C., David, A. S., Reichenberg, A., & Hultman, C. M. (2010). Excellent school performance at age 16 and risk of adult bipolar disorder: National cohort study. *British Journal of Psychiatry, 196*(2), 109–115.

Mankad, M., & Beyer, J. L. (2010). *Clinical manual of electroconvulsive therapy.* Washington, DC: American Psychiatric Publishing.

Martell, C., Dimidjian, S., & Herman-Dunn, R. (2013). *Behavioral activation for depression: A clinician's guide.* New York, NY: Guilford Press.

McCullough, J. P. (2003). *Treatment for chronic depression: Cognitive behavioral analysis system of psychotherapy.* New York, NY: Guilford Press.

Meador, K. J., Baker, G. A., Browning, N., Cohen, M. J., Bromley, R. L., Clayton-Smith, J., . . . Loring, D. W. (2014). Breastfeeding in children of women taking antiepileptic drugs: Cognitive outcomes at age 6 years. *JAMA Pediatrics, 168*(8), 729–736.

Messaoudi, M., Violle, N., Bisson, J. F., Desor, D., Javelot, H., & Rougeot, C. (2011). Beneficial psychological effects of a probiotic formulation (Lactobacillus helveticus R0052 and Bifidobacterium longum R0175) in healthy human volunteers. *Gut Microbes, 2*(4), 256–261.

Meyer, T. D., Pell, J. P., & Mackay, D. (2015). Childhood IQ and risk of bipolar disorder in adulthood: Prospective birth cohort study. *British Journal of Psychiatry Open, 1,* 74–80.

Micallef-Trigona, B. (2014). Comparing the effects of repetitive transcranial magnetic stimulation and electroconvulsive therapy in the treatment of depression: A systematic review and meta-analysis. *Depression Research and Treatment, 135049.*

Miklowitz, D. (2010). *Bipolar disorder: A family-focused treatment approach,* 2nd ed. New York, NY: Guilford Press.

Mischoulon, D., & Rosenbaum, J. (2008). *Natural medications for psychiatric disorders: Considering the alternatives,* 2nd ed. Philadelphia, PA: Lippincott, Williams and Wilkins.

Mockenhaupt, M., Messenheimer, J., Tennis, P., & Schlingmann, J. (2005). Risk of Stevens-Johnson syndrome and toxic epidermal necrolysis in new users of antiepileptics. *Neurology, 64*(7), 1134–1138.

Moore, S. C., Patel, A. V., Matthews, C. E., Berrington de Gonzalez, A., Park, Y., Katki, H. A., . . . Lee, I. M. (2012). Leisure time physical activity of moderate to vigorous intensity and mortality: A large pooled cohort analysis. *PLoS Medicine, 9*(11), e1001335.

Morris, M. E., Martin, C. L., & Schenkman, M. L. (2010). Striding out with Parkinson disease: Evidence-based physical therapy for gait disorders. *Physical Therapy, 90*(2), 280–288.

Muhonen, L. H., Lönnqvist, J., Juva, K., & Alho, H. (2008). Double-blind, randomized comparison of memantine and escitalopram for the treatment of major depressive disorder comorbid with alcohol dependence. *Journal of Clinical Psychiatry, 69*(3), 392–399.

Mukai, T., Kishi, T., Matsuda, Y., & Iwata, N. (2014). A meta-analysis of inositol for depression and anxiety disorders. *Human Psychopharmacology, 29*(1), 55–63.

Norris, E. R., Burke, K., Correll, J. R., Zemanek, K. J., Lerman, J., Primelo, R. A., & Kaufmann, M. W. (2013). A double-blind, randomized, placebo-controlled trial of adjunctive ramelteon for the treatment of insomnia and mood stability in patients with euthymic bipolar disorder. *Journal of Affective Disorders, 144*(1–2), 141–147.

Nurnberger, J. I., Jr., Koller, D. L., Jung, J., Edenberg, H. J., Foroud, T., Guella, I., . . . Kelsoe, J. R. (2014). Identification of pathways for bipolar disorder: A meta-analysis. *JAMA Psychiatry, 71*(6), 657–664.

NutritionData.com. (2009). Retrieved from http://nutritiondata.self.com

Opie, R. S., Itsiopoulos, C., Parletta, N., Sanchez-Villegas, A., Akbaraly, T. N., Ruusunen, A., & Jacka, F. N. (2015, August 28). Dietary recommendations for the prevention of depression. *Nutritional Neuroscience.*

Pacchiarotti, I., Bond, D. J., Baldessarini, R. J., Nolen, W. A., Grunze, H., Licht, R. W., . . . Vieta, E. (2013). The International Society for Bipolar Disorders (ISBD) task force report on antidepressant use in bipolar disorders. *American Journal of Psychiatry, 170*, 1249–1262.

Pedersen, B. K., & Saltin, B. (2015). Exercise as medicine—Evidence for prescribing exercise as therapy in 26 different chronic diseases. *Scandinavian Journal of Medicine and Science in Sports, 25*, 1–72.

Perretta, P., Akiskal, H. S., Nisita, C., Lorenzetti, C., Zaccagnini, E., Della Santa, M., & Cassano, G. B. (1998). The high prevalence of bipolar II and associated cyclothymic and hyperthymic temperaments in HIV-patients. *Journal of Affective Disorders, 50*(2–3), 215–224.

Perugi, G., Quaranta, G., & Dell'Osso, L. (2014). The significance of mixed states in depression and mania. *Current Psychiatry Reports, 16*(10), 486.

Perugi, G., & Vannucchi, G. (2015). The use of stimulants and atomoxetine in adults with comorbid ADHD and bipolar disorder. *Expert Opinion on Pharmacotherapy, 16*(14), 2193–2204.

Phelps, J. (2011). Tapering antidepressants: Is 3 months slow enough? *Medical Hypotheses, 77*(6), 1006–1008.

Phillips, M. L., & Kupfer, D. J. (2013). Bipolar disorder diagnosis: Challenges and future directions. *Lancet, 381*(9878), 1663–1671.

Poradowska-Trzos, M., Dudek, D., Rogoz, M., & Zieba, A. (2007). Comparison of social networks of patients with unipolar and bipolar disease. *Psychiatria Polska, 41*(5), 665–677.

Porcelli, S., Fabbri, C., & Serretti, A. (2012). Meta-analysis of serotonin transporter gene promoter polymorphism (5-HTTLPR) association with antidepressant efficacy. *European Neuropsychopharmacology, 22*(4), 239–258.

Post, R. M., & Leverich, G. S. (2008). *Treatment of bipolar illness: A casebook for clinicians and patients.* New York, NY: W. W. Norton.

Post, R. M., Leverich, G. S., Nolen, W. A., Kupka, R. W., Altshuler, L. L., Frye, M. A., . . . Walden, J. (2003). A re-evaluation of the role of antidepressants in the treatment of bipolar depression: Data from the Stanley Foundation Bipolar Network. *Bipolar Disorder, 5*(6), 396–406.

Ranjbar, E., Memari, A. H., Hafizi, S., Shayestehfar, M., Mirfazeli, F. S., & Eshghi, M. A. (2015). Depression and exercise: A clinical review and management guideline. *Asian Journal of Sports Medicine, 6*(2), e24055.

Rethorst, C. D., & Trivedi, M. H. (2013). Evidence-based recommendations for the prescription of exercise for major depressive disorder. *Journal of Psychiatric Practice, 19*(3), 204–212.

Rief, W., Barsky, A. J., Bingel, U., Doering, B. K., Schwarting, R., Wöhr, M., & Schweiger, U. (2016). Rethinking psychopharmacotherapy: The role of treatment context and brain plasticity in antidepressant and antipsychotic interventions. *Neuroscience and Biobehavioral Reviews, 60,* 51–64.

Roehrs, T. A., Randall, S., Harris, E., Maan, R., & Roth, T. (2012). Twelve months of nightly zolpidem does not lead to rebound insomnia or withdrawal symptoms: A prospective placebo-controlled study. *Journal of Psychopharmacology, 26*(8), 1088–1095.

Rosenbaum, S., Tiedemann, A., Sherrington, C., Curtis, J., & Ward, P. B. (2014). Physical activity interventions for people with mental illness: A systematic review and meta-analysis. *Journal of Clinical Psychiatry, 75*(9), 964–974.

Roshanaei-Moghaddam, B., Pauly, M. C., Atkins, D. C., Baldwin, S. A., Stein, M. B., & Roy-Byrne, P. (2011). Relative effects of CBT and pharmacotherapy in depression versus anxiety: Is medication somewhat better for depression, and CBT somewhat better for anxiety? *Depression and Anxiety, 28*(7), 560–567.

Salvadore, G., Machado-Vieira, R., & Manji, H. (2010). Neuroprotective agents in mood disorders: Pathophysiological and therapeutic implications. In M. S. Ritsner (Ed.), *Brain protection in schizophrenia, mood and cognitive disorders* (pp. 417–449). New York, NY: Springer.

Samamé, C., Martino, D. J., & Strejilevich, S. A. (2012). Social cognition in euthymic bipolar disorder: Systematic review and meta-analytic approach. *Acta Psychiatrica Scandinavica, 125*(4), 266–280.

Saroukhani, S., Emami-Parsa, M., Modabbernia, A., Ashrafi, M., Farokhnia, M., Hajiaghaee, R., & Akhondzadeh, S. (2013). Aspirin for treatment of lithium-associated sexual dysfunction in men: Randomized double-blind placebo-controlled study. *Bipolar Disorder, 15*(6), 650–656.

Schiele, J. T., Schneider, H., Quinzler, R., Reich, G., & Haefeli, W. E.

(2014). Two techniques to make swallowing pills easier. *Annals of Family Medicine, 12*(6), 550–552.

Schiffman, J., Davis, M., & Pierre, J. (2011). Hydroxyzine: Rational choice for inpatients with insomnia. *Current Psychiatry, 10*(3), 88.

Schoeyen, H. K., Kessler, U., Andreassen, O. A., Auestad, B. H., Bergsholm, P., Malt, U. F., . . . Vaaler, A. (2015). Treatment-resistant bipolar depression: A randomized controlled trial of electroconvulsive therapy versus algorithm-based pharmacological treatment. *American Journal of Psychiatry, 172*(1), 41–51.

Schuch, F. B., Deslandes, A. C., Stubbs, B., Gosmann, N. P., Silva, C. T., & Fleck, M. P. (2016). Neurobiological effects of exercise on major depressive disorder: A systematic review. *Neuroscience and Biobehavioral Reviews, 61*, 1–11.

Scott, J., Colom, F., & Vieta, E. (2007). A meta-analysis of relapse rates with adjunctive psychological therapies compared to usual psychiatric treatment for bipolar disorders. *International Journal of Neuropsychopharmacology, 10*(1), 123–129.

Simeonova, D. I., Chang, K. D., Strong, C., & Ketter, T. A. (2005). Creativity in familial bipolar disorder. *Journal of Psychiatric Research, 39*(6), 623–631.

Simon, N. M., Otto, M. W., Fischmann, D., Racette, S., Nierenberg, A. A., Pollack, M. H., & Smoller, J. W. (2005). Panic disorder and bipolar disorder: Anxiety sensitivity as a potential mediator of panic during manic states. *Journal of Affective Disorders, 87*(1), 101–105.

Sinn, N., Milte, C., & Howe, P. R. (2010). Oiling the brain: A review of randomized controlled trials of omega-3 fatty acids in psychopathology across the lifespan. *Nutrients, 2*(2), 128–170.

Slavin, J. (2013). Fiber and prebiotics: Mechanisms and health benefits. *Nutrients, 5*(4), 1417–1435.

Sobczak, S., Honig, A., Nicolson, N. A., & Riedel, W. J. (2002). Effects of acute tryptophan depletion on mood and cortisol release in first-degree relatives of type I and type II bipolar patients and healthy matched controls. *Neuropsychopharmacology, 27*(5), 834–842.

Srivastava S., & Ketter T.A. (2011). Clinical relevance of treatments for acute bipolar disorder: balancing therapeutic and adverse effects. *Clinical Therapeutics, 33*(12):B40-48.

Stanley, B., Sher, L., Wilson, S., Ekman, R., Huang, Y. Y., & Mann, J. J. (2009). Non-suicidal self-injurious behavior, endogenous opioids and monoamine neurotransmitters. *Journal of Affective Disorders, 124*(1–2), 134–140.

Stern, J. (2014, October 7). The best sleep-tracking devices to mind your Z's. *The Wall Street Journal.*

Stranahan, A. M., Khalil, D., & Gould, E. (2006). Social isolation delays the positive effects of running on adult neurogenesis. *Nature Neuroscience, 9*(4), 526–533.

Strejilevich, S. A., Martino, D. J., Marengo, E., Igoa, A., Fassi, G., Whitham, E. A., & Ghaemi, S. N. (2011). Long-term worsening of bipolar disorder related with frequency of antidepressant exposure. *Annals of Clinical Psychiatry, 23*(3), 186–192.

Sublette, M. E., Ellis, S. P., Geant, A. L., & Mann, J. J. (2011). Meta-analysis: Effects of eicosapentaenoic acid in clinical trials in depression. *Journal of Clinical Psychiatry, 72*(12), 1577–1584.

Suez, J., Korem, T., Zeevi, D., Zilberman-Schapira, G., Thaiss, C. A., Maza, O., . . .Elinav, E. (2014). Artificial sweeteners induce glucose intolerance by altering the gut microbiota. *Nature, 514*(7521), 181–186.

Sundgot-Borgen, J., Rosenvinge, J. H., Bahr, R., & Schneider, L. S. (2002). The effect of exercise, cognitive therapy, and nutritional counseling in treating bulimia nervosa. *Medicine and Science in Sports and Exercise, 34*(2), 190–195.

Teasdale, J. D., Scott, J., Moore, R. G., Hayhurst, H., Pope, M., & Paykel, E. S. (2001). How does cognitive therapy prevent relapse in residual depression? Evidence from a controlled trial. *Journal of Consulting and Clinical Psychology, 69*(3), 347–357.

Terman, M., & McMahan, I. (2013). *Reset your inner clock: The drug-free way to your best-ever sleep, mood, and energy.* New York, NY: Avery.

Terman, M., & Terman, J. S. (2006). Controlled trial of naturalistic dawn simulation and negative air ionization for seasonal affective disorder. *American Journal of Psychiatry, 163*(12), 2126–2133.

Tomiyama, A. J., Mann, T., Vinas, D., Hunger, J. M., Dejager, J., & Taylor, S. E. (2010). Low calorie dieting increases cortisol. *Psychosomatic Medicine, 72*(4), 357–364.

Torrens, M., Fonseca, F., Mateu, G., & Farré, M. (2005). Efficacy of antidepressants in substance use disorders with and without comorbid depression. A systematic review and meta-analysis. *Drug and Alcohol Dependence, 78*(1), 1–22.

Tracy, N. (2013, September 3). Keeping a job when you have bipolar disorder. Retrieved from http://www.healthyplace.com/blogs/breaking-bipolar/2013/09/keeping-job-bipolar-disorder

Trivedi, M. H., Rush, A. J., Wisniewski, S. R., Nierenberg, A. A., Warden, D., Ritz, L., . . . Fava, M. (2006). Evaluation of outcomes with citalopram for depression using measurement-based care in STAR*D: Implications for clinical practice. *American Journal of Psychiatry, 163*(1), 28–40.

U.S. Food and Drug Administration. (2012, July 12). Letter to Lithia Mineral Water, Inc. Retrieved from http://www.fda.gov/ICECI/EnforcementActions/WarningLetters/2012/ucm313934.htm

Uguz, F., Sahingoz, M., Gungor, B., Aksoy, F., & Askin, R. (2015). Weight gain and associated factors in patients using newer antidepressant drugs. *General Hospital Psychiatry, 37*(1), 46–48.

van der Loos, M. L., Mulder, P. G., Hartong, E. G., Blom, M. B., Vergouwen, A. C., de Keyzer, H. J., . . . Nolen, W. A. (2009). Efficacy and safety of lamotrigine as add-on treatment to lithium in bipolar depression: A multicenter, double-blind, placebo-controlled trial. *Journal of Clinical Psychiatry, 70*(2), 223–231.

Vázquez, G., Tondo, L., & Baldessarini, R. J. (2011). Comparison of antidepressant responses in patients with bipolar vs. unipolar depression: A meta-analytic review. *Pharmacopsychiatry, 44*(1), 21–26.

Vestergaard, P. (2015). Effects of antiepileptic drugs on bone health and growth potential in children with epilepsy. *Paediatric Drugs, 17*(2), 141–150.

Vieta, E., & Torrent, C. (2014). *Functional remediation for bipolar disorder.* Cambridge, UK: Cambridge University Press.

Virtanen, M., Stansfeld, S. A., Fuhrer, R., Ferrie, J. E., & Kivimäki, M. (2012). Overtime work as a predictor of major depressive episode: A 5-year follow-up of the Whitehall II Study. *PLoS One, 7*(1), e30719.

Voderholzer, U., Riemann, D., Hornyak, M., Backhaus, J., Feige, B., Berger, M., & Hohagen, F. (2001). A double-blind, randomized and placebo-controlled study on the polysomnographic withdrawal effects of zopiclone, zolpidem and triazolam in healthy subjects. *European Archives of Psychiatry and Clinical Neuroscience, 251*(3), 117–123.

Vogel, M., Braungardt, T., Meyer, W., & Schneider, W. (2012). The effects of shift work on physical and mental health. *Journal of Neural Transmission (Vienna), 119*(10), 1121–1132.

Volkow, N. D., Baler, R. D., Compton, W. M., & Weiss, S. R. (2014). Adverse health effects of marijuana use. *New England Journal of Medicine, 370*(23), 2219–2227.

Vural, E. M., van Munster, B. C., & de Rooij, S. E. (2014). Optimal dosages for melatonin supplementation therapy in older adults: a systematic review of current literature. *Drugs and Aging, 31*(6), 441–451.

Wang, S. M., Han, C., Lee, S. J., Patkar, A. A., Masand, P. S., & Pae, C. U. (2014). A review of current evidence for acetyl-l-carnitine in the treatment of depression. *Journal of Psychiatric Research, 53,* 30–37.

Wartofsky, L., & Dickey, R. A. (2005). The evidence for a narrower thyrotropin reference range is compelling. *Journal of Clinical Endocrinology and Metabolism, 90*(9), 5483–5488.

Weaver, M. (2016, January 8). New tough alcohol guidelines not scaremongering, says chief medical officer. *The Guardian.*

Wehr, T. A., Turner, E. H., Shimada, J. M., Lowe, C. H., Barker, C., & Leibenluft, E. (1998). Treatment of rapidly cycling bipolar patient by using extended bed rest and darkness to stabilize the timing and duration of sleep. *Biological Psychiatry, 43*(11), 822–828.

White, T. M., Terman, M., Musa, G. J., & Avery, D. H. (2005). Incidence of winter depression varies within time zones. *Chronobiology International, 23,* 743–745.

Wignall, N. D., & Brown, E. S. (2014). Citicoline in addictive disorders: A review of the literature. *American Journal of Drug Alcohol Abuse*, 40(4), 262–268.

Wirz-Justice, A., Benedetti, F., & Terman, M. (2013). *Chronotherapeutics for affective disorders: A clinician's manual for light and wake therapy*, 2nd ed. Basel, Switzerland: S. Karger.

Woo, Y. S., Seo, H. J., McIntyre, R. S., & Bahk, W. M. (2016). Obesity and its potential effects on antidepressant treatment outcomes in patients with depressive disorders: A literature review. *International Journal of Molecular Sciences*, 12(17).

Wozniak J., Faraone S. V., Chan J., Tarko L., Hernandez M., Davis J., . . . Biederman J. (2015). *Journal of Clinical Psychiatry*, 76(11), 1548-1555.

Yang, Q. (2010). Gain weight by "going diet?" Artificial sweeteners and the neurobiology of sugar cravings. *Yale Journal of Biology and Medicine*, 83(2), 101–108.

Yildiz, A., Ruiz, P., & Nemeroff, C. (Eds.). (2015). *The bipolar book: History, neurobiology, and treatment*. New York, NY: Oxford University Press.

Zimmerman, M., Posternak, M. A., Attiullah, N., Friedman, M., Boland, R. J., Baymiller, S., . . . Chelminski, I. (2005). Why isn't bupropion the most frequently prescribed antidepressant? *Journal of Clinical Psychiatry*, 66(5), 603–610.

REFERENCES FOR TABLE 22.1

Baldwin, D. S., den Boer, J. A., Lyndon, G., Emir, B., Schweizer, E., & Haswell, H. (2015). Efficacy and safety of pregabalin in generalized anxiety disorder: A critical review of the literature. *Journal of Psychopharmacology*, 29(10), 1047–1060.

Baniasadi, M., Hosseini, G., Fayyazi Bordbar, M. R., Rezaei Ardani, A., & Mostafavi Toroghi, H. (2014). Effect of pregabalin augmentation in treatment of patients with combat-related chronic posttraumatic stress disorder: a randomized controlled trial. *Journal of Psychiatric Practice*, 20(6), 419–427.

Delahanty, D. L., Gabert-Quillen, C., Ostrowski, S. A., Nugent, N. R.,

Fischer, B., Morris, A., . . .Fallon, W. (2013). The efficacy of initial hydrocortisone administration at preventing posttraumatic distress in adult trauma patients: a randomized trial. CNS Spectrurms, 18(2), 103–111.

Greist, J. H., Liu-Dumaw, M., Schweizer, E., & Feltner, D. (2011). Efficacy of pregabalin in preventing relapse in patients with generalized social anxiety disorder: Results of a double-blind, placebo-controlled 26-week study. International Clinical Psychopharmacology, 26(5), 243–251.

Ostrowski, S. A., & Delahanty, D. L. (2014). Prospects for the pharmacological prevention of post-traumatic stress in vulnerable individuals. CNS Drugs, 28(3), 195–203.

Pande, A. C., Davidson, J. R., Jefferson, J. W., Janney, C. A., Katzelnick, D. J., Weisler, R. H., . . .Sutherland, S. M. (1999). Treatment of social phobia with gabapentin: A placebo-controlled study. Journal of Clinical Psychopharmacology, 19(4), 341–348.

Vázquez, G. H., Baldessarini, R. J., & Tondo, L. (2014). Co-occurrence of anxiety and bipolar disorders: Clinical and therapeutic overview. Depression and Anxiety, 31(3), 196–206.

Vieta, E., Manuel Goikolea, J., Martínez-Arán, A., Comes, M., Verger, K., Masramon, X., . . .& Colom, F. (2006). A double-blind, randomized, placebo-controlled, prophylaxis study of adjunctive gabapentin for bipolar disorder. Journal of Clinical Psychiatry, 67(3), 473–477.

REFERENCES FOR TABLE 22.2

Haghighi, M., Jahangard, L., Mohammad-Beigi, H., Bajoghli, H., Hafezian, H., Rahimi, A., . . . Brand, S. (2013). In a double-blind, randomized and placebo-controlled trial, adjuvant memantine improved symptoms in inpatients suffering from refractory obsessive-compulsive disorders (OCD). Psychopharmacology, 228(4), 633–640.

Maglione, M., Maher, A. R., Hu, J., Wang, Z., Shanman, R., Shekelle, P. G., . . . Perry, T. (2011). Off-label use of atypical antipsychotics: An update. AHRQ Comparative Effectiveness Reviews, Report No. 11-EHC087-EF.

Sarris, J., Oliver, G., Camfield, D. A., Dean, O. M., Dowling, N., Smith, D. J., . . . Ng, C. H. (2015). N-Acetyl Cysteine (NAC) in the treatment of obsessive-compulsive disorder: A 16-week, double-blind, randomised, placebo-controlled Study. *CNS Drugs, 29*(9), 801–809.

Sahraian, A., Bigdeli, M., Ghanizadeh, A., & Akhondzadeh, S. (2014). Topiramate as an adjuvant treatment for obsessive compulsive symptoms in patients with bipolar disorder: A randomized double blind placebo controlled clinical trial. *Journal of Affective Disorders, 166,* 201–205.

Soltani, F., Sayyah, M., Feizy, F., Malayeri, A., Siahpoosh, A., & Motlagh, I. (2010). A double-blind, placebo-controlled pilot study of ondansetron for patients with obsessive-compulsive disorder. *Human Psychopharmacology, 25*(6), 509–513.

REFERENCES FOR TABLE 22.3

Horrigan, J. P., & Barnhill, L. J. (1999). Guanfacine and secondary mania in children. *Journal of Affective Disorders, 54*(3), 309–314.

McDonagh, M. S., Peterson, K., Thakurta, S., & Low, A. (2011). Drug class review: Pharmacologic treatments for attention deficit hyperactivity disorder: Final update for report. *Drug Class Reviews.* Portland: Oregon Health & Science University.

Vaisman, N., Kaysar, N., Zaruk-Adasha, Y., Pelled D., Brichon, G., Zwingelstein, G., & Bodennec, J. (2008). Correlation between changes in blood fatty acid composition and visual sustained attention performance in children with inattention: Effect of dietary n-3 fatty acids containing phospholipids. *American Journal of Clinical Nutrition, 87*(5), 1170–1180.

REFERENCES FOR TABLE 22.4

Burdick, K. E., Braga, R. J., Nnadi, C. U., Shaya, Y., Stearns, W. H., & Malhotra, A. K. (2012). Placebo-controlled adjunctive trial of pramipexole in patients with bipolar disorder: targeting cognitive dysfunction. *Journal of Clinical Psychiatry, 73*(1), 103–112.

Dean, O. M., Bush, A. I., Copolov, D. L., Kohlmann, K., Jeavons, S.,

Schapkaitz, I., . . . Berk, M. (2012). Effects of N-acetyl cysteine on cognitive function in bipolar disorder. *Psychiatry and Clinical Neurosciences, 66*(6), 514–517.

Ghaemi, S. N., Gilmer, W. S., Dunn, R. T., Hanlon, R. E., Kemp, D. E., Bauer, A. D., . . . Harvey, P. D. (2009). A double-blind, placebo-controlled pilot study of galantamine to improve cognitive dysfunction in minimally symptomatic bipolar disorder. *Journal of Clinical Psychopharmacology, 29*(3), 291–295.

Kaye, N. S., Graham, J., Roberts, J., Thompson, T., & Nanry, K. (2007). Effect of open-label lamotrigine as monotherapy and adjunctive therapy on the self-assessed cognitive function scores of patients with bipolar I disorder. *Journal of Clinical Psychopharmacol, 27*(4), 387–391.

REFERENCES FOR TABLE 22.5

Brownley, K. A., Von Holle, A., Hamer, R. M., La Via, M., & Bulik, C. M. (2013). A double-blind, randomized pilot trial of chromium picolinate for binge eating disorder: Results of the Binge Eating and Chromium (BEACh) study. *Journal of Psychosomatic Research, 75*(1), 36–42.

Gelber, D., Levine, J., & Belmaker, R. H. (2001). Effect of inositol on bulimia nervosa and binge eating. *International Journal of Eating Disorders, 29*(3), 345–348.

Ramoz, N., Versini, A., & Gorwood, P. (2007). Eating disorders: An overview of treatment responses and the potential impact of vulnerability genes and endophenotypes. *Expert Opinion on Pharmacotherapy, 8*(13), 2029–2044.

Index

how to think about not sleeping, 99
if you don't fall asleep after 20
minutes, get up, 98
relaxation technique, 97–98
steps in, 94–99
train your body to expect sleep
when in bed, 95
wake at regular time, 96
sleep medications, 100, 283–84
sleep monitors
in bipolar disorder, 135–36
sleep restriction, 99–100
CBT-I in, 100
goal of, 100
Sleep Time, 136
Smiling Mind, 137
SNRIs. *see* serotonin norepi-
nephrine reuptake inhibitors
(SNRIs)
social activities
for depression, 292–94
social interactions
neurohormones impact on, 82
specialist(s)
finding, 140–48
inability to find/afford/get,
142–43
preparing for first visit, 143–45
strategies for working with,
145–47
working with over time, 147–48
specialty centers
finding, 142
speech

pressured, 20–21, 29t
spice
in people with mood disorders,
129–30
SRT genes. *see* serotonin transporter (SRT) genes
SSRIs. *see* selective serotonin
reuptake inhibitors (SSRIs)
Stanford University, 136
statin(s)
for depression, 187t
steroid(s)
uses of, 176
Stevens Johnson syndrome
causes of, 154
lamotrigine and, 154
stimulant(s), 183–85, 185t
1stimulant(s)
for ADHD, 192–93
described, 183–84
facts about, 185t
modafinil, 184–85, 185t
novel, 183–85, 185t
traditional, 184
types of, 184, 284
uses of, 176
STOP-BANG questionnaire,
230–31, 230t
street drugs
bipolar disorder effects of, 63
stress
flexible way of adapting to, 73
mood disorders effects of, 62
stretching
in overcoming depression, 108